The Island Motif in the Fiction of L. M. Montgomery, Margaret Laurence, Margaret Atwood, and Other Canadian Women Novelists

Studies on Themes and Motifs in Literature

Horst S. Daemmrich
General Editor

Vol. 68

PETER LANG
New York • Washington, D.C./Baltimore • Bern
Frankfurt am Main • Berlin • Brussels • Vienna • Oxford

Theodore F. Sheckels

The Island Motif in the Fiction of L. M. Montgomery, Margaret Laurence, Margaret Atwood, and Other Canadian Women Novelists

PETER LANG
New York • Washington, D.C./Baltimore • Bern
Frankfurt am Main • Berlin • Brussels • Vienna • Oxford

Library of Congress Cataloging-in-Publication Data

Sheckels, Theodore F.
The island motif in the fiction of L. M. Montgomery, Margaret Laurence, Margaret
Atwood, and other Canadian women novelists / Theodore F. Sheckels.
p. cm. — (Studies on themes and motifs in literature; v. 68)
Includes bibliographical references and index.
1. Canadian fiction—Women authors—History and criticism.
2. Islands in literature. 3. Women and literature—Canada—History—20th century.
4. Montgomery, L. M. (Lucy Maud), 1874–1942—Settings.
5. Atwood, Margaret Eleanor, 1939-—Settings.
6. Laurence, Margaret—Settings. I. Title. II. Series.
PR9192.6.I75S54   813′.50932142—dc21   2003004890
ISBN 0-8204-6792-8
ISSN 1056-3970

Bibliographic information published by **Die Deutsche Bibliothek**.
Die Deutsche Bibliothek lists this publication in the "Deutsche
Nationalbibliografie"; detailed bibliographic data is available
on the Internet at http://dnb.ddb.de/.

For Kath, dear friend
and kindred spirit

Contents

Preface

I have been teaching Canadian literature for twenty years: every other year, I'd do my best to introduce American undergraduates to the literature of our nearest neighbor to the north. I was drawn to Canadian literature myself in the early 1980s because I began reading the early novels by Margaret Atwood. Not surprisingly, my reading Atwood led to my reading Margaret Laurence and Alice Munro and, then, other Canadian women. These writers were always a part of the course I taught, as well as a "special topics" course I twice taught focused exclusively on Canadian women writers.

As I read more and more fiction by these writers, I began discerning a pattern. I noticed that islands—sometimes figurative but more often literal islands—played a major role in these novels. Female protagonists either went off to an island or were already there—usually trapped there. Sometimes the "island experience" was a positive one; sometimes it was not. Sometimes the island was quite literal and quite easy to spot; sometimes the island was more veiled; sometimes the island was figurative. Regardless, whether it is the obvious small island in Margaret Atwood's *Surfacing*, the less obvious United Kingdom in Margaret Laurence's *The Diviners*, or the insularity of the small town of Jubilee in Alice Munro's *Lives of Girls and Women*, the motif seemed the same. The island as escape; the island as trap; the island as, paradoxically, both.

This book, *The Island Motif in the Fiction of L. M. Montgomery, Margaret Laurence, Margaret Atwood, and Other Canadian Women Novelists*, explores this motif in a range of twentieth-century Canadian novels by women. The motif is explored primarily by attending to their texts.

However, a curious critical lens is often noticeable as I attend to the texts. I say "curious" because it is derived from the work of what many in literary studies might think to be an "odd couple": Northrop Frye and Julia Kristeva. Frye's "green world" blends with Kristeva's emphasis on retreating from the symbolic to the semiotic to offer a structure that facilitates one's understanding of what underlies the "island experience" common to these novels. I do not allow this critical lens to dictate what I see in the books; however, I do find that patterns and images and issues described by Frye and Kristeva emerge from these works of fiction, giving the stories and the island motif in them a special resonance.

As this preface has already suggested, *The Island Motif* considers novels by Margaret Atwood (*Surfacing* and *Bodily Harm*), Margaret Laurence (*A Jest of God* and *The Diviners*), and Alice Munro (*Lives of Girls and Women*). The study also treats two very important novels, Marian Engel's controversial *Bear* and Audrey Thomas's *Intertidal Life*. The study assumes, as do many, that L. M. Montgomery is not *just* a writer of juvenile fiction and treats her work quite seriously, examining the classic *Anne of Green Gables* as well as the later novels focused on three other young heroines, Jane Stuart, Patricia Gardiner, and Marigold Lesley. Finally, the study considers two very different Quebecois works, Gabrielle Roy's ground-breaking novel *The Tin Flute* and Marie-Claire Blais's rather recent *These Festive Nights*. These works are not treated chronologically or geographically; rather, they are treated in terms of their optimistic vision. Thus, we begin in Chapter 2 with the unlikely trio of Montgomery's *Anne of Green Gables*, Montgomery's *Jane of Lantern Hill*, and Marian Engel's *Bear*, and we end in Chapter 7 with the frightening trio of Gabrielle Roy's *The Tin Flute*, Margaret Atwood's *Bodily Harm*, and Marie-Claire Blais's *These Festive Nights*.

There are, of course, some Canadian women writers not discussed by this study—most notably, Anne Hébert, Carol Shields, and Joy Kogawa. There may well be ways to relate these authors to the motif. For example, the claustrophobic Gothic villages in Hebert's fiction are as insular as Laurence's Manawaka and Munro's Jubilee. But whether these other Canadian writers "fit" or not is not of concern, for I am not trying to argue that the motif this book traces is *the* defining theme or mythos of *all* Canadian women writing. In much the same way as Margaret Atwood saw a pattern and presents it in *Survival* and D. G. Jones saw a pattern and presents it in *Butterfly on Rock*, I am presenting a dominant theme or mythos, so dominant that it is noteworthy. Recognizing it could lead to reductive readings of individual works of literature, but that, of course, is not the goal. The goal is for the motif to serve as a touchstone, providing a general focus as we explore individual literary works that play variations on the theme. Ultimately, it is those variations that are truly significant; nonetheless, seeing the motif does draw one's attention to how escape and entrapment define Canadian women's writing, to how mirror images and intense bodily experiences work in many of the works, and to the dialectic relationship between language and whatever is not in language.

These ideas about Canadian women's fiction have evolved through the years, and I need to acknowledge the roles played by many students over those years in helping me shape my thoughts as I taught these and other novels. More particularly, I'd like to acknowledge the assistance of the librarians of the McGraw-Page Library at Randolph-Macon College. Over the years, several of these fine people have helped me to acquire through inter-library loan services the materials I needed to consult to see how others were treating these texts. I would also like to acknowledge the assistance of Peter Lang Senior Editor Heidi Burns, who copy-edited this work, thereby sharpening the prose on many occasions; Randolph-Macon College Faculty Secretary Susan Timberlake, who assisted in the preparation of the final copy; and Peter Lang Production Coordinator Sophie Appel, who steered the manuscript through the stages preceding actual publication. Finally, I'd like to acknowledge the assistance of a grant from the Walter Williams Craigie Endowment that funded the earliest work on this project. That early work led to a paper I presented at the Third International L. M. Montgomery Symposium at the University of Prince Edward Island. That paper is the core of Chapter 1.

Permissions

1

Introduction

One does not read for patterns, but, sometimes, they are inescapable. Thus was Margaret Atwood led to her "classic," although frequently criticized (as reductive), study of Canadian literature in *Survival* (1972). Much in the spirit of that study is this book—a book that suggests that a defining trait of much fiction by Canadian women is their heroines' retreats to islands. An initial critical gloss on this retreat is provided (appropriately enough for works Canadian) by Northrop Frye, for the island is much like the green world he sketches in exploring the mythoi of spring and summer, the genres of comedy and romance. In terms derived from Frye, retreating once more to the island serves as a recurring mythos in Canadian fiction by women.[1]

Frye spent years during his stellar career studying the structure of those literary kinds he termed "comedy" and "romance." Although the formalistic, analytic rigor evident in his *Anatomy of Criticism* (1957), which would have one talking in terms of "phase four comedy" and "phase five romance," is certainly passé, many of the observations Frye offers in that classic treatise are still relevant. So are the later observations he offers on romance in *The Secular Scripture* (1976). One thing that makes these observations still relevant is the way they are consonant with the more avant-garde thoughts on literature offered by Julia Kristeva in *The Revolution of Poetic Language* (1974, 1984)

and elsewhere. Together, Frye and Kristeva offer a theoretical founda-
tion for understanding numerous works of fiction authored by Canadian women such as L. M. Montgomery, Margaret Laurence, Marian
Engel, Audrey Thomas, Margaret Atwood, Alice Munro, Gabrielle
Roy, and Marie-Claire Blais.

Kristeva, following Lacan, traces human development from the semiotic to the symbolic. From a psychoanalytic perspective, this
movement into language is premised on the ability to differentiate the
self from the other. Dealing with one's mirror image—be it the literal
image or a double—is a crucial preparatory stage to grasping the con-
cept of the other. Seeing one's mother as other is a crucial first step.
This mirroring and this separation, which Kristeva terms castration,
serve as dual landmarks along the course of development. That
course into the symbolic does not, however, leave the semiotic entirely behind. Because of the symbolic realm's inherent limitations, the
semiotic chora pulses through in imaginative writing, especially at
points of extreme emotional intensity. These pulsions, Kristeva observes, exist apart from language and seem of the body. They constitute *jouissance*.

Development and identity are, of course, related. As one develops
into the symbolic, one acquires what serves as one's identity in language. But within the undifferentiated space of the semiotic chora, a
prelanguage identity is also available. Experiencing *jouissance* may
then represent an escape from identity in language to this unarticu-
lated, of-the-body identity. This escape is more essential for females
than males because the symbolic realm is male-defined, and, therefore, any identity rendered in language is necessarily defined in patriarchal terms. According to Frye, the comedy/romance genre he explores in the *Anatomy of Criticism* and *The Secular Scripture* is just such
an escape from identity in language, an escape Frye says is accompanied by erotic intensity. *Jouissance* seems part of what Frye finds in the
genre, even though the particular term was not part of Frye's critical
lexicon.

If the narrative pattern Frye describes in his discussion of com-
edy/romance is a return to the semiotic, then much of Frye's detailed

description is relevant. Frye notes that the escape is figured as that into another world, characterized by its festive and pensive shadings. Whether in celebration or contemplation (or both), the central character seems safe. Surrounding the locus of escape is chaos, often figured as the sea. Thus, the locus of escape is often figured as the island. The heroism the central character exhibits is that of enduring, patiently suffering. The retreat itself, if not the reflections offered during moments of contemplation, reflects social protest. Thus, the genre is appropriate for expressing dissatisfaction with the identity society (and its language) foists upon one. Women, whose identity is often patriarchically defined, and Canada, whose identity has been—arguably—determined by its colonization and its neocolonization, might thus find the genre of comedy/romance especially appropriate for their escapes.

According to Frye in *The Secular Scripture*, escapes can be either ascents or descents, paradisial or demonic. Even so, Frye, although captive a bit within his spatial metaphor, does admit that much about these escapes is ambiguous. Paradises prove demonic; hells prove heavenly. To the extent an escape is predominantly an ascent, Frye sees the recognition scene and the throwing off of animal disguises as conventional. To the extent an escape is primarily a descent, Frye sees caves or shadows or dark forests and separation and false accusations of crime as conventional. However, an ambiguous mixture would not only mix these conventions but present them in a surreal haze. These conventions are apparent in the works of fiction discussed in this study, so are "conventions," if one can call them that, borrowed from Kristeva, such as castration, mirroring, unease-in-language, and *jouissance*.

In accordance with Frye, who sees these escapes as paradisial, ambiguous, and demonic, this book proceeds through a large number of novels by Canadian women, beginning with the most positive, L. M. Montgomery's Anne of Green Gables (1908), and ending with the most hellish, Marie-Claire Blais's These Festive Nights (1998).

Chapter 2 brings together two rather unlikely authors, L. M. Montgomery and Marian Engel. Montgomery, once thought to be nothing more than a writer of books for adolescent girls, has finally been treated quite seriously by scholars—most notably by Elizabeth Epperly in *The Fragrance of Sweet-Grass* (1992). Montgomery's output was large: She wrote far more than the several books focused on her most famous creation, Anne Shirley. In this chapter, I will deal with these "Anne books" as a group as well as with the much later *Jane of Lantern Hill* (1938).

Anne Shirley's "escape" in L. M. Montgomery's *Anne of Green Gables* (1908) is not a radical one. She is obviously on an island, but its insularity and its surrounding seas are not stressed. Prince Edward Island offers safety, but the threat that necessitates safety is not clear. For Anne herself, the safety seems to be from her orphan's life in Nova Scotia and the association's disreputability. Being labeled "orphan," Anne has a reason to rebel against language, but, rather than reject words or indict words, she appropriates them, renaming places and even trying to rename herself. She also represents social protest against various constraints imposed upon girls and women, but her protest is quiet, and it is conducted largely within the social structures established by the patriarchy. Within her Prince Edward Island escape, she deals with doubles in Gilbert Blythe, her intellectual "twin," and Diana Barry, her bosom friend. With them and other "kindred spirits," she experiences a joy, a *jouissance* in so far as it is from deep within and not expressible in language—no matter how hard she tries. She has a moment of recognition when she realizes her similarity to Marilla; this same moment gives her a mother to replace her lost mother. Now, Anne can negotiate her degree of separation. In fact, she does, as the successively more distancing titles of *Anne of Green Gables, Anne of Avonlea* (1910), and *Anne of the Island* (1915) suggest. As she matures on (and occasionally off) the island, she loses the less-than-human identity of "orphan" (orphans being those who poison and commit arson) and becomes fully human.

In Montgomery's later *Jane of Lantern Hill*, the heroine's escape is more radical. The island is emphasized more; and, if the surrounding waters *per se* are not, the long train journey to Prince Edward Island is. The train journey serves to emphasize the remoteness—both literally and psychologically—of the island world. Once Jane embraces the island and her father, the island offers safety—safety from the tyranny of 60 Gay Street, Toronto. On Prince Edward Island, Jane embraces values that serve as a protest against the stuffiness and oppressiveness of her Grandmother Kennedy's Toronto household, figured by playmate Jody, who functions in her victim status as a mirror image of Jane-in-Toronto. These island values find expression in the quaint rustic names of places and people and in domestic chores. In this paradisial environment, she experiences a joy, an out-of-language *jouissance*. As in *Anne of Green Gables*, it is not erotic, but perhaps its incipient erotic quality is what has led a few to note (I think, incorrectly) a disturbing incestuous quality to Jane's relationship with her father. In any event, her delight in the island is viewed negatively by those in her grandmother's Toronto world; in enjoying it, she shares in the sin of the father they say. From this false accusation, she arises, revivifying her father and reuniting him with his estranged wife. Once they are safely together, Jane becomes daughter, and they live off the island but in an island-like green world on the outskirts of the urban.

Montgomery's works are read more by young girls than by adults. Conversely, Marian Engel's *Bear* is undoubtedly thought to be totally unsuitable for young girls. Thus, Montgomery and Engel are indeed an unlikely duo to be discussed together. However, the island Engel's central character Lou escapes to in *Bear* is rather similar in its redemptive power to Montgomery's Prince Edward Island.

Lou's escape is far more radical than those of Anne and Jane. In Marian Engel's *Bear*, a novel Engel coincidentally wrote while summering on Prince Edward Island, Lou's life in Toronto is described in the novel's opening pages as being that of a mole. As we move farther into her story, we learn just how stultifying urban life has been for her—paling her skin, reducing her sex life to a weekly encounter on her boss's desk, killing her self-esteem. At the root of this pathology is a separation of mind and body. Once on her island, she is driven into her mind and body—the octagonal house full of books representing her mind; the bear in the outbuildings her body. Soon, Bear enters the house, and the mind-body dichotomy begins to be obliterated. However, Lou still has farther to go on her journey. She must see in Bear a mirror image of her physical self and embrace it. As readers of Engel's novel know, she does, and the *jouissance* is highly erotic. Certainly some readers will reduce the relationship to bestiality. Giving it this label is highly inaccurate, but so is giving it just about any label. The relationship is symbolic, and hence it defies categorization because it largely exists in semiotic space.

Lou's escape ends with her return to Toronto. She recognizes Bear as bear, no longer a symbol, after she crosses the line sexually with him and he claws her back. However, she embraces within her being the bear's essence just as she often, while on Cary Island, absorbed the bear's scent. When she returns, her body is healthy, she commits herself to no more sexual objectification, and she has sufficient self-esteem to contemplate quitting her job. She has become redeemed from a world in which mind and body become so separate that the definition of human has become problematic.

It is rather obvious that Anne, Jane, and Lou all go to islands and are in some sense redeemed there. Chapter 3 will deal with two works in which the redemption is late in coming and much more tentative: Margaret Laurence's *The Diviners* (1974) and Audrey Thomas's' *Intertidal Life* (1984). In these novels, the central characters enter what feels like a holding pattern as they experience their islands.

In reading Laurence's masterful last work, we learn a great deal about the life of Morag Gunn. We travel with her on journeys through relationships that take Laurence's heroine from Manitoba to Toronto and Vancouver and, then, to the island of Great Britain. As self-assertive as young Morag is, she nonetheless finds herself in a love relationship and then a marriage where not only her role but also her identity is defined by her older husband. She escapes this relationship, but, in its aftermath, finds passion and bears a daughter. Nevertheless, she still cannot realize herself and be the artist she is destined to be. Frustrated, Morag flees to the island.

There, in Great Britain, her new lover becomes a mirror. In London, their relationship is shadowed by her awareness that he has a family and a home. When she sees him at home in Scotland, she realizes that he belongs there and, more importantly, that she also belongs at her home back in Canada. The fact that he is home—with his wife and family—makes him untouchable, distances him. She can only look on, as if at a mirror.

After considerable reflection, she returns to her girlhood home in rural Canada. She seeks reconciliation with the dying man (and the deceased woman) who raised her, a couple she had grown to think were socially and culturally beneath her. She embraces the Scottish heritage this man had celebrated with her as she grew up. She renews her acquaintance with perhaps the one lover, Jules, who did not try to define her. She comes to terms with their daughter Pique, who has, much like Morag, been struggling to find her own separate identity. Pique, the daughter, serves as mirror to Morag, the mother—reversing the typical Lacanian psychodrama. Once Morag has re-embraced her home, she begins, much like the diviner seeking and then finding wellsprings by folk magic, to seek and find creative inspiration in her native earth. Throughout Morag's story, words are her passion, but they bring her no fulfillment. Her island sojourn, insofar as it led her home, brings her finally to the point where the words work, and she is fulfilled as artist and person. Coincidentally, she ends up working and living on another island-like place, but it is one that brings her both time to contemplate and time to connect with visiting others

Morag wrestles with language. Anne and Jane re-name, refusing to accept the pre-existing labels of the symbolic realm. Lou, in exploring the lore of bears, pierces beneath the surface of the symbolic to its mysteries. None of these characters, however, truly rebel against language. Thus, their islands are only implicitly semiotic. Audrey Thomas, in *Intertidal Life*, gives us a more fully semiotic island.

Thomas's heroine, Alice, struggles with the collapse of her marriage and, then, the aftermath of divorce. She does so in a cottage on Vancouver Island. She and her husband Peter bought the cottage as (unbeknownst to her) the marriage was collapsing. In retrospect, Alice wonders if Peter did not envision the island home as a place to put her while he carried on his illicit affairs back on the mainland. It is on this island that she struggles to cope with life between—between her marriage and what might follow, between that first high tide and the next. She does not struggle alone, for, in the various male and female characters who visit the island and her, she has many mirror images of aspects of herself. Not surprisingly, the female characters and her three daughters prove the more crucial mirrors in her quest for identity.

Alice also struggles with language. As a writer, she struggles: too many things—her thoughts and unwanted visitors—are interfering with her work; far too often, the words themselves become unglued. She makes this process explicit in the novel. Before our eyes, we can see the symbolic fading back into the semiotic. As this fading occurs, we seem to be in the womb. The dominating spirit of the island is maternal, and water—like the amniotic fluid—seems all-present.

Thomas's novel is both poignant and poetic. Style holds the reader, not plot, for there is not much plot per se. Just as time brings the return of the tide, time brings healing and, perhaps, the beginnings of the ability to work within the symbolic once more. We leave Thomas's heroine still fragile, leaving the island (she hopes temporarily) for minor surgery. We do not find out if she survives and returns. We are also left puzzling over the possible symbolic meanings of both the surgery and the surviving intertidal sea creatures Thomas writes of. Words of explanation and words of clear association are not provided, for the semiotic is still dominant. Alice's return to the symbolic is still ahead.

Both Great Britain and Vancouver Island offer the necessary shelter while time takes its course. A kind of redemption occurs. For Morag, it occurs after she realizes that she must leave the island; for Alice, it occurs only after the book ends, perhaps through the very agency of writing the book. The island to which Atwood's un-named narrator escapes in *Surfacing* (1972), however, is not as safe as Alice's—or Anne's or Jane's or Morag's or Lou's. Nor is the redemption as sure. Chapter 4 deals exclusively with this rich, puzzling masterpiece.

The two interconnected evils of *Surfacing*, the unnatural and language, have affected the island to which Atwood's unnamed narrator and central character travels. As the narrator lashes out at these evils, she voices a strong protest against a host of values and actions she labels "American." But just as the others' uses of language prove inadequate, so does hers, for, by the time the novel is two-thirds done, it is clear that the evils are not American as much as they are, unfortunately, human. Thus, she must return to nature, to communion with its semiotic spirit in ways that transcend human communication. As she escapes into the island within the island, she sees the mirror images arrayed around her as having been falsely construed by her. David seems to share her leftist politics, but he is just as imperious as those he indicts. Anna seems, as a woman, to share her oppression, but she is just as petty and jealous and vicious as those who abuse her. Joe seems to share her appreciation of art and the animal, but he is, at least for the moment, incapable of being redeemed from the unshaped emptiness suggested by his pottery. Through her dead father's clues and her dead mother's visions, the narrator becomes whole again, perhaps reconnecting her head and body. By admitting her crime of abortion, by conceiving a life to replace the one she destroyed, and by ritualistically purifying herself at nature's unworded commands, she readies herself for an uneasy return to the world. Very much a part of this readiness is a re-embracing of language. She culminates her many reflections on the artificiality and tyranny of the symbolic and her ritualistic return to the semiotic by commenting that, "For us it's necessary, the intercession of words" (224). As she throws off her animal disguise and puts on her human attire, she acquires an identity that will allow her to endure, although we do wonder for how long, for she admits that, once back in the symbolic, "we will probably fail, sooner or later,
more or less painfully" (224).

Surfacing climaxes several times: near the end, when the narrator emerges purified from the water; earlier, when the narrator dumps the exploitative film "the boys" had shot into the water; still earlier, when the narrator dives into the lake to read cave paintings, has a vision, and surfaces. The water, as medium, frees—from guilt, exploitation, complicity. However, the water is also unnaturally high, killing waterside vegetation, and the water is also that upon which the vacationing, killing fisher-hunters ride. Atwood strongly suggests, through a swirl of images in language, that the narrator's retreat to the island has been redemptive. At the same time, Atwood suggests that the threat has affected and rendered problematic the watery medium's ability to suggest either the baptismal or the amniotic.

One cannot therefore help but feel uneasy about this unnamed character's future back in the world. Similarly, one cannot help but feel uncertain about Patricia Gardiner's future beyond L. M. Montgomery's *Pat of Silver Bush* (1933) and *Mistress Pat* (1935) or Marigold Lesley's future after Montgomery's *Magic for Marigold* (1929). These novels, supposedly written for young girls to read, depict characters who become so absorbed in island-like worlds that their departures from them offer not even the qualified hopeful prospects Atwood's unnamed narrator in *Surfacing* faces back in Toronto. Chapter 6 deals with these fairly late, surprisingly disturbing books by Montgomery.

Throughout both "Pat books," Pat shelters herself from the storms often associated with the sea—at Silver Bush, her island within the island of Prince Edward. Change is the enemy: it is bad when it is the cutting of a prized tree; it is worse when it is the departure through marriage or higher education or death of a mirroring other.

There is much that is lighthearted in Montgomery's "Pat books," even though Epperly's description of Mistress Pat as "one of the saddest books Montgomery ever wrote" (217) is apt. The sadness is to some extent produced because celebrations in the gardens and groves of Silver Bush almost always turn pensive, because celebrations cannot last. Time progresses; others change. Pat, however, clings to her child-like existence, resisting beau after beau, suitor after suitor, until she stands falsely accused of being flirtatious and haughty when she is really simultaneously trying to resist change and resist the ways the suitors and the world want to foist a new identity on her. The "old maid" she is on the verge of becoming is indeed a proto-feminist, but that woman is still very much the child obsessed with Silver Bush and determined to stay there, with her weak mother, in a semiotic retreat.

The island escape has become a trap in Mistress Pat. Writing at least partially for an adolescent audience, Montgomery seems to have felt compelled to escape the trap she had written herself into. Thus, suddenly, mother gets well, Silver Bush burns down, and Hillary Gordon returns from his architectural studies and "rescues" Pat. He says, "I know what this tragedy of Silver Bush must have meant to you...but I've a home for you by another sea, Pat. And in it we'll build up a new life and the old will become just a treasury of dear and sacred memories...of things time cannot destroy?" Hilary is offering a new escape, a new island—one that can resist change, or so he claims. There, they will be "two children again" (239). Pat's seemingly happy move into the future is in many ways another retreat. Moreover, it is difficult to accept Hillary's assessment of that retreat, just as we have a difficult time accepting the book's ending as anything other than the author's way out of the trap of the plot.

Places are, of course, special in Montgomery's work—Green Gables, Lantern Hill, Silver Bush. As her Old Grandmother tells Marigold Lesley in Magic for Marigold, places are human and need love—and make demands. Like Pat Gardiner, Marigold Lesley is devoted to her island within the island--to "Cloud of Spruce." However, Marigold's true devotion takes her deeper: The house named "Cloud of Spruce" offers comfort but the magic land (also known as "Cloud of Spruce") through the Magic Door, through the Green Gate, accessible only if one recites The Rhyme, is Marigold's true escape.

There she has Sylvia, her imaginary mirror-like playmate. For years, over Young Grandmother's objections, Marigold retreats to this place. When she is denied it, she falls ill; when she is allowed back through the Magic Door, she is restored. Her Young Grandmother and her shy mother try to find her a "real" playmate to supplant imaginary Sylvia. However, all of them are mirror images but for a moment. They show their true colors—almost always dark ones, and Marigold returns to Sylvia. With Sylvia, Marigold can celebrate and contemplate— protesting the real world's duplicity.

Montgomery does not burn down Cloud of Spruce, or plow under the field through the door and the gate. Montgomery's way of ending Marigold's retreat, however, is just as sad. Montgomery has Marigold grow up. Attracted to a boy playmate Budge, she becomes jealous over his friendship with another boy Tad. To win Budge away from his mate, she reveals—she puts into words (into the Symbolic)—the secrets of the Magic Door, the Green Gate, the Rhyme, and Sylvia. What was shared only within the maternal semiotic with Mother, Young Grandmother, and Old Grandmother was for the first time verbal-ized to an-other. Budge responds, "'Aw, that sounds awful silly,'"(269). Then, when Marigold rejects these hurtful words and re-turns to her island within island within island, "Her lovely dream was gone" (269–70); "The old magic was gone forever—gone with Sylvia and the Hidden Land and all the dear, sweet fading dreams of childhood" (273). Even so, in a moment quite Wordsworthian, Mont-gomery tells us "there were compensations" (273) insofar as Marigold now knew that her ground—her place—was not to rival a boy's friends but, rather, to "be here for him to come back to" (274). But what kind of substitute is such stasis for the lost magic?

Of course, neither Silver Bush nor the Hidden Land through the garden door was literally an island. Although there are literal islands aplenty in Canadian women's writing, there are also places that seem sufficiently island-like to be worth noting. The rural small town is one such. Both the Manawaka of Margaret Laurence's *A Jest of God* (1966) and the Jubilee of Alice Munro's *Lives of Girls and Women* (1971) are is-land-like. They seem to offer protection from the chaos beyond; how-ever, they are smothering places. Chapter 5 examines these small town islands.

Both Rachel Cameron and Del Jordan feel smothered. As if to stress this smothering, Laurence houses Rachel with her aging mother on the second floor of what was once the father's funeral parlor and has the scent of embalming fluid waft in occasionally. Conversely, Munro offers the vivid scene in which Del's lover, Garnet French, nearly drowns her as he tries to baptize her forcibly in the river where they've been skinny-dipping after making love.

The two novels, furthermore, show Rachel and Del, through mirror images, what they might have become if they had allowed themselves to be trapped. Rachel's fellow teacher Calla and Del's girlhood friend Naomi succumbed completely to the insularity. For Rachel, teaching, enthusiastic religion, and casual sex--the escapes from suffocation of others--offer her little. She must literally escape. So, in the end, she leaves Manawaka (with her mother) aboard a bus bound for Vancouver and the expansive Pacific. For Del, Garnet French was a trap-- although an erotically pleasurable one. She flees the river he tried to baptize her in, runs through the graveyard where Jubilee's youth— symbolism ignored—make out and make love, and leaves Jubilee to pursue a career as a writer.

Just as the small rural town can be thought of as an island, so can Montreal, which literally is one, although the geographic fact is often overlooked when one scans the metropolis. Thus, Gabrielle Roy's *The Tin Flute* (1945) can be seen partially as an escape from the small town island to another island. Interestingly, this movement parallels that of Quebecois fiction in which Roy's 1945 novel represents the move from the oppressive provincial settings of Louis Hemon's *Maria Chapdelaine* (1916) and its progeny to the possibilities of the urban as well as that of many literal Quebecers who were heading for the island city. Although Roy's novel has these larger literary and social implications, it is more immediately the story of Roy's heroine, Florentine Lacasse. She is the daughter of Rose-Anna Lacasse, who had moved upon marrying from the rural village to the urban island, only to find that Montreal offered no escape. Daughter Florentine tries to escape from the urban poverty of Montreal's very insular Saint-Henri district to the glamour of the slightly less insular St. Catherine Street area in centre-ville. Although the novel focuses on Florentine, its structure compels the reader to draw the experiences of mother and daughter together and assess whether Florentine's escape to her island within the island of Montreal is any more successful than Rose-Anna's to the island city.

A similar retreat from an oppressive environment is made by Margaret Atwood's character Rennie in *Bodily Harm* (1982). She leaves Toronto, where she has been victimized in several ways, for peace and quiet on an obscure Caribbean island. Another similar retreat is made by Marie-Claire Blais's character Renata in *These Festive Nights* (1997), who also flees for the Caribbean. What links Florentine's story to Rennie's and Renata's is not geography, for Florentine's escape is nei-ther from urban terror nor to Caribbean tranquility. Rather, what links Florentine's story to that of Rennie and Renata is the horrifying fact that the islands all three escape to, Montreal's Rue St. Catherine, the twin islands of St. Antoine and St. Agathe, and Blais's unspecified spot, prove anything but idyllic. These three novels are the subject of Chapter 7.

The glamour proves illusory for Florentine. Pregnant, her lover gone, she marries a man she does not love. She thereby gains money, but not happiness. She seems just as trapped as she had been back in St. Henri. Back in St. Henri, her mother, Rose-Anna, serves as a mir-ror, suggesting what Florentine might have become and, despite her riches, probably did become. As the novel ends, Florentine "dazzled by their [her and her child's] prospects," "delighted at the turn of events"(383). However, Roy shifts the focus on the novel's last page to her new husband Emmanuel's very different vision—tortured tree branches, shriveled leaves, the dark clouds of an impending storm. He will suffer death in World War II; Florentine will suffer entrap-ment on the urban island that seemed to offer her and her mother and other Quebecers so much.

Floretine's fate is sad. Much more nightmarish is the island that traps Rennie in Atwood's *Bodily Harm*. Similarly to Lou in Engel's *Bear*, Rennie is oppressed in Toronto—by her kinky boyfriend, by a potential rapist, by her editor, by her surgeon/lover. So, to escape op-pression and recover from her mastectomy, Rennie travels to a remote Caribbean island—ostensibly to write a travel piece for her magazine. Once there, words fail her: Not only can't she find the words to write, but she can't read the words being spoken to her. She unwittingly be-comes immersed in the island's tumultuous politics, not knowing what anything or anyone stands for. The symbolic is collapsing all around her.

Eventually, Rennie becomes victimized by those politics when she thrown into a filthy third world prison. There, she realizes that Lora, a woman she had initially scorned, is her mirroring double. She furthermore sees in Lora's forced prostitution to earn them their keep and in Lora's beating and murder a mirror image of her own fate.

In contrast to Anne, Jane, Lou, Morag, Alice, and Atwood's unnamed narrator in Surfacing, Rennie's escape from the symbolic to the semiotic, from the oppressive more urban world to the green one, is not redemptive or even faintly so. Rather than distancing herself from language either playfully or critically (or somewhere in between), Rennie becomes lost in its collapse. Rather than *jouissance*, Rennie experiences violence, in which the erotic has been blasted by the pornographic. Rennie's island does not offer redemptive ascent; rather, it is a descent into the prison's cave-like shadows, falsely accused of crimes, separated from all who might help.

Strikingly similar to Atwood's Bodily Harm is Marie-Claire Blais' *These Festive Nights*. Blais's character is also named Renata, the long form of Rennie. Similarly to Rennie, she retreats to a Caribbean island after cancer surgery. She drinks in the pleasures of the seeming paradise, for "such was life, always demanding, distracting, numbing us with its pleasures" (279). However, she encounters many mirrors: socially aware artists, political activists, women torn between career and children, who, like her, struggle to find a role—an identity—in the world. Blais's canvas is larger than Atwood's: she manages to examine the criminal justice system in the U.S., revolution on Caribbean islands, white racism, black anger, American imperialism, war crimes against women in Bosnia, AIDS, nuclear accidents.

The world—the symbolic space—Renata, as a lawyer and woman, must deal with is deadly; Blais's tone is often apocalyptic. "...those dark January mornings would soon be here when, waking, they would weep endless tears, tears like those butterflies..., [which] would crumple silently in a candle flame, in lethal dust that would issue from the sky..." (155). However, the tone of Blais's book sometimes veers from that of apocalypse to that of carnival. Blais's prose-poem style blends the two, however, transforming a dichotomy of the symbolic into a wholeness of the semiotic. When Renata attempts to act, the symbolic rises and forces of society oppress; when Renata simply allows life to be, the symbolic recedes and a kind of *jouissance* emerges. When Renata (or the narrator) looks at past or present, the symbolic rises and forces of society oppress; when Renata (or the narrator) looks toward the future, especially at the children, the symbolic recedes and a kind of *jouissance* emerges. However, once recorded, "the faces of the innocent children seemed to harden" (284): the *jouissance* fades.

Style and meaning coalesce. In the semiotic, there is life; but fight as Renata and the book might, the semiotic yields to the symbolic. More precisely, it is in the symbolic that Rennie must find an identity that allows her to sustain life despite being surrounded by death. Escaping to the island is, only at moments, a refreshing retreat from this problem: the island cannot keep the terrors at bay.

The novel ends in song-and-prayer. Two children—one Black, one white; one female, one male; sexually attracted but in a pre-verbal way—sing, "O let my joy endure, O let my joy endure" (293). However, childhood ends, vacations end, escapes must end. The last several pages of Blais's novel contain some of the book's most hideously violent descriptions of Hiroshima, Dachau, prisoners used as human guinea pigs in Washington and Oregon. Renata, it seems, will go back and assume the role of jurist, one she at a gut level had found objectionable from the novel's first pages.

The fuller readings offered in the chapters that follow suggest that critical lenses as seemingly different as those provided by Frye and Kristeva can merge in a way that reveals much about Canadian women authors such as Montgomery, Laurence, Engel, Thomas, Atwood, Munro, Roy, and Blais. This list is certainly of diverse women—English and French, native-born and American-born, popular writers and elite writers, older and younger. That the island proves to be a recurring motif across this diversity is striking, leading me to assert the dominance of this mythos in Canadian women's writing. Clearly, different dimensions of theisland as symbolic place—as revealed through the critical lens of Frye and Kristeva—show up in the different works. The green world is especially striking in *Jane of Lantern Hill, Bear* and *Surfacing;* the semiotic-symbolic dialectic in *Anne of Green Gables, Intertidal Life,* and *Surfacing.* Mirror images are noteworthy in almost all, whereas the mother figure is especially compelling in *Mistress Pat, A Jest of God,* and *The Tin Flute. Jouissance* is a strong element in books as different on the surface as *Jane of Lantern Hill, Bear,* and *These Festive Nights.* Despite the varied ways Frye's island and Kristeva's semiotic space reveal themselves, there seems to be a core story implicit in all.

Audrey Thomas superimposes on the very personal narrative of *Intertidal Life* the story of explorers, discovering their islands. Their questions are at the core of these Canadian women's novels: does the island offer fresh water, does it pose new unanticipated obstacles, or is the journey in vain. This is the essence of the epigraphs from The Spanish Voyage to Vancouver that Thomas begins the three sections of her novel with. They will do nicely as a summary of the range of things the island proves to be in Canadian women's fiction—from a site for fresh water to the vanity of human wishes, from the true (albeit quite different) idylls of Montgomery's Anne and Jane and Engel's Lou to the disturbingly false idylls of Roy's Florentine, Atwood's Rennie, and Blais's Renata.

Notes

1. The structure of motif has been the subject of critical inquiry in the study of
    many literatures. Horst S. Daemmrich and Ingrid G. Daemmrich's two-
    volume *Spirals and Circles: A Key to Thematic Patterns in Classicism and Realism*
    (New York: Peter Lang, 1994) offers a good overview. E. R. Curtius's *Essays
    on European Literature* (Princeton, N.J.: Princeton UP), as well as other works
    by this critic, exemplify how the structure of motif illuminates a wide range
    of literary works. Very useful is Daemmrich and Daemmrich's *Themes and
    Motifs in Western Literature: A Handbook* (Tübingen: Francke, 1987), for it dis-
    cusses motifs such as "island" and "mirror" and how they generally func-
    tion in literature. Discussions of these particular motifs may be found in
    Gaston Bachelard's *Poetik des Raumes* (München: Carl Hanser, 1960); Bern-
    hard Blume's "Die Insel als Symbol in der Deutschen Literatur," which ap-
    peared in *Monatshefte* 41 (1949): 239–47; Horst Brunner's *Die poetische Insel:
    Inseln und Inselvorstellungen in der Deutschen Literatur* (Stuttgart: J. B.
    Metzlersche, 1967); and Ingrid G. Daemmrich's *Enigmatic Bliss: The Pardise
    Motif in Literature* (New York: Peter Lang, 1997).

2

Redemptive Retreats

L. M. Montgomery's "Anne Books";
L. M. Montgomery's *Jane of Lantern Hill*;
Marian Engel's *Bear*

Lucy Maud Montgomery is one of Canada's foremost authors, but literary historians have conspired—it would seem—not to give her her due. W. J. Keith's *Canadian Literature in English* (1985), for example, does not discuss Montgomery's work at all. Montgomery's problem with the literary historians is akin to her problem with both her readers and her initial publisher, L. C. Page of Boston, from 1908 on. In 1908, she published *Anne of Green Gables*. It was popular, especially with adolescent girls. Thus, she became identified in the minds of her public and her initial publisher as a writer of a lesser kind, as a writer of "young adult fiction." Then, though, both the public and her initial publisher wanted more books like *Anne of Green Gables*, preferably books that featured that novel's iconoclastic heroine Anne Shirley.

Thus began the series of "Anne books," which end with *Rilla of Ingleside* in 1920, a novel that focuses on Anne's daughter, not Anne.

Montgomery's correspondence, compiled in several volumes by Mary Rubio and Elizabeth Waterston, reveal how vehemently the author was opposed to writing more books about Anne. In August 1913, for example, she writes that she "began work on a third 'Anne' book. I did not want to do it—I have fought against it. But Page gave me no peace and every week brought a letter from some reader pleading for 'another Anne book'" (2, 133). In fact, she was under contract and desirous of pleasing her readers, and, therefore, along came *Anne of Avonlea* (1909), *Anne of the Island* (1915), *Anne of Windy Poplars* (1936), *Anne's House of Dreams* (1917), *Anne of Ingleside* (1939), *Rainbow Valley* (1919), and *Rilla of Ingleside*. (As the dates of publication reveal, she did not write the eight "Anne books" in the precise order Anne "lived" them.) As the correspondence also makes clear, Montgomery's level of engagement varied considerably from book to book. Sometimes, she "bit the bullet" and wrote a good piece of fiction; sometimes, she generated words and scenes and let the process drive her to the brink of an emotional breakdown. As a result, the "Anne books" vary enormously in quality. Furthermore, although perhaps none but the very first rise to the level of *Emily of New Moon* (1923), *Emily's Quest* (1925), and *Emily Climbs* (1927), three rather autobiographical novels Montgomery cared very much about and wrote between the initial six "Anne books" and the final two, there are good moments in all of the "Anne books," and both *Anne of the Island* and *Rilla of Ingleside* are noteworthy for their architectonics and their themes.

One of the themes that Montgomery sounds to varying degrees in all of the "Anne books" concerns Prince Edward Island as place. This message is so pronounced that, thanks to Montgomery and Anne, Prince Edward Island has become a major tourists' destination. Although Charlottetown is quaint and has a beautiful waterfront, many tourists quickly pass through the province's capital en route to Cavendish on the island's north shore. They flock to Cavendish because it is the real life version of Montgomery's Avonlea. Once there, they can stay in the Anne Shirley Motor Lodge or the Kindred Spirits Inn; they can eat at Marilla's pizza and tidy their things up at Matthew's laundromat, and they can visit a replica of the house Green Gables and tour a replica of Avonlea village. Kevin Sullivan's television adaptations of the "Anne books" as well as his CBC-produced television series "Avonlea" (which developed characters in

Montgomery's *The Story Girl* [1910] and *The Golden Road* [1910]) have certainly helped attract tourists to the Cavendish area, but the tourists were there long before Sullivan brought Montgomery's characters to a larger audience. Anne's popularity was accelerated not engendered by Sullivan's television productions.

These tourists flock to Prince Edward Island in general and Cavendish in particular because they want to see what was in Montgomery's famous books and because they want to absorb some of the magical atmosphere Montgomery attributes to the place. In *Anne of the Island*, the atmosphere helps Anne regain her bearings when the world of college and courtship off the island on Nova Scotia overwhelms her. In *Anne of Windy Poplars*, the atmosphere is desired— almost like punctuation marks—in the account Anne offers of her three years as principal at Summerside High School. She waxes grandiloquently about Avonlea's beauties; she longs for vacation times so she can be "a part of it again as if I had never been away" (12). In the later "Anne books," the atmosphere consoles many who are facing the pain of the losses suffered because of World War I. The island's power to comfort is present, however, from the very beginning of the series in *Anne of Green Gables*.

In that 1908 novel, Anne Shirley arrives at the farm home of Marilla and Matthew Cuthbert by mistake. They, an aging sister and brother, had requested an orphan boy who might help Matthew out with the farm chores. Anne manages to charm them, and she stays on. Anne wants so very much to be allowed to remain at the Cuthbert farm because it is beautiful and because it offers her redemption from what she has been since her parents' death, an orphan. She has lived a rather lonely life for a good number of years at an orphanage in Halifax with her mirror friends "Katie" and "Violetta." From there, she was sent to poor families who treated her as a domestic servant and denigrated her as an orphan. When the last family breaks apart and the orphanage does not want to take her back in, she is "posted" to Green Gables. The "posting" represents another chance, perhaps her last, to escape loneliness, find beauty, and overcome the stigma of an orphanage upbringing.

That stigma follows Anne to the island. Mrs. Rachel Lynde, presented as "the voice" of the Avonlea community, warns Marilla about orphans. She recalls the story of an orphan boy who "set fire to the house at night—set it on purpose, Marilla—and nearly burnt them to a crisp in their beds." She recalls the story of an orphan girl who "puts strychnine in the well…and the whole family died in fearful agonies" (15). She also taunts Anne with another verbalization that has evidently long haunted the girl—that she has very red hair. Given how Anne has been abused by words, one would think that perhaps she would be distrustful of them or negative toward them. One might even expect her to attack words in whatever manner a turn of the century pre-teen "deconstructionist" might. Anne's attitude toward words, however, is quite different.

Anne delights in words. She reads voraciously, and she tries to use words garnered from her literary explorations to color her ordinary life. She renames the path from the Bright River train station to Green Gables the "White Way of Delight"; she renames a pond she and Matthew pass as the "Lake of Shining Waters." She even wants Marilla and Mathew to call her "Cordelia," because of that name's beauty. When they refuse, she insists that they call her "Anne with an 'e,'" and they tolerate this tiny bit of beautifying by renaming. Later, she delights in declaring Diana Barry her "bosom friend," and, when they must part, she melodramatically asks Diana for "a lock of her raven tresses." She delights in referring to those who are attuned to the magical beauty of the island (and, thereby, to her) as "kindred spirits."

Anne's playful fascination with language never ceases, but it does become less effusive as she matures because "[t]here's so much to learn and do and think that there isn't time for big words" (253).

However, throughout her life, she refuses to surrender to the symbolic. Rather, she challenges it with her namings and renamings, lending something of the joy—maybe even the *jouissance*—of the semiotic to her inscriptions and reinscriptions. There may be implicit in what she does with language at least an attitude toward the patriarchy that has not seen the opportunity to impart beauty to things by naming them and has, instead, relegated much that might impart joy to the realm of the mundane or the ordinary, a realm that Marilla, who uses language spartanly, has accepted.

Anne's proto-feminist attitude toward male-inscribed language is also very much apparent in her actions. She does not acquiesce to an inferior place in the Avonlea classroom. Instead, she takes Gilbert Blythe on and ends up—a bit to her surprise—just as often ahead of him as right behind him at Avonlea School and then tied with Gilbert for the highest scores on the Queen's College admission test. She is at least partially motivated to challenge Gilbert in this manner because he verbally assaulted her early in her Avonlea schooldays by hurling the word "carrots" at her, making fun of her very red hair. She responded by breaking a slate over his head and, then, challenging Gilbert academically at every turn. This "battle" is softened somewhat by the fact that a romance is budding between the two of them—although readers and others in Avonlea see that long before Anne does. Nonetheless, she refuses to accept the place to which society has assigned her--as orphan and as female.

A similar spirit is apparent in her accepting Josie Pye's challenge to walk a house's ridgepole from which she falls and sprains her ankle. A similar spirit is also apparent in her excelling—perhaps even beyond the level of the guest "professional" elocutionist—in her interpretive reading of "The Maiden's Vow" and in her quick-thinking when the Barry baby fell gravely ill and Diana and the French Canadian babysitter did not know what to do to save the child.

Anne, in all of these scenes, is structurally the hero in Montgomery's novel. However, the time is the turn of the century. So it is not altogether surprising that Anne's heroism is somewhat limited to arenas that one might label as "feminine." In the scene in which she saves the

Barry baby, Anne does exactly what the male doctor would have done; however, she is depicted in more of the stereotypical nurse's role, soothing the feverish child as she fights throughout the night against the upper respiratory congestion that is threatening the infant's life. In Anne's schoolroom encounters with Gilbert, she excels in English while he excels in mathematics. At Queen's, she wins a prize in English literature while he wins an overall prize for scholarship. Moreover, her triumphant reading of "The Maiden's Vow," although lauded, falls nonetheless in the stereotypically feminine realm of "culture." Anne is heroic; Anne is iconoclastic. However, just as her "battle" with Gilbert is softened by the budding romance between them, so are the heroism and iconoclasm softened by the times the novel is set in.

Finally, an iconoclastic spirit is apparent in her refusal to enter into a romantic relationship with Gilbert Blythe despite her rather obvious attraction to the boy. She resists his overtures and scorns his attempts to express his admiration of and fondness for her. Even in the end of *Anne of Green Gables*, when Gilbert gives up the job at the Avonlea school so that Anne might take it and be able to stay at Green Gables and help Marilla, who, eyesight failing, is now alone after Matthew's sudden death, Anne treats the gesture as generous but very much retreats from acknowledging the love that is at its root. She knows that Gilbert's further education will be slowed by his having to pay for a room while serving the school in White Sands, but she avoids fully recognizing the sacrifice Gilbert has made for her out of love by affirming their friendship and suggesting that they might, on occasion, help each other along with the studies they will both pursue via correspondence. She is determined to succeed, and she is not going to let romance and marriage get in the way of that success. She will, books later, marry Gilbert Blythe, but before she accedes to becoming his wife, she will acquire a college education, pursue a career as a teacher, and achieve some success as a published author. Once married, she will be Gilbert's equal. Together they will raise their children. He will pursue his career as a physician with Anne's support;

she will play a leading role in the communities they inhabit with his support.

Looking back on Anne's story from our perspective at the beginning of the twenty-first century, we may not find Anne's social protest all that striking. In the terms of turn of the century Canada, it would have been. She was doing things few girls, especially from rural Prince Edward Island, did; she was making choices few would think to make. Anne, however, always did what she did without rocking the social structure of her community: her iconoclasm was of a restrained sort. She availed herself of the support of two of the community's respected women, Miss Stacy, the school teacher, and Mrs. Allan, the minister's wife, to help her get where she wanted. She refused to do anything against the wishes or the interests of Marilla and Matthew, earning begrudging respect from Mrs. Rachel Lynde. There was just something about the atmosphere of the Avonlea community that made this restrained iconoclasm possible. After a bit, Anne was Avonlea's Anne; therefore, if she wanted to do the atypical, well then, of course she could. The community members might shake their heads a little, but Anne was, after all, their Anne and therefore to be cheered-on. Such was the magic of this island place—that it would encourage not just tolerate her eccentricities and that it would (eventually) embrace in love someone who came to them a scorned orphan.

As Anne lived her island life, she had mirrors to look at in the persons of Gilbert Blythe and Diana Barry. She also had mirrors to look at in the older persons of Miss Muriel Stacy and Diana's Aunt Jo. In Gilbert, she saw the reflection of her own potential for academic excellence. This mirroring is reinforced by the times she and Gilbert were almost twinned in achieving academic successes. Their names were always, together, at the top of Avonlea School achievement lists. They tied for the highest score on the admission test to Queen's College; and once there, they each won a prestigious academic prize—prizes announced and cheered, within minutes, on the same day. In addition, they both ended up with teaching job offers in or near their home Prince Edward Island village. Once Gilbert began studying for a career in medicine, the twinning and the mirroring ceased. By then, though, Anne did not need the mirror image to help push her along.

In Diana Barry, Anne saw the personal warmth she was also herself capable of. As "bosom friends," they were linked together for a long time—even after Diana chose to steer a more domestic course than Anne was. This course suggests to Anne what she, one day, might do. As Gilbert mirrors the academic Anne that will blossom first, Diana mirrors the domestic Anne who will blossom books later in *Anne's House of Dreams*. The mirroring image of Muriel Stacy showed Anne that a single woman could pursue a career in education and achieve success and respect. The mirroring image of Josephine Barry worked in a somewhat similar manner: It showed Anne that a single woman could achieve a different kind of success, a financial one. These two mirroring images were necessary for Anne because the social pressure in the community was, of course, to marry. Anne needed to see that a husband was not necessary. However, the mirroring image of Aunt Jo also showed her that, if there was not eventually a man in her life, her single life could be quite lonely. Jo's image then served a dual purpose is guiding Anne's life. It inspired, but it also cautioned.

The most important mirror image for Anne is the missing maternal one. As an orphan, Anne does not have such an image available. Once she is at the Cuthbert farm, Anne might well look to Marilla to become a surrogate mother and become this necessary mirror image. Unfortunately, Marilla does not cooperate. She is stern, seemingly unloving, always on the verge of regretting her decision not to send Anne back. Marilla, we find out later in the novel, is actually a very loving person who was driven into her stern shell by a combination of her pride and an ill-fated romance. The romance was with John Blythe, Gilbert's father, who married another when Marilla's pride prevented her from responding favorably to John's attention. "We had a quarrel," Marilla tells Anne. "I wouldn't forgive him when he asked me to. I meant to, after awhile—but I was sulky and angry and I wanted to punish him first" (297–98). As we discover Marilla's past, we begin to see her as a rather exact mirror of Anne, for Anne is, perhaps, about to repeat Marilla's mistake and let her pride stand in the way of a loving relationship with John Blythe's son. Curiously, Marilla serves as a mirror in other ways as well. Early in both of their lives, Anne and Marilla were mocked for their unattractive appearance, something that Marilla was fifty before "the sting had gone out of that memory" (73); later, both Anne and Marilla will give up something to help a loved one along, Anne giving up the Avery scholarship to Redmund to stay at Green Gables and help Marilla; Marilla giving up marriage and motherhood to stay at Green Gables and help her unmarried brother along.

The scene where Marilla reveals some of this past to Anne moves their relationship forward closer to the point where it is a mother-daughter one. That scene occurs after Matthew dies and Marilla responds emotionally to Anne's decision to forego her university education and stay at Green Gables to help Marilla tend the farm. Marilla talks about how she had been over the years "kind of strict and harsh" and how she perhaps had not come across as being as loving as Matthew had. She adds that "[i]t's never been easy for me to say things out of my heart," and then tells Anne that "I love you as dear as if you were my own flesh and blood and you've been my joy and comfort ever since you came to Green Gables" (295).

As Marilla gradually opens up, Anne gains finally the mother image she never had. She is able to profit immensely from looking in the mirror Marilla provides. She sees in Marilla's strength and in Marilla's intense devotion to Green Gables qualities of character that she desires to make her own. She also sees that pride can prevent her, as it did Marilla, from blending fierce individualism with the sincere affection she and Gilbert clearly feel for each other. Thus, shortly thereafter, she will tell Gilbert she had long since forgiven him for taunting her years before at Avonlea School.

All of this drama occurs on the island. It is a place in *Anne of Green Gables* for the nurturing of Anne's being as well as the redemption of her spirit from the curse of being an orphan and, perhaps, the curse of having hair too red. I have already mentioned Anne's returns to the island in *Anne of the Island* and her return to the island within the island of Avonlea in *Anne of Windy Poplars*. These returns offer Anne necessary magic. Similarly, Anne and Gilbert choose to live their married life on the island to partake of that magic and to raise their children bathed in it.

The magic in Anne's life as an eleven-year-old orphan is very much contained within Green Gables, the farmhouse she arrives at desperately and passionately at the beginning of *Anne of Green Gables*. All of Montgomery's "Anne books" have geographical references in the titles. They form an interesting progression that is worth noting. Although they all associate Anne with her magical Prince Edward Island, they broaden and then they focus again as Anne's life does. The titles go from the house Green Gables to the village Avonlea to the entire island. Then, they go elsewhere on the island to Windy Poplars, and then they focus on Anne and Gilbert's House of Dreams and the Ingleside community they and their children inhabit. No matter though, whether it is Green Gables or the House of Dreams, Avonlea or Ingleside, or the island as a whole, there is a magic that continually both consoles and redeems.

One recalls Montgomery's "Anne books" as "light," but some of the problems raised in them are not. Matthew's death in *Anne of Green Gables* and what that might mean for Marilla and the farm is a serious matter, as is World War I, which is very much in the background of later books such as *Rainbow Valley* and *Rilla of Ingleside*. The background of Montgomery's much later book *Jane of Lantern Hill* is similarly ominous: instead of death and war, it features an oppressive older woman and potential divorce as the problems to be dealt with. The island, P.E.I again, offers redemption that is so powerful that it can overcome these problems and eventually be imported into Toronto to serve as a counterpoint to the older woman's city mansion.

Given both this uplifting message and the tight construction of *Jane of Lantern Hill*, it is surprising that readers and critics have turned to it only recently. The several "Anne books" held readers captivated so very long, and, then, the rather autobiographical Emily trilogy drew interest. *Jane of Lantern Hill*, as commentators have noted, deserves attention too.

Writing in the initial volume of *Canadian Children's Literature*, Jean Little asks "But What about Jane?" Her 1975 answer, however, represents only a small portion of her article. The article attempts to categorize all of Montgomery's fictitious children. After developing several categories, Little notes how Jane does not seem to fit because she is more "real" than Montgomery's other creations. Elizabeth Epperley's 1992 *The Fragrance of Sweet-Grass* focuses on the stories of Anne and Emily; then, in the study's last thirty-some pages, Epperley considers the rest of Montgomery's fiction and the other Montgomery heroines, including Jane. The character Jane as well as the novel's structure seem to be too much out of a fairy tale to suit Epperley's taste. Nonetheless, Epperley does extract some of the mythic elements of the story, for example, P.E.I. as a new Eden, and she does draw attention to the structural use Montgomery makes of houses in Jane of Lantern Hill as well as other Montgomery novels. My 1993 essay in *The American Review of Canadian Studies* treats all of Montgomery's fiction in chronological order. That order was necessary to show how the proto-feminist author struggles to find a nonpatriarchal form for her stories of girls and women. I treat *Jane of Lantern Hill* as a late failure. It is well-structured, unlike other late Montgomery works; however, its structure represents a concession to the marketplace. Montgomery chose a familiar structure that would appeal; unfortunately, in so doing, she chose a structure that reinforced many patriarchal assumptions. Diana Arlene Chlebek, writing in the 1999 collection *L. M. Montgomery and Canadian Culture*, which Epperly and Irene Gammel edited, focused on how Jane deals with marital discord and divorce, topics not common in juvenile literature. Chlebek is alert to both the autobiographical resonance of the novel (Montgomery's marriage was not a happy one) and the ways in which the island environment Jane creates on P. E. I. (and later in metropolitan Toronto) corresponds with some of what Northrop Frye writes about in *The Bush Garden* and elsewhere.

These critical assessments, although they seem different, offer a coherent picture of the book as the story of a real child facing real problems posed by characters both real and fairy tale-like who escapes to a magical, Edenic green world that redeems her and allows her to solve those real problems bringing about a happy ending that is structurally and emotionally satisfying but, perhaps, unrealistic. This reading of *Jane of Lantern Hill* suggests that Montgomery's use of the redemptive magic of Prince Edward Island "walks" a tightrope between real and fantasy that gives the book its particular tone.

The problem in *Jane of Lantern Hill* predates the novel's actual events. Something has soured the marriage between Robin Kennedy and Andrew Stuart. One gets the impression that four factors can be pointed to as bringing about the demise of this marriage. First, Andrew was too "romantic." He was a creature of a magical island, devoted to his writing, and unable to deal with some of the practical issues that necessarily surface in a relationship. Second, the younger Robin was immature, unable to know what she really wanted in life let alone to assert it. There was a beauty to the couple, but his idealism and her immaturity doomed the marriage almost from the outset. Third, their relationship was weakened by various jealousies: Robin's of Drew's work and his close relationship with his sister Irene; Drew's of the intimacy between Robin and their baby Jane. Fourth, Robin's mother, Mrs. Robert Kennedy, was opposed to the relationship from the beginning. Although she could not prevent the marriage, she could exacerbate the problems in the relationship so as to end it once her daughter was back in her Toronto household. Mrs. Kennedy reveals the pathological depths of her possessiveness when she declares "She [Robin] is my daughter…no outsider shall ever come between us again…" (207).

This Toronto household at 60 Gay Street is depicted in Montgomery's novel as horribly oppressive. Gay Street is described as "the most melancholy street in Toronto," as "dark and dingy, lined with forbidding, old-fashioned brick houses, grimy with age, whose tall, shuttered, blinded windows could never have thought of winking at anybody" (1). The house itself is described as having "towers and turrets wherever a tower or turret could be wedged in" and "surrounded by a high iron fence with wrought-iron gates" (1). It looks like an old castle in which Jane had "a very nasty feeling that she was a prisoner" (1). In this environment, daughter Robin is also trapped. In fact, it seems as if this entrapment is precisely what Mrs. Kennedy wants, for, if Robin stays put, Mrs. Kennedy can pretend as if time has stopped and she is not falling into the old age she fears. Andrew Stuart is, of course, a threat to this stagnant order, for he has encouraged Robin to fly away with him to his island. His imagination and his joy are also a threat, for 60 Gay Street is so strictly ordered that imagination is suppressed and joy is denied there.

Sixty Gay Street, serving symbolically as Montgomery's critique of urban life, is certainly not a very pleasant environment for a young girl. However, being very strongly attached to her mother, Jane feels secure there. She thinks she is happy, for she has her mother, her playmate Jody, and the physical comforts that money can buy. So, when Andrew exercises his right to have Jane spend the Summer with him on Prince Edward Island, Jane reacts in dismay. "Three months of absence from a beloved mother and three months' presence with a detested father seemed like an eternity to Jane" (51). Facing this prospect, Jane declared that "'God…is no good'" (48). Her dismay very much mirrors that of her grandmother. This mirroring suggests the extent to which Jane's mind has been shaped by Mrs. Kennedy's influence, even though Jane detests her g randmother.

Jane's journey to Prince Edward Island is described at some length and in considerable detail—right down to the names of the trains she takes. Perhaps Montgomery does so in order to have several opportunities to depict how Jane's spirits have sunk as she takes this forced journey. The long train journey, however, also establishes a psychological and physical distance between the world of 60 Gay Street that Jane has left and the world of Prince Edward Island that she is entering.

Once on Prince Edward Island, Jane's attitude toward the place gradually changes. She initially sees the island as "this rain-drenched land where the trees cringed before the wind and the heavy clouds seemed almost to touch the fields" (54). The next morning, however, she discovers many "lovely surprises": "far-off hills that seemed made of opal dust"; "brooks that appeared from nowhere and ran off into green shadowy woods where long branches of spicy fir hung over the laced water"; "a hollow of tipsy buttercups"; "a tidal river unbelievably blue" (65). She declares Prince Edward Island "a lovely place" and decides "that I should apologize to God" (69). Then, as she hunts with her father for a house for the two of them to live in, she discovers her own beautiful place on this beautiful island. They discover the little cottage on Lantern Hill that she will help her father fix up as their abode: It has the magic that he insists upon; for her, it "had a feeling of home" (76).

Once settled there, she takes on the house's domestic duties, and, in her free time, she explores the neighboring farms and nearby seashore and meets the country folk who reside nearby who, she thought, "were nicer, or at least more neighbourly, than the Toronto people" (86). She delights in all that she sees and in all whom she meets. She gradually acquires a magic herself that allows her to weave a strong sense of community among the folk who live close to Lantern Hill. In the novel, we read much about their adventures and games, and we hear various interpolated tales of their lives. Throughout it all, a joy suffuses, a palpable joy. This joy dominates the middle third of the novel, and although we can line up the events and the tales that help produce the joy, we sense that the joy is there even if we and Jane participated in no adventures and heard no words. We seem to have receded into semiotic space, and the joy that suffuses the space is that of *jouissance*.

In the countryside setting of Lantern Hill, Prince Edward Island, *jouissance* might seem the wrong word. After all, the word is rife with sexual suggestion. Even so, *jouissance* need not be sexual. It is a joy that emanates from being and from the body's being, and on Prince Edward Island Jane and her father are and as they work and play their bodies are. The innocent joy they experience may be closely allied to the sexual joy many associate with the word *jouissance*. Thus, critics have questioned the incestuous closeness that seems to develop between Jane and her father in their cottage where she, in many ways, plays the wife and he the husband. It is important, however, to note that, in the idyllic, Edenic island world Montgomery offers us, any such suggestion is clearly off the mark.

When in Toronto, Jane had a "moon secret." She had "buil[t] for herself an existence in the moon, where she ate fairy food and wandered through fairy fields, full of strange white moon-blossoms, with the companions of her fancy" (22). Jane "was supported through many a dreary day by the hope of going on a moon spree at night" (23). On Prince Edward Island, "the moon life had lost its old charm" (93), for the joy Jane had found through her imaginary sprees was available in the island's less rarefied atmosphere. Living on the island "was all like a fairy-tale come true" (100). Before the summer was out, "She and her Island understood each other," and she felt that she "belong[ed] here" (141) on P.E.I.

Jane returns to Toronto a very different person. She dreaded Prince Edward Island when she took her long journey eastward. Now she dreads the city on her long train journey back to 60 Gay Street. "She was reentering prison," she felt, as "[t]he great, cold, still house struck a chill to her spirit" (144). She returns to the city hoping to save her mother Robin from the oppression of the city and dreaming of the possibility of completing the family unit at Lantern Hill by adding her mother to it. However, rumors of various sorts get in the way—rumors about why Robin and Drew separated; rumors about a pending American divorce and a new marriage for her father. Then, once she is back on the island for the following summer, she falls ill and Andrew summons Robin to the child's bedside. In terms that come from fairy tales, they drink "from some deep well of life, and the draught had made them young lovers again" (216). They then defeat the evil grandmother, "stalking about 60 Gay, like a bitter old queen, her eyes bright with venom" (217). The princess-like Robin and princely Andrew can now live in the sunny cottage on the magical island. Jane, having herself been redeemed, has now served as the unwitting agent of her mother's redemption and the restoration of her mother and father's joy.

Robin in many ways mirrors Jane. Robin is child-like, under her mother's control, at 60 Gay Street. Robin is also trapped there as Jane had been: "There is no escape for either of us now" (33), she says early in the novel. However, that early, young Jane sees herself but not really her mother in this manner. Once Jane has been to Lantern Hill, she sees her mother's mirror image clearly. Then, having acquired a fuller understanding of who her mother is, she can separate her identity from that of her mother. In doing so, she not only defines herself as daughter to both Robin and Andrew, but she redefines her mother as not only her mother but Andrew Stuart's beloved wife and Mrs. Robert Kennedy's oppressed daughter. If there had been any incipient incestuous hints in the father-daughter relationship at Lantern Hill, then this process of separation and definition ends them by restoring Jane and Robin to their proper roles.

Robin is not the only mirror image Jane learns from in *Jane of Lantern Hill*. Her Toronto playmate Jody also mirrors Jane. Jody is the orphaned daughter of the former cook at 58 Gay Street, a boarding house. After her mother's death, the owners of the house allow Jody to stay on. "She slept in a little attic cubby-hole which was hot in the summer and cold in the winter, she wore cast-off things the boarders gave her" (17). She worked for her keep for the new cook. Her oppression is obvious to anyone who sees her bedraggled physical being. As a young child, however, Jane cannot conceive Jody's situation. A playmate is a playmate. However, Jane "was conscious of ...those appealing eyes," eyes that were "very dark and very sad" (15). Gradually, Jane sees Jody's plight more clearly. Then, she comes to see Jody's oppression as analogous to her own. Jody then functions in the novel as a physical analogue to Jane's more psychological oppression. Jane cannot fully see this connection—cannot clearly see what the mirror image is—until she has been to Prince Edward Island and experienced the island's redemptive joy. Upon her return from the island, Jane more clearly understands Jody's tragic situation. Then, when it looks as if Jody is bound for the orphanage, Jane tries to act on Jody's behalf and arrange an island adoption for her. Jody's redemption through this adoption by two spinsters takes her to the magical island. It mirrors Jane's earlier redemption on P.E.I. and Robin's future redemption there.

The plot of *Jane of Lantern Hill* is such that Robin and Andrew and Jane cannot live happily ever after on Prince Edward Island. Despite the novel's fairy tale elements, reality does intervene and complicate matters as Andrew accepts a job as assistant editor of Saturday Evening in Toronto. Thus, the final question in the novel is whether the renewed relationships among Robin, Andrew, and Jane can be sustained in the urban environment. The question is answered through their choice of place to reside in the Toronto area. They reject close-in houses, such as 60 Gay Street. Rather, they choose a very wooded home on the outskirts of the city, a home Jane had long admired and "knew at first sight...belonged to her" (164). "It was built of grey stone and had casement windows...some of them beautifully unexpected...and a roof of shingles stained a very dark brown. It was built on the edge of the ravine overlooking the tree tops, with five great pines just behind it" (164). The choice of this lakeside home is clearly an attempt to lend something of the rural magic on Prince Edward Island to their city abode. They cannot reside on their island; however, they can make their off-the-island home as much like an island home as possible. In fact, they can make it live as Lantern Hill lived and as 60 Gay Street, as passersby noted early in the novel, did not.

Montgomery's novels, whether written for adolescent girls or for a larger audience, offer an innocent beauty—so much so that one feels that the charge of incipient incest directed at Andrew and Jane at Lantern Hill is just plain wrong. Sex is simply not an issue in Montgomery's fiction. Marian Engel's 1976 novel *Bear* is a very different story. As most know, the novel, written curiously while Engel was summering on Prince Edward Island, chronicles the increasingly intimate relationship between a thirty-some year old woman named Lou and a bear. Most read—at least partially—to see how far this relationships goes. The novel has inevitably evoked prurient snickers, but it has also evoked serious commentary.

Engel rather heavy-handedly signals that Lou is changing as the story progresses and has changed by the time she leaves the bear behind and returns to Toronto. Thus, most commentary has focused on the nature of this transformation. Playing off the few comments Engel offers about Lou's life as librarian in the city, many commentators have defined the change as movement along a bipolar course: from fragmented to integrated (Hair), from unnatural to natural (Cameron), from methodically rational to unmethodically irrational (Hutchinson), from controlled to wild (Harger-Grinling and Chadwick), from love as defined within phallocentric discourse to love as defined outside it (Rubenstein, "Animal" 124, 133). Just a bit different from these approaches at pinpointing the transformation is Osachoff's, for she sees Lou pursuing the wrong course by reading the human into the bear. Lou then must admit "the bearness of bear," retreat from his embrace, and pursue a third course toward nature as nature (19-20). Within most of these structures offered to describe Lou's journey, the bear acquires a symbolic presence that, once grasped, transforms the novel itself from border-line pornography to literature. Along the way, commentators have noted other dimensions of symbolism in *Bear*, most notably how the bear and the late Colonel Cary are Lou's doubles (Cameron 86; Hair 42) and how the octagonal house on Cary Island represents the perfect merging of circle and square and all those geometric configurations might represent (Hair 36). The symbolic possibilities of the island setting, however, have only been glanced at by Osachoff, who notes Lou's desire for isolation, on Cary Island and in her life in Toronto (15).

Commentators have discussed Engel's novel within various contexts. Its thematic concerns link it to other works of Canadian literature (Cameron 88; Hair 34-35; Osachoff 21). The way the novel positions itself parodically vis-á-vis oppressive or potentially oppressive genres link it to women's writing in general which often is double-voiced, following the conventions of a genre while undermining it (Fee 20; Howells, "On Gender" 72; Rubenstein, "Animal" 123-24). Bear has not, however, been contextualized within the territory one gets if one focuses on the intersection of these two contexts, Canadian women's writing. Many have been quick to note connections between Engel's novel and Margaret Atwood's *Surfacing* (Cameron 86, 92-93; Hair 35; Osachoff, 13, 18; Rubenstein, "Animal" 131). The connections discussed are, strangely, that of theme (both deal with the natural versus the unnatural) and that of plot (both heroines mate or attempt to mate with very hairy creatures). Commentators, however, have not noted how both Engel's novel and Atwood's share a similar setting—that of an island—with many other novels by Canadian women. This setting—and how female characters retreat to it—is not incidental, as this study attempts to demonstrate.

Finally, commentators have seen in Engel's story elements that evoke Frye and Lacan, although these critics have not pushed the evocations very far. Harger-Grinling and Chadwick place the novel's bear, as an instance of "the figure of the wild animal,""[i]n Lacanian terms...in the realm of the Symbolic," thereby shutting the door on the possibility that the novel leads Lou into the Semiotic, which is the argument I will shortly offer (55). Cameron sees the contrasting urban and rural worlds of the novel in wintry and summery terms and evokes a bit of what Frye's says, for example, about midsummer's eve, in discussing Lou's summer adventure on Cary Island (84-85, 93). Cameron does not, however, very thoroughly explore Frye's mythos of summer or the late phases of his adjoining mythoi, spring and fall, which also seem relevant to the novel's story. The argument I will offer will be more fully attentive to Frye's observations about the patterns of literature.

Bear begins with its heroine Lou in Toronto. However, in the course of the novel, we are taken further back into Lou's life. These glimpses help explain why she is the way she is at the novel's beginning. The novel is in some ways a puzzle. These glimpses are clues,casually dropped into the story the third person narrator offers us.

As Lou makes her way to Cary Island, she remembers once upon a time being in a similar scene. She recalls "something sad happening," "some loss" (19). Once she is on the island and has had her first physical contact with the bear, she remembers a time when, so very lonely, she picked up a man in the street—a total stranger—and took him home for sex. She vaguely recalls that "he had turned out not to be a good man" (64). Much later, not too long before she attempts to have sexual intercourse with the bear, she remembers when she was "a half child" at a school dance. She recalls "being held to a man's body" and feeling "flushed, confused, and guilty" (114). Finally, right before she attempts sexual intercourse, she remembers a charming lover who abandoned her for someone smaller, neater, more energetic, and more subservient. She also recalls how this elegant lover forced her to have an abortion, causing her genitalia—as he saw them—to lack the neatness of his new younger lover. She recalls her rage at his desertion; she also recalls her sexual frustration afterwards.

The reader cannot be certain; however, there are clues in these flashbacks of sexual abuse—perhaps even rape—when Lou was young. These early experiences of her body—in particular, its sexuality—would have inevitably left her with a negative sexual self-image. Her later experiences with the stranger she picked up and brought home and the lover who forced her to have an abortion would have deepened this image. Nonetheless, she has strong sexual desires. Thus, she finds herself, as a young woman, disliking her body but nonetheless satisfying its sexual needs but in degrading ways that lower her sexual self-image even further.

Thus, when we meet her at the novel's beginning, we are told that "she lived like a mole" in the basement of the Historical Institute (11). Her skin was "slug-pale"; her fingers "grained with old, old ink" (12). She was "lonely, inconsolably lonely," for men were not drawn to her for they "knew that her soul was gangrenous" (92). Her sexual yearnings caused her to yield weekly to the Institute's director on her desk. She felt no affection for the man, and "it horrified her to think of" sex with him (93). She describes it as masturbation, and, having tried cucumbers and other devices suggested in Aristophanes' *Lysistrata*, she found the director's penis preferable.

This mole-like, self-deprecating, libidinous woman is the Lou who heads off to Cary Island at the beginning of *Bear*. The Historical Institute had just inherited the estate of the late Colonel Cary. Lou's task on the island was to catalogue the estate. Since the Historical Institute was short on funds, the Director's hope was that Lou would find valuable treasure. Ironically, Lou will find such treasure, but it will not be anything of use to the Director or the Institute. She will find the natural, beautiful body and the natural, beautiful sexuality she had long ago lost.

As Lou approaches Cary Island, she is struck by its new greenness. Engel is not at all subtle when it comes to symbolism. Thus, the reader rather readily sees that the island is a place of potential rebirth. She recalls vacations to northern Canada with her parents; she recalls going out in a large ship to an island on one of these excursions. The paths were "obscured by poison ivy plants as tall as herself." She remembers being "riveted by the skeleton of the biggest dragonfly in the world, caught in a spider web in a cabin window, sucked dry"(18). The island as a place then may just as readily be a place of poison and death as of rebirth. The island is ambiguous: it might be Eden, but it might be Hell.

Thus, when Lou finally arrives on Cary Island in the dusk, we know neither what kind of island nor what kind of story to expect. There is an eerie quality to the darkening island and the dank atmosphere of the octagonal house a previous Colonel Cary had built. There is also, Lou finds out after she's escorted to the island and is on the verge of being left alone there, a bear.

The dawning of the next day dispels the ominous hints of the night before. Lou and the reader begin to become acquainted with Cary Island. It is a fecund place, not to be readily regulated by any gardener. The wild growth is lush, exhaling earthy smells. Mushrooms, described as phalluses, pop up here and there. A muskiness—described by Lou as "good" (24)—pervades the house. The "muskiest" thing of all was, of course, the bear. Just as the island itself seems incipiently sexual, so does the bear—at least as Lou sees him. The earthiness of both place and its furry inhabitant draw Lou to them. Gradually, she becomes increasingly comfortable with this earthiness.

Engel signals this progression in at least three ways. First, she depicts Lou as becoming increasingly at ease on the island. Second, she has Lou comment explicitly several times on the transformation she was undergoing. Third, she has Lou become more and more intimate with the bear. If we trace the second and third progressions together, we acquire a good sense of where Engel is taking her heroine.

Before Lou even arrives on Cary Island, she notes that she has "an odd sense...of being reborn" (19). This rather heavy-handed forecast is followed by her meeting the bear, unchaining him, swimming in the nude with him, and letting him into the house. The bear, through this sequence of events, is serving very much as a mirror image for Lou. In his physicality, he emblematizes the bodily side of her being that Lou loathes even as she tends to its needs. As she sets the bear free, she sets this side of her being free; as she swims in the river with him, she cleans away the objectionable earthiness of his body, leaving behind a natural muskiness she will wrap herself in. She will wrap herself in it as she absorbs the scent into her flesh from the animal's fur. As she lets the bear into the house, she merges a dichotomy signaled in the novel by the estate's two buildings.

The elder Colonel Cary built a two-story octagonal house, the top story of which housed his extensive library. This house seems structured along human lines: The intellectual functions at the top; the spoken-of bodily functions (e.g. eating, sleeping) on the ground level; the unspoken-of bodily functions in the out-buildings. Of course, the bear was out among the out-buildings, the placement suggesting his identification with those bodily functions. Lou, of course, gravitates to the upper level, for her work at the Historical Institute is cerebral. Then, one night as she's working, the bear finds his way into the house and up to the library. Symbolically, the physical—even its coarser dimensions—and the intellectual merge at this point. Lou is initially uncomfortable with the bear's intrusion. Gradually, she becomes comfortable with him and the physical side of her life that the bear mirrors—so comfortable she even dances with him.

The novel will very soon turn quite sexual. Before we follow that turn, we should note how this coming to terms with one's body is presented in androgynous not male-female terms. The bear is described in the novel as female more than as male. As later scenes will make apparent, the bear is anatomically male. However, at this stage in the novel, Lou describes him as "a middle-aged woman" (36) and "a large-hipped woman" (69). Lou's name suggest her androgyny. We find out that the last Colonel Cary was a female who legally acquired the first name "Colonel" because her father's will stated that only a "Colonel Cary" could inherit the estate. Lou's guide-to-the-island Homer (named ironically after the poet who guided and misguided Odysseus from island to island) termed the last Colonel Cary "an imitation man, but a damned good one" (81). Engel's insistence on androgyny—in depicting Bear, Lou, and the late Colonel Cary—alerts us to the fact that it is the body in all of its physical manifestations as well as in its physical and intellectual wholeness that Lou first becomes comfortable with. Once she acquires this comfort, she is ready to continue on her redemptive journey.

Once she is comfortable, then she can truly love. The novel is far too rich to be reduced to cliché, but the novel does demonstrate, at this juncture in the story, that one cannot love others until one loves one's self. Lou's dancing and playing with the bear is emblematic of her joy in her own physical being insofar as the bear serves as a mirror. Still alive with this joy, Lou thinks of some of bear lore that is sprinkled, like clues to a puzzle, through the Cary books she is cataloguing and how bears have been historically "baited, flayed, pursued." The thought was "agony" to her, so she prayed for her bear. Through that prayer she demonstrated her love of her fellow creatures. To highlight the moment, the narrators tells us that Lou "had not prayed in years" (65).

Now comfortable with her body and now able to love, Lou is ready for the next step: to form a relationship based on love. Given her previous experiences with men, this step will prove to be very difficult for her. She recognizes the maleness of her androgynous bear and chooses him as partner. Why? Despite the danger he poses because he is, after all, a wild animal, he seems much safer than the men she has known. He also, unlike the men in her life, offers much and asks for so very little. He gives her the warmth of his pelt; he gives her the length and texture of his tongue. He "asks" for food, a place to rest, and—perhaps—a degree of freedom. The relationship is thus a very comfortable one for Lou to embrace; however, it does not answer all of her needs, as she demonstrates when she attempts to have sexual intercourse with the bear.

Afterwards, she felt "guilty"; she felt "empty and angry" (122). She knew that she had crossed a line. Moreover, like Adam and Eve, after they sin in their paradise, Lou "knew she had to hide" (123). She chooses to hide in the water. She identifies the water as that of the womb; she tries desperately to be reborn out of this water. She wants to enter the world anew from the semiotic space she has retreated to; she also desires a baptism that will wash away the sin of bestiality she has tried to commit. The narrator tells us she spent her time in the water "pretending to be born" (123). The phrase suggests imaginative play, but it also suggests that she has not really achieved either rebirth yet.

It is at this point in the novel that Lou turns to Homer for sex. Engel makes it easy to see that he is substitutes for the bear. When they kiss as they have sex, she note the ridge of his upper dental plate and how it is like the palate of the bear. She also notices Homer's two missing teeth, much like those of the bear. The narrator tells us, seemingly contradictorily, that sexual intercourse with Homer "excited" her and that "she felt nothing with him, nothing" (126). We are supposed to read that seeming contradiction as meaning she felt physical but not emotional pleasure. Afterwards, Lou goes back to the island and cries. She laments that she "only want[s] to love him," and the "him" was the bear, not Homer. However, that night, because the bear "smelled man on her" (127), he would not come near her.

Then, the story poses another puzzle. Summer is yielding to autumn, and the bear is readying his body for hibernation. Her quest for a relationship with the bear seems to have reached its end. Then, suddenly, the bear's penis grows erect and Lou gets down on all fours before him, offering her vagina to him. However, rather than enter her, he swipes at her back with his claw, tearing her flesh from her shoulder to her buttock. She becomes enraged and scared. In addition, very clearly, in her mind the bear becomes very much just a bear. One would think that she would re-experience the guilt she felt after she tried to mount the bear's flaccid penis days before. She experiences a swirl of emotions, but Engel's language after this incident is anything but negative.

No longer needing bear (or Homer) as mirror, Lou looks in a real mirror and sees herself. She sees that she is "different" from what she was before she journeyed to Cary Island. "She seemed to have the body of a much younger woman. The sedentary fat had gone, leaving the shape of ribs showing" (134). Also showing was the mark the bear had made with his claw on her back. She notes that she "shall keep that," and she also notes that "it is not the mark of Cain." Her thoughts imply that being clawed by the bear taught her something worth holding on to; furthermore, her thoughts imply that what she has learned is not the costs of sin.

On the islands Frye discusses, the islands of romance, the throwing off of animal disguises is a conventional way of symbolizing the return from the retreat. Throughout *Bear*, we see Lou enveloped in the fur of the bear almost as if wearing his fur as a disguise. When he claws her, she orders him out. It is almost as if she is at that point throwing the disguise aside. That moment is, in Frye's terms, a moment of profound recognition. So what has she recognized? What does the scar down her back suggest to Lou?

It is important to keep in mind that whatever has happened (and whatever has been learned) happened in the semiotic realm, a realm that is by definition outside language. Thus, it is not altogether surprising that Lou cannot and we cannot put what was recognized and what was learned into words. The narrator tells us that "What had passed to her from him [Bear] she did not know" (136). However, she did, within her body, feel it. "She could feel in her pores and the taste of her own mouth that she knew what the world was for" (137). As a result of this unvoiced knowledge, she felt "[c]lean and simple and proud" (137). Later, she recalled the bear's clawing as "heal[ing] guilt" and felt "strong and pure" (140).

3

Holding Patterns

Margaret Laurence's *The Diviners;* Audrey Thomas's *Intertidal Life*

Montgomery's Prince Edward Island and Engel's Cary Island are indeed places of redemption. As the remainder of this study will discuss, islands do not always figure in the writing by women of Canada in such an unambiguously positive way. As later chapters will suggest, islands can be traps, as well as very ambiguous places—offering hints of redemption, possibilities of entrapment, and other things. Two of the richest portrayals of this ambiguity are Margaret Laurence's *The Diviners* and Audrey Thomas's *Intertidal Life.*

Other female characters who write are discussed in this study: Anne Shirley of L. M. Montgomery's *Anne of Green Gables* and Rennie Wilford of Margaret Atwood's *Bodily Harm.* However, their wrestling with words is not foregrounded the way it is in *The Diviners* and *Inter-*

tidal Life. Laurence's Morag Gunn and Thomas's Alice Hoyle truly wrestle with language, with the symbolic realm. This wrestling gives these novels part of their richness. Morag and Alice feel compelled to come to terms with language, if not control it. That need drives them back into the semiotic realm. They both seem to think that the semiotic is to be found in an island retreat. They both come to realize that the island is at best a way station until they are capable of finding the semiotic through solidarity in opposition to oppression, through non-hierarchical relationships, through the maternal, through the frankly sexual, and by coming to terms with the problems posed by the symbolic and the world it defines.

Laurence's Morag Gunn spends close to thirty years of her life trapped. She has just a few vague memories of her early life as the daughter of a middle-class couple living in the prairie town of Manawaka. In many ways, this early life was Edenic, but what was Edenic was less the day-to-day life with her parents, which Morag cannot really recall, and more the imaginary backyard playland populated with imaginary playmates that Morag retreated into. Her need for this retreat is a disturbing sign that there are incipient threats in life that a young girl simply "feels," threats that necessitate fleeing into fantasy, a fantasy that can become debilitating (as we'll see in L. M. Montgomery's two "Pat" books and her *Magic for Marigold*). In Laurence's novel, the fantasy world is not allowed to become debilitating, for it is abruptly shattered when young Morag's parents die in a polio epidemic. Morag then leaves her middle-class Manawaka world and goes to live "on the other side of the tracks" with Prin and Christie Logan. Prin is sweet, but slovenly and "slow"; Christie is the much-abused "scavenger" —or trash collector—of Manawaka. Prin and Christie offer Morag what they can, but, a social outcast at school and in the town, Morag desperately wants to get away from Manawaka. Using a plot device that some have found improbable, Morag finds her way out: Using money that just happened to be set aside for her by a family friend when her parents died, she goes off to the university in Winnipeg.

Free at last, Morag finds a way to entrap herself once again. She allows herself to be seduced into marriage by her thirty-some year-old English professor, Brooke Skelton. With him, she goes off to Toronto, where he has secured a more prestigious academic appointment as he begins his rise to a university presidency.

Marriage gives Morag many of "the things" she never had growing up; it also gives her status. The marriage, however, does not give her fulfillment. Brooke treats her like a child—even referring to her as such during sex. Furthermore, he acts as if she were clay that he might mold into whatever he wants in a wife. She is compelled to abandon her education and devote herself to maintaining Brooke's home and helping along Brooke's career by looking and acting the role of an aspiring academic's wife. As their married life progresses, Morag begins to resent the way she is treated and is being shaped. She is not a child, she tells Brooke; and she wants something in life more than being *his* image of the model wife. She wants to be a mother, and she wants to be a writer. The first he denies her, without offering much by way of explanation; the second he "allows" her, intent upon controlling her "career" by belittling her work. Control is very much what Brooke feels he must have—in all aspects of his life. He even controls Morag's sexual fulfillment by ritualistically asking her if she's been "a good girl" before allowing her to experience orgasm. His need to control Morag suggests that he may be, at base, a very insecure man. In fact, as Wainwright notes, he seems to finding Morag's writing career unusually threatening, and it is her "good news" that her first novel has been accepted for publication that leads to their most violent fight.

Morag plays an innocent role when Brooke first courts her. However, she has had a lover prior to Brooke, "half-breed" Jules Tonerre, who comes from a segment of the Manawaka population inferior to Prin and Christie, the *Metis* who trace their origin to an intermingling of French and Native North American blood in the days before Confederation. As Morag approaches the breaking point in her relationship with her husband Brooke, she meets Jules again in Toronto. Morag leaves Brooke for the many reasons outlined in the previous paragraph, but the catalyst is Brooke's rude, racist treatment of Jules. Perhaps that treatment of Jules as inferior "other" —as an "Indian" to whom it might be illegal to give a glass of his Scotch whiskey—made her see that she, as a woman, was also an inferior "other" in Brooke's eyes. Jules may then serve as one of the many mirrors with whom Laurence populates the novel. Upon leaving Brooke's posh penthouse apartment, she chose Jules's bed in a shabby rooming house. She also chooses to conceive a child with Jules, thereby sealing her departure from entrapment in marriage to Brooke.

Jules's story is rather fully told by Laurence in *The Diviners*. We learn about his *Metis* ancestors who nobly resisted the Canadian desire to control the plains; his father, who worked desperately to provide very little for his many children; and his sister, who died with her children when their shack caught on fire. We follow Jules through school, where he maintained a rebellious aloofness; through military service in World War II, where he earned glory but not recognition; and through a career as an itinerant folk singer and folk song writer. He offers Morag little stability, but he never claims he would or could. He allows her to decide about conceiving a child, and, as their daughter grows up, he is involved in her life only occasionally. He offers Morag little as life partner or father of daughter Pique; however, he does liberate her, for he gives her back control of her body (Buss 104).

So the story of *The Diviners* is not the story of Morag's departure from one man—Brooke—for another—Jules. In fact, as Greene notes, Laurence seems to rather consciously reject the "two suitors" convention of much of women's fiction, making Morag's choice be between the controlling Brooke and the terrifying unknown, not between Brooke and Jules ("Margaret Laurence's *Diviners*" 170). *The Diviners* then is the story of Morag's departure from the traps of, first, Manawaka and, second, marriage. What Morag ultimately departed *to* is less clear: many, many pages will show us Morag trying to craft this destination for herself.

As far as literal place is concerned, Morag leaves Toronto for Vancouver—passing through but not stopping in Manawaka en route. In

Vancouver, she tries to raise a child and make enough money to get by by writing. Some of the writing she is proud of; some of it, however, is hack work, taken on solely to pay the bills. While in Vancouver, Morag interacts with exotic dancer Fan Brady. Fan serves as a mirror for Morag insofar as they are both doing what they can to get by and trying to give their work as creative a touch as possible. Interacting with Fan seems to prompt Morag to reflect on other women's stories, those of her childhood friend Eva, her high school acquaintance Julie Kazlik (who is in Vancouver), and her college friend Ella. This section of the novel more than any other tells the stories of the lives of girls and women. In fact, this section departs in style from the preceding one. The preceding one, as Hunter notes, was flat, and it was focused rather narrowly on Brooke and Morag's troubled marriage. It lacked the intertextuality of the earlier parts of the novel; it lacked a sense of community gained by telling more stories than just those of the central character. After leaving Brooke Skelton, both the intertextuality and the multiplicity return. So does a touch of Morag's slangier Manawaka language, something she suppressed when she was with the more cultured Brooke.

Although Morag learns a great deal about the common plights experienced by women in a male-defined world during her time in Vancouver and although she regains the openness implicit in the "freer" prose style, she feels that what she must learn, about writing and about herself, is ultimately not to be acquired in Canada. So, she and her young child go off to England. On that island, she hopes to be surrounded by writers and artists and, from them, learn a great deal about her chosen craft. Furthermore, on that island, she hopes to track down her ancestral origins in the Sunderland district of Scotland and find out about who she is.

Quite a few who have commented on Morag's trip to England talk about it, quite explicitly, as a trip to an island. However, it is easy to overlook it as such. Unlike Prince Edward Island, it is not called one, and, unlike the fictitious Cary Island, it is neither called one nor easily navigable, by canoe or by foot. That it is easy to overlook the off-to-the-island pattern in Laurence's novel should not diminish the pat-

tern's presence in the book. In fact, what Frye says about "displace-
ment" of myths suggests that, as literature becomes more sophisticated, patterns and conventions he associated with the basic *mythoi*
that define literary expression will become increasingly obscured. It is
well worth noting, however, that Laurence herself draws attention to
Morag's island journey by titling one of the memorybank movies
"Sceptr'd Isle" (293).

The U. K. does not, however, prove to be the inspiring island Morag
had anticipated. She is not immersed in a colony of highly cultured
writers. Instead, she's pretty much on her own. She does, however,
find time to write. The job she takes in a bookstore is not *that* time-
consuming. Her only significant interactions while there, other than
those with daughter Pique, are with lover Dan McRaith. He is a
painter, not a writer. Nonetheless, he is a fellow creative soul. Like
Morag, he journeys to London so that he can paint. Most commentators on the novel devote much more attention to Jules than to Dan.
Because Jules has a presence throughout the phases of Morag's life
and because he is Pique's father, this attention is warranted. However, Dan may play a more important role in directing Morag's life
than Jules.

Whereas Jules mirrors Morag's social marginalization, Dan mirrors
her artistic longings. Dan's story reveals the paradox that the artist
needs both rootedness and rootlessness. The artist must be connected
to a place, and that place will provide the artist with both subject matter and a sense of identity. Conversely, the artist needs distance from
that place. While they are in London, Morag recognizes Dan's—and
thus the artist's—rootlessness. When they go to his home in Scotland,
Morag discerns the rootedness. She had thought that perhaps her
roots were to be found in the Sunderland district of Scotland. In fact,
she and Dan had planned a side trip to the ancestral land of clan
Gunn. Seeing the extent to which Dan's roots were entangled with the
people in Crombruach makes Morag realize that the Sunderland district is merely a place. The people with whom her roots are entangled
went to Canada and are in Canada. These people have kept Scotland
alive as myth, and that myth is important to them. However, it is not

to be found by journeying to Scotland; rather, it is to be found in the hearts and souls of these Canadians (Carolan-Brozy & Hageman; Greene, "Margaret Laurence's *The Diviners*"; Thieme 155-57). "'It's a deep land here, all right,' Morag says. 'But it's not mine, except a long long way back.'" When Dan asks her what land is, she replies "Christie's real country. Where I was born" (319).

Morag certainly would have found it difficult to return to London and resume the affair with Dan. She could no longer easily push aside "Dan's wife," for she now has etched in her mind an evocative picture of Bridie. However, this inability to resume the affair is not the reason Morag leaves England. She leaves because Canada, its myths and realities, is home. The British island does not offer her what she has hoped—what she has thought—it would. The island is probably not the "psychic shelter" Wainwright describes it as either (305). Although it did keep her safe and sane, it also taught her a great deal about where her art and her being were rooted.

So, she returns to Canada and—more precisely—to Manawaka. Once there, she begins the process of re-embracing. Growing up there, she has scorned her adoptive parents Prin and Christie. She now re-embraces the memory of Prin, who has died in the intervening years, and the person of Christie Logan, who was dying. She tells him, "'Christie—I used to fight a lot with you, Christie, but you've been my father to me'" (323). She especially re-embraces the Scottish heritage she had been offered by Christie. What is factually true and what is not about this heritage really does not matter; it is the story that matters: the forced departure from Scotland, the arrival on the Hudson Bay's shore, the trek overland from near Churchill to near Winnipeg, the valorous fighting in battles noble and ignoble. Jules's legends—passed to him by his father Lazarus—contradict both Christie's and those in the schoolroom history books. Facts aside, Jules's story is, like Christie's, a story of dispossession and, in the face of it, heroic survival. So Morag merges Jules's story with Christie's and embraces this as that of the people—all of them—her roots are entangled with. They are all Manawaka, and, although the different social classes and ethnic groups there try to pretend they are separate,

they are really linked. The fiery death of Jules's sister Piquette, for example, of course, affects the Tonerres, but it also affects Niall Cameron, who buries her; and Morag, who covers the tragedy for the Manawaka newspaper; and Morag's daughter Pique, who is named in
Piquette's honor.

Back in Canada, Morag re-embraces Jules as he is dying of throat
cancer. At the riverside cabin in Ontario that she has chosen to live
and write in, she also re-embraces Pique. *The Diviners* is structured
around parallel stories: one in the present; the other in the past. The
"past" story has drawn my attention thus far, but, in each chapter, before we are taken back to Morag's past in "Memorybank movies," we
are told about the present, especially about the strained relationship
that exists between mother and daughter in this present time. Pique
is a late teenager dealing with all of the issues a late teenager does —
and then some. This is, after all, the early 1970s, and Pique is experiencing adolescence at a time when a counter culture was pronounced,
drug use and uninhibited sex were common, and "traditional" values
and authorities were scorned. On top of all of this, Pique is struggling
with what her mixed (*Metis* and Scottish-Canadian) heritage means
for her. She may represent, as several have claimed, a perfect Canadian blend (Bader 43; Howells, "Storm" 474; Thieme 157; Warwick,
River 61), but, for the moment, she is more confused about what her
roots truly mean than anything else. She certainly does not see herself
as a perfect anything. Furthermore, she is none too happy to be there
in a cabin in the woods with a lady the nearby townspeople think is a
bit "crazy."

Coming to terms with Pique means at least two things for Morag.
First, she must see the extent to which Pique is just like she was when
she was a late adolescent (Greene, "Margaret Laurence's *The Diviners*"
197). Pique is rebellious, just as Morag was; Pique wants to "get out,"
just as Morag did; Pique has "issues" with her parents, just as Morag
did with her step-parents; and Pique is creative, just as Morag was —
and is. In these many ways, mother and daughter merge, with Pique
serving as a mirror to Morag (Wagner 6-7). Coming to terms with this
mirror image entails, second, letting her be free. Jules tells Morag as

much. Perhaps he intuits that Morag herself will never totally be free until she ceases being obsessed with Pique's life and lets the girl steer her own destiny and find out who she is.

Once back in Canada, Morag also ceases moving around. The first two-thirds of the novel has her move from Manawaka to Winnipeg to Toronto to Vancouver to London. This movement is, of course, in the "memorybank movies" portions of the novel's chapters—the part that takes us back into Morag's life. Now, the movement stops, as the past catches up with the present and the two parts of the chapters merge somewhat. The result is a relatively stable Morag. The stability is literally true: She is in one spot, the cabin by the Otonabee River that, like the bulk of the book, flows both ways. The stability is also figuratively true, for Morag can now cease flitting hither and yon because she has come to terms with all that she must to know herself. She has come to terms with Prin and Christie, with her heritage, with her sometimes lover Jules, and with her daughter Pique.

At this point in the novel, knowing herself for the first time, Morag can also comes to terms with her creativity. She will learn its fragility, but, more importantly, she will be able to take it to a peak it has never reached before. She will be able to do what others have been able to do—to divine, a metaphor at the core of the novel (Besner, "A World" 42). Christie, somewhat comically, was able to do so with people's "muck." He extracted people's secrets. Jules was able to do so through the folksongs he wrote about his ancestors, his father, and his sister. He extracted the meaning of their sad lives. Royland was able to do so, most literally, by finding the water hidden beneath the Canadian soil and rock. He helped people extract life-giving water, although he did not know, for the life of him, how he did what he did and he knew that his gift was fading. Fragility is one common thread that runs through the stories of all of these diviners, so is the paradoxical mixture of "the foul rag-and-bone shop of the heart" (to quote Yeats's "The Circus Animals' Desertion") and the redemptive. Redemption is not to be found through flights of fancy—or flights; rather, it is to be found by focusing on where one's being, physically and psychologically, is rooted.

Royland perhaps represents the redemptive potential more strikingly than the others. He is, as his name suggests, a king of the land insofar as he knows its secrets, i.e., where the life-giving water lurks beneath it. Royland does enable people to bring that symbolic water forth from the depths where it has hidden itself. Thus, it is not entirely suprising that the geographic area we associate with Royland becomes, in some ways, a new Eden for Morag. As Warwick notes, she began her story in the paradise of her childhood home's backyard (*River* 72); she ends it here at McConnell's Landing in a new paradise. Moreover, both are fragile: The first was lost when polio took the lives of her parents; this second may be as fleeting as Royland's gift as literal diviner or her gift as writer. However, Morag learns to let it be, just as she learns to let Pique be. As Godard has suggested, Morag's writing and Morag's Pique are linked, as the woman's creations. She must let both her daughter and her fictive characters be. She must be a new kind of Prospero, creative but not controlling (Godard, "Caliban's" 224). As Lindberg has noted, Morag graciously accepts this limit as the novel ends (197).

There is one crucial dimension of Morag Gunn's story that has only, thus far, been glanced at. It is a dimension that requires more thorough discussion—because it is important in her story and because it has been, I think, widely misunderstood. This dimension is her progress as a writer.

Morag, from very early in her life, is fascinated with words; therefore, it is not surprising that language is foregrounded in the novel (Nicholson 167). Throughout her life, she asks "What means" followed by a word that has come to intrigue her. For example, as a very young child told she must attend school, she asks "What means *Law?*" (25). When she asks these questions, she is not, as one might initially expect, asking about the word's dictionary definition. Rather, she has become alert to the word's ambiguities, and she is probing them. Sometimes, the probing is comic, as when she spends several sentences reflecting on the phrase "Frog in my throat," thinking about "[t]hose clammy clambering teeny saurian legs in you *gullet*" (163). Sometimes, it is poignant, as when she struggles with the words "love" and "know" in relation to Jules, saying to her daughter that she "find[s] words more difficult to define than I used to" (192). This probing represents two instincts: First, she is acutely aware of how slippery the symbolic realm is; and, second, she is simultaneously intent on exposing this slipperiness and then gaining a degree of control over the verbal situation. She is, perhaps, motivated to do so partially because, when she was young, words were used to oppress her (Lindberg 189). Back then, Christie was taunted in rhymes such as "Christie Logan's the Scavenger Man— / Gets his food from the garbage can" and Morag was taunted in rhymes such as "Mo-rag! Morag / Gets her clothes from an ol' flour bag" (31). In other words, she wishes to deconstruct and reinscribe the symbolic. Morag's critical "game" is not entirely in line with a feminist agenda; however, as Verduyn has noted, many times it is: many times, the words she probes are ones that the patriarchy has defined in such a way so as to deny or marginalize women's experiences (53). Furthermore, as Lindberg has observed, Morag seems attuned to those experiences that cannot find their way into the symbolic: her feelings at Prin's funeral and her feelings about Jules, for example.

At the same time Morag critiques the symbolic, she also is very attuned to the semiotic (Bok 80-81). Denied a close bonding with her mother because of her mother's death and, then, her uppity attitude toward Prin's social class, Morag develops a very close bonding with her daughter. In some ways that are, quite appropriately—because from within the semiotic, beyond the ability of language to easily describe, this relationship has dimensions of both the mother-daughter relationship and the daughter-mother relationship. In other words, Morag is mother to Pique, while, in a peculiar way, Pique is mother to Morag. These relationships are, of course, played out in prelanguage terms, terms heavily imbued with the bodily realities of the womb, of birth, of nurturance, of mirroring, of necessary separation. The semiotic chora pulses through the story of Morag and Pique.

The semiotic chora also pulses through the story of Morag and her several lovers. Her climaxes during intercourse with Jules find expression outside of language, for, as Verduyn has noted, words cannot capture sexual pleasure for Morag (64): "The pulsing between her legs spreads and suffuses all of her. The throbbing goes on and on, and she does not know if she has spoken until it stops, and then she does not know if she has spoken words or only cried out somewhere in someplace beyond language" (112). With a candor that disturbed some readers, Morag is an intensely sexual being. At her first sexual experience, "She feels not shyness at all" (112), and she rouses quickly. With Jules, "She is…aroused quickly, surprised at the intensity of her need to have him enter her" (222). With Brooke, "Morag responds, as usual, instantly, but more so than ever before. If he should ask her to strip in the exposed and icy car and make love with him here and now, no holds barred, she would do so" (158). And even with a stranger she picks up in a Vancouver bar, she finds "Her need for him, for the pressure of his sex, is so great that she finds it difficult to hold back enough to accommodate his time" (263). In fact, one of the barriers in the way of Morag's coming to terms with Pique at the end of the novel is Morag's deeply felt jealousy of her daughter's youthful sexuality. Morag is uneasy sleeping the same house as Pique and her lover, not because she disapproves of their adolescent sexual activity but because she is aroused by it.

Morag's distrust of the symbolic and deep awareness of the semiotic mark her as a potential female artist of some talent. She needs to remain aware of the symbolic realm's dangers as she learns to work in it; she needs to remain attuned to the semiotic as she finds ways—albeit inadequate—to bring the semiotic into something like words. Morag then is very much the prototypical feminist writer, although, in a time before theory, she could not articulate her position but only feel it.

The last sentence I wrote is typical of what is said about Morag in a way I wish to expose as deceptive. That last sentence could just as easily have been a statement about Margaret Laurence as about Morag Gunn. In fact, that last sentence may be truer for Laurence than for Gunn because we would probably talk about Laurence in terms of what she might or might not know about literary theory. Would we really talk in those terms about Morag? Recall her background: she dropped out of university when she married Brooke Skelton; she took up writing "on the side." We very much dislike the way Brooke condescendingly views her writing; however, given Morag's background at that point, Brooke's perspective might be more accurate than we'd like to admit. His sexist condescension is certainly one of the reasons we become angered at what he says; another—I'd like to suggest—is that we have become trapped in an identification between Morag Gunn and Margaret Laurence that may be only partially valid.

Morag's story sets this trap. Laurence is from Manitoba, and so is Morag. Laurence wrote three Manawaka novels (*The Stone Angel, A Jest of God,* and *The Fire-Dwellers*) and a collection of Manawaka-based short stories before writing *The Diviners*; Morag wrote *Spear of Innocence, Prospero's Child, Jonah, Shadow of Eden* (four not three), and a collection of short stories before writing the novel we presume to be *The Diviners*. Any attempt, however, to map Laurence's works onto Morag Gunn's is doomed to fail. Not only do the numbers not quite work out, the plots and themes don't. Yes, there are some similarities. *Jonah* does deal with a troubling father-daughter relationship, as does *The Stone Angel,* and *Prospero's Child* does deal with a suffocating marriage, as does *The Fire-Dwellers.* However, what does Gunn's historical chronicle of the Sunderlanders in *Shadow of Eden* match up with? One might try to salvage the comparison by complicating it: by arguing that it is a three-way comparison: among Laurence's novels, Gunn's novels, and Gunn's fictitious life. Conceived of in this manner, the inconsistencies between Laurence and Gunn can be explained by the need to integrate Gunn's life. Saving the comparison in this manner strikes me, however, as a denial of the obvious: that Gunn's novels were never intended to parallel Laurence's. In fact, the only place where Laurence hints at a parallel is at the end of *The Diviners* when she seems to assign this novel to Morag Gunn. Laurence may well be making her sometimes narrator the nominal author, much as Jonathan Swift assigns *Gulliver's Travels* to Lemuel Gulliver on the title page of that work of fiction or John Barth would have us believe George Giles is the author of *Giles Goat Boy.* Swift and Barth are using a literary convention. We are not to assume that Lemuel Gulliver served Queen Anne or wrote *A Tale of a Tub* when reading *Gulliver's Travels* just as we are not to assume that George Giles taught creative writing at Johns Hopkins University or wrote *The Floating Opera* when reading *Giles Goat Boy*.

So, if we are not to read Morag Gunn's fiction as analogous to Margaret Laurence's, how are we to read it. Let's return to some threads left dangling a few paragraphs back: a possibly talented young writer with protofeminist inclinations but very little formal training. We should then read Morag's work asking ourselves if she will be able to become the writer she has the potential to become. Some have noted how "bad" some of Morag's work seems to be (Keith, "Margaret"), but they have seen this as either a flaw in the book or a flaw in the comparison between Morag as writer and Laurence as writer. These critics have swerved the wrong way, I think. These works are "bad" because Morag does not quickly or readily succeed. Let's consider Morag's four novels prior to *The Diviners*.

Morag's first two novels *Spear of Innocence* and *Prospero's Child* deal with the oppression of women by the patriarchy. In the first, a young woman goes off to the city, much as Morag does, and becomes corrupted. We do not know much about the text. However, it would seem to be a piece of social realism because Morag, when she meets Fan in Vancouver and hears her story, is struck by the extent to which Fan's real story is like the heroine of *Spear*. We also do not know much about the text of *Prospero's Child*. What we do know suggests that it is more of a Gothic romance in which a young woman marries the rich, powerful ruler of an island state and then finds herself trapped in that marriage on that island. The novel seems to be a fairy tale turned nightmare version of Morag's own marriage to Brooke Skeleton. (This novel could have been more—a paradigmatic story of colonialism and Canada's place in that story, but there is no evidence Morag's book is much more than shallow romance.)

Both of these novels reveal Morag's sensitivity to the plight of women in a male-dominated world. However, we doubt that there is much else in them to suggest that Morag is developing into much of a writer. Morag does not seem to be especially aware of the "tyranny" of the symbolic realm. She resists Brooke's editing, but she resists it more because it is Brooke's, not because it is patriarchal. She tries to incorporate some of the rhythms of speech she remembers from Manawaka, giving her prose style less of an academic feel than Brooke would prefer (Verduyn 62). Even so, she does not see this resistance as being directed at more than just her imperious husband. Perhaps to signal Morag's *not* seeing her resistance in larger terms, Laurence has her character play-off Shakespeare's *The Tempest* in the second book. *The Tempest,* of course, has been the point of departure for both postcolonial revisions of the play and postcolonial theorizing, both of which stress how Prospero as imperialist regulates the colonized Caliban—and, to a lesser extent, the old magician's daughter Miranda. None of these ideas about oppression find their way into Morag's novel. Laurence was aware of Mannoni's work, having read it and been profoundly influenced by it while residing in Africa (Godard, "Caliban's" 216; Morley 255), but this awareness does not seem reflected in Morag's story. Prospero is mentioned in the title but hardly—it would seem—in the novel, which focuses on a daughter other than Miranda. She experiences oppression, but no link seems to be made between what she experiences at the hands of her husband and what Caliban and others experience at the hands of her supposed father. Morag's novel has a strikingly limited focus: it's Gothic fiction with Prospero in the title either to give it a cultured air, an exotic site, or both.

With *Jonah* and *Shadow of Eden*, Morag's work seems to mature. She gets beyond what one might term the standard fare of women's fiction in these books, focusing the first on a father-daughter relationship that has been marred by the daughter's embarrassment at her father's work and life and the second on a highly mythologized episode in Scottish-Canadian history. Both of these topics are, of course, important to Morag: *Jonah* allows her to deal with her strained relationship with Christie Logan through the medium of fiction; *Shadow of Eden* allows her to get into print the legends Christie had shared with her about the expulsion of the Sunderlanders from their lands in Scotland and their journey westward to Canada. Although the latter book glances at oppression and it implicitly raises the question of how accurate the received written versions of the Sunderlanders' story might be, neither it nor *Jonah* truly wrestle with the tyranny of the symbolic realm.

So, Morag's novels touch on oppression as a theme, but she does not seem to probe the symbolic much at all. Furthermore, in none of these works of fiction is there a sense of the semiotic emerging and destabilizing her texts. Morag Gunn may have been able to scrape together enough money so that she can now, at age forty-seven, be just a writer. However, she is certainly not a celebrated author. Her work, although interesting, seems quite inferior to Laurence's Manawaka novels that preceded *The Diviners*. Morag has a long way to go before she is capable of being even the fictitious author of Laurence's last novel. *The Diviners*, in ways I have already suggested, tries to take us through Morag's process of becoming a writer sufficiently in tune with her past, with who she is, and with the inherent limitations of language to pen the novel.

Critics can—and will—disagree about whether what we see of Morag's growth in the course of *The Diviners* justifies the fiction that she is its author. Perhaps Laurence herself had doubts and that is why she deleted the title *The Diviners* from the novel's concluding sentence and left it with the vague "her title." Perhaps Laurence felt that she had in Morag Gunn an author who could now, finally, write up to her potential, not an author capable of a masterpiece such as *The Diviners*.

However, if we are to accept the fiction that *The Diviners* is a novel by Morag Gunn, what does the novel reveal about Morag Gunn, the writer? First, the novel reveals that she has acquired a broad understanding of oppression. It is far more than what she experienced trapped in the tower of Brooke Skelton's posh apartment. Oppression embraces many women as its victims, just as it embraces the underclass, regardless of gender. Oppression has victimized her Scottish ancestors; it has victimized her lover Jules's *Metis* ancestors in western Canada. Furthermore, in some measure, in that case, the Scottish victims of oppression sadly and ironically turned around and proved to be the oppressors of the *Metis* (Rocard, "The Dispossession" 110). As Spriet has noted, Morag gradually develops a resistance to—perhaps even a revolutionary attitude toward—the accepted ideologies that underpin this oppression (323-25).

Second, the novel reveals that Morag has come to question the symbolic, as her frequent "What means" probes suggest. Her questioning, however, goes beyond interrogating words. The novel exhibits her interrogation—and, at times, explosion of that larger unit of discourse. *The Diviners* very much challenges the realistic tradition of the novel, a tradition valorized by the patriarchy (Bok 90). She proceeds in a nonlinear manner, circling back to the present at the beginning of each chapter before presenting increasingly more immediate stories from the past. She at times gives the visual primacy over the verbal (Verduyn 53, 67; Warwick, "The Dispossession" 32). For example, she foregrounds the snapshots of her childhood in the initial chapter, shifting then to the "memorybank movies" that dominate the other chapters. She uses a third person narrator that "feels" like first person (Beckman-Long 64-65), and finds ways to let all of the characters, major and minor, speak. She thereby creates a heteroglossia that grants independent voices to her characters (Godard, "Caliban's" 214; Lacombe 151; Warwick, "The Dispossession" 32). She thereby sometimes raises socially low discourse to the level of the high, creating a carnivalesque mood (Godard, "*The Diviners*" 43). She also thereby creates on her pages an interconnectedness among people that strikes one as genuine community. In order to accomplish this feat, Laurence refuses to be the stereotypical ego-involved author: She does not control her creations; she lets them go (Greene, "Margaret Laurence's *The Diviners*" 197).

The novel then is strikingly nonpatriarchal. It may not be a radical assault on the patriarchal tradition such as that launched later by some Quebecois writers. Nonetheless, *The Diviners* is a feminist text. It is highly metafictional (Thieme 154), and, as Godard has noted, it uses references to other texts to achieve explosive ends ("*The Diviners*"). It challenges several patriarchal literary forms, including the epic (Greene, "Margaret Laurence's *Diviners*"; Lacombe 155-56) and the *künstlerroman* (Bok 88-89); it also challenges the fantasy narratives found in much women's fiction (Howells, "Margaret Laurence" 99). It alludes to Joyce's *Portrait of the Artist as a Young Man*, Milton's *Paradise Lost*, and, of course, Shakespeare's *The Tempest*. These allusions are neither decorative nor straightforwardly enriching. Rather, they are questioning, subverting, challenging (Godard, "Supplement" 55-57; Greene," Margaret Laurence's *Diviners"*; Greene, "Margaret Laurence's *The Diviners"*). We therefore get a view of the artist as joined to community not isolated from it (Greene, "Margaret Laurence's Diviners" 175; Greene, "Margaret Laurence's *The Diviners*" 197); a view of a new Eden where to name is not to regulate; and a view of how not to play Prospero through Brooke Skelton as well as a view of how to play a better Prospero through Morag at the novel's end, without enthralling either one's agents or one's subjects. As Laurence's novel parodies the works of male writers, it also searches for model works by female authors (Carolan-Brozy and Hageman 149; Howells, "Inheritance" 61-63). Virginia Woolf is alluded to; more strikingly, Catherine Parr Traill is resurrected so that Morag can benefit from her wisdom while, eventually, steering her own course (Boutelle; Godard, "Caliban's" 217-23; Godard, "*The Diviners"*; Sparrow).

One needs to ask why Laurence proceeds as she does in crafting this novel. Like all of her Manawaka novel's, Laurence is concerned in *The Diviners* with a woman's identity. The forces that deny that identity vary from book to book, but independent identity always seems in jeopardy. As Clara Thomas has suggested, in focusing on this theme, Laurence is dealing with what may be *the* dominant theme of Canadian literature, for, just as women must seek identity in a society in which they are often marginalized, Canada must seek identity in a world in which they have been colonized, first, by Great Britain and, later and in a less literal way, by the United States. According to Thomas, language plays a major role in this marginalization/colonization. Women writers and Canadian writers and, especially, Canadian women writers, must wrestle with that language. *The Diviners,* I think, has disappointed some insofar as it is not more "postmodern" than it is. As the foregoing analysis should suggest, one should not let the fact that the novel presents a compelling, realistic story distract one from noting the extent to which the novel calls attention to itself as artifact and challenges the dominant discourse. Certain subject positions, for women, for men, and for nations, are authorized within that discourse. Laurence's novel challenges it because the dominance of these positions stands in the way of identity and fulfillment.

Besides thematizing oppression and challenging the symbolic, the novel—in a manner that surprised some readers, perhaps leading to its being banned in some schools (Livesay 236)—also foregrounds Morag Gunn's sexuality. At age fifteen, we see her masturbating after nervously running away from Jules's boastful attempted seduction:

> When she is back home, she goes to her room and locks the door. Hating herself for having been so scared. Slips one hand between her legs and brings herself, with her eyes closed, imagining his hard flesh bones skin on hers, pressing into her, feeling her tits, putting his cock there there there. (105)

Then, we witness her adolescent fumblings with Jules and her adult relationships with Brooke, Jules, and Dan and her jealous yearnings at age forty-seven inspired by her daughter Pique's sexuality. Throughout, Morag exhibits her sexual being and exhibits it without shame or inhibition. With a stranger, "she cannot stop herself, and her consciousness is submerged, drenched in this spasm of gladness" (163); with Brooke, sex was at one point "an unworded conversation and connection" (214); with Jules, sex was an "urgent meeting and grappling, [a] brief death of consciousness" during which, at climax, when Morag does "cry out,...he stops her cry with his mouth" (280). What these moments have in common, besides Morag's passion, is their being somehow outside of language, beyond the ordinary symbolic. Morag's sexuality then is a part of her being, a part that is still in touch with the semiotic. As noted earlier, she cannot always put her sexual feelings into words, just as she cannot always put the maternal ones discussed previously. She manages nonetheless to bring them into the novel. In fact, as Gandesbery has noted, the maternal

and the sexual are linked throughout Laurence's fiction and are manifestations of the semiotic chora that pulses through *The Diviners* (68).

These characteristics of *The Diviners* suggest that it is a sophisticated
book, one very much in accord with what feminist literary theoreti-
cians have said about writing and the novel, largely after the novel's
1974 publication. So, the novel in many ways anticipates this body of
theory. That the novel is not as radical as some that consciously reflect
the theory is partially explained by its publication at the advent of the
feminist movement and partially by Laurence's rooting in modernism. Radical or not, the novel seems far beyond where Morag Gunn
was at when she wrote *Jonah* and *Shadow of Eden*. The remembered
events of *The Diviners* show how Morag Gunn acquired a distrust of
the symbolic, an awareness of the interconnectedness of (primarily
women's) lives, and a comfort with her sexuality. So, it is plausible
that Morag Gunn has acquired the wherewithal to be the author of
The Diviners. If there is a flaw in the fiction that Laurence creates, it is
that the novel does indeed seem "a reach" for Morag Gunn, given
what we know and can infer about her earlier fiction.

If readers remain unconvinced that Morag could write the novel
they have read, they are at least convinced that her attitude toward islands has changed. When Morag went off to England, she went off to
an island that, in her mind, offered both escape and the potential of
self-realization. By the time she is living by the river, she has become
aware that England was, at best, a way station. She tells us that she no
longer believes in islands: "Islands are unreal....Islands exist only in
the head" (292), she says. Her comment is perhaps ironic, for what
she has created for herself in rural Ontario is in many ways island-
like. In fact, she herself talks about it in island terms, telling Royland
"I've made an island," before quickly asking "Are islands real?" (192).
It is not surrounded by the river that flows both ways, but that river
does seem to provide some degree of separation for Morag, separation that is necessary so that she might write. Although visitors come
to the cabin—perhaps more often than the writer Morag would like,
the cabin is sufficiently isolated from the nearby town and other rural
residents to provide her with a retreat that seems to offer her far more

inspiration than either the way station of England or the entrapment of Brooke's tower apartment. I have already suggested how, within the framework of the novel, this riverside retreat seems to be a new paradise to replace the one Morag was expelled from when her parents died. If we merge the suggestions in the text that Morag has found an island-like retreat with those that Morag has found a new Eden, then we end the novel on quite a positive note. We have an Eden that is really not a new Eden, but functions as one; a retreat that (as Fabre has noted) is not disconnected enough to be one, but functions as one (64); an island that is really not an island, but functions as one.

Less positive—more ambiguous—is the ending of Audrey Thomas's *Intertidal Life*. However, although the endings might be different, Laurence's *The Diviners* and Thomas's novel are strikingly similar. Both are about writers; both are about writers who are constantly interrogating the very medium they work in. Both have problematic relationships with the men in their lives, and, for both, the mother-daughter relationship is crucial. Both find their island retreats to be nothing more than temporary ones, where their lives are on hold until they are ready to take the next step.

One plotline difference is, however, apparent from the outset of *Intertidal Life*: Alice, Thomas's heroine, does not escape to the island; she is already there when things in her life start collapsing. Her marriage collapses, and, because that relationship so structured her existence, its collapse resonates outward causing everything else in her life—friendships, relationships with her children, writing—to become shaky. What prolongs the shakiness is husband Peter's charismatic influence over other characters in Alice's life. They—even her female friends—are drawn to him. At one point, Alice even describes Peter as "the sun" and these women as "moons" that are drawn into orbits around him: "Peter was the sun, the hub, around which first Alice, then Anne-Marie, then Penny, now Stella and Trudl, revolved" (239). What also prolongs the shakiness is that Peter periodically reenters Alice's life, further convincing her that his desire for sexual freedom is either because of the era (the sexually "free" '60's) or his inability, like his namesake Peter Pan, to grow up. She thinks the era will change, and Peter Pan might mature, so she holds onto hope that her life will soon be put back together again the way it was before he left her and the island retreat they, ironically, bought for the both of them and the children to enjoy.

From the onset, this island—literally, Galiano Island in Vancouver Bay—is ambiguous. Was the cabin-like home there acquired not as a retreat for them but, rather, as a place where Peter could conveniently stash Alice while pursuing his sexual adventures back on the mainland? As she tells Peter, she imagines, "You and Anne-Marie having long talks about old Alice and what to do about her. Can't exactly put her down like an old dog, but at least we can make sure she's over there on the island" (21). Now that it is ruined as a retreat for them, can it still function as a retreat for her—a retreat away from the problems the collapse of her life has brought? Conversely, does the place—cabin and island—hold too many memories of the two of them together? If it is to be her retreat—a place where she can regain herself and a place where she can write, how must she alter it— literally and in her mind? In many ways, Alice is like her namesake, Alice in Wonderland: confused, alternatively delighted and threatened. The link to Lewis Carroll's character is not explicit in the novel; however, Thomas does make explicit use of Alice in Wonderland in an earlier novel, and she does note in an interview that Carroll's novel is her favorite book (Wachtel 39).

Alice at times wishes she were more alone in the cabin on the island, for she needs solitude to write. She needs time away from the children; thus, she relishes the hours when they are at school. She also needs time away from friends; thus, she inwardly cringes when friends intrude into her privacy. She even goes so far as to announce that, during certain hours, she will not be interrupted, even posting a sign saying, "NOT OPEN TO THE VISITING PUBLIC BEFORE 3:30 MON – FRI" (60).

These friends, especially the female ones, serve as mirrors of Alice's condition. They are struggling with relationships. Some are even struggling with the artistry they believe is budding within them. Almost all are trying to come to terms with a decade that offers freedoms that do not mesh well with the strait-laced Canadian society that had kept sexuality, drugs, and the like hidden away. At times, Alice's immediate environment resembles more a hippie commune than a single mother's household or a writer's retreat. A room of her own Alice rarely has. These friends swirl about Alice, offering her glimpses of her own condition. So do her daughters, who are dealing with some of the same issues, which might be summed up in the question, who is a woman to be in the world now before us. Interestingly, Alice has her daughter Flora read both gothic romances (titles such as *Nurse Prue in Ceylon*) and Flaubert's *Madame Bovary* as she tries to answer the question. These polar reading selections suggest that, for women in general, as well as for Alice in particular, it is a time in between. Alice is in between life with Peter and life on her own; women are in between life defined by the patriarchal expectations reflected in the gothic romances (which Thomas has confessed to know well and to find "very dangerous" [Wachtel 60]) and life defined in starkly realistic, iconoclastic terms by Flaubert's heroine. In the Harlequins, as daughter Flora notes, "People...eat oysters and stuff like that" and the stories "always end when [the man and the woman] both admit to one another they they're madly in love" (260–61). Not so in Flaubert—or, the book suggests, life.

The novel's title suggests this in-betweeness. Alice is drawn to the intertidal life she finds on the island. (In fact, the conversation between Alice and Flora about Harlequins and life occurs in the midst of Alice's discussion of the intertidal life.) Between one high tide and the next, there are pools. In these pools, there are sea creatures. Their lives, however, are fragile. The water is low; the sun may be warm enough to evaporate the little there is. And some of these creatures have been battered by the surf or attacked by predators and are wounded. "Many have legs missing: one, two, three, testimony to narrow escapes from whatever it is that eats them" (268). This intertidal life, which Alice feels compelled to study, becomes a rich metaphor for the life Alice is trapped in and women more generally are trapped in.

The word *trapped*, however, is not entirely accurate, for the in-betweeness is womb-like. The warm water of the pools suggests the amniotic fluid. On a larger scale, the island is also surrounded by water, water that protects it from the helter-skelter of life on the mainland. "Water imagery again—I can't escape it" (165), Alice says, perhaps warning us against resting too easily with the idea of island as womb. The image is given and, in a way, taken away, in keeping with the novel's characteristic ambiguity. Nonetheless, the island itself is at times womb-like. Certainly the life that we see depicted on the island is strikingly maternal, reinforcing the island as womb. As womb, the island is a place of rest and time: "There seemed to be more time to talk to [the children], to play with them. It wasn't Peter's absence, really, although of course that had something to do with it. It seemed to be the island itself and the simple life they were living" (147).

The womb then is a safe place. However, just as the next tide comes and carries the intertidal sea creatures outward, birth comes and carries the being safe in the womb out into the world. While in the womb, that being acquires what is necessary to survive in the world. So, if the island serves in some sense as a protective womb for Alice, what does she acquire while semi-safe within it?

The novel does not have much of a plot *per se*: it is more interesting as a fabric composed of people. Hutcheon ("'Shape-shifters'") has noted that these people are overwhelmingly female, so much so that she suggests that the island is a place of female community with the mutual support one would expect in such a community. Stella says, "This island isn't a very good place to meet men"; Alice replies, "But a good place in every other way....It's a bit as though Adam had been banished from the garden and Eve's punishment had been to stay there all alone" (212). There certainly are more women than men, and some of the men on the island, such as Raven, are markedly feminine. Furthermore, the members of this community do lend Alice their emotional assistance:

> Sometimes Alice saw, growing between her and the other three women, a
> great twisted vine, or rope. So that, if she had to step out into the dark, she

could, as she had once done on a small ship caught in the tail end of a hurricane, pull herself forward safely, even in the most severe of storms. Could move from her cabin, to Trudl's, to Stella's, even over to Selene's in the most awful storm of blind despair or self-hatred and know that so long as she held on tightly to the friendship she would be *all right*. (164)

However, as Coldwell ("Natural" 143) notes, this community often fails Alice. Peter snaps his fingers, and supposed friends betray Alice. Alice felt "the dark pull of the man…who was taking her friends away from her, gathering them in under his magician's cape" (218). "'I wish he would leave my friends alone,' Alice said. '*I really wish he would leave my friends alone!*'" (220). They not only accept patriarchal assumptions about their roles, they enact them—with the slightest provocation—despite any language of solidarity they might voice when just among women.

What Alice begins with then is not really community or solidarity but, rather, her acute awareness of language. As Tiger has noted, very much like Morag Gunn but more often, Alice is interrogating the words that constitute the symbolic realm. She does much of this work in "a commonplace book, where I would finally bring together all the words and definitions and phrases I have copied out for years on scraps of paper." She expresses her "need to sprawl, to scrawl, to pull out from myself the great glistering sentences full of hate and fury and fling them, still wet and steaming onto these white pages" (30). Whereas Morag asks "What means," Alice offers definitions that do not quite seem to work. She thereby suggests that the symbolic is inexact. Alice also offers puns, playing with the symbolic so as to suggest her control—her mastery—of it. In her commonplace book, she plays with the meanings of "mother," finding implicit in it her role and hysteria; and she plays with the meanings of "mummy," finding implicit in it her role and death. She notes how she liked "languid," until now, when she associates the word with "Peter tasting the cool juice from Anne-Marie's cunt on his exploring tongue." She plays in ways witty and obscene with Peter's name, and she notes how easy it is to change "Lover" to "over" by simply crossing out the "L." She plays outside of the confines of her book as well, leading the children in word games, creating female characters whose first names are the prefixes "Una" (as in "Una Verse. A poet" [118]) and "Anti" (as in "Auntie Christ" [118]). As Hales has observed, she often regenders language through this play (77). To the extent that the symbolic is a male-defined realm, Alice reduces its patriarchal power by pointing to its weaknesses and, then, dancing in empowered circles about it. Thomas, in a published interview, has observed that, "language was my enemy for a long time." According to Thomas, in response, "You wrestle it to the ground" (Wachtel 39). Alice in *Intertidal Life* is wrestling—and often winning her matches.

Words represent the symbolic at its most fundamental level. *Intertidal Life* also deals with larger examples of the symbolic. Like Laurence's *The Diviners*, Thomas's novel challenges the genre as a form of patriarchal discourse. She challenges the valorized conventions of formal realism by destabilizing the text. She interrupts the flow; she begins but fails to finish. She narrates using a third- person omniscient narrator. However, she interjects close to thirty first-person segments, most of which are metafictional insofar as they talk about language or writing. In addition, as Irvine has noted, in defiance of narratological conventions, she merges the two perspectives toward the novel's end ("Sailing" 287). The result is that Alice is neither here nor there, as the subject positions authorized by conventions become destabilized (Buckman 80-81). Further destabilization is achieved by the metafictional commentary (Hutcheon, "'Shape-shifters'" 224) and the many intertexts (Coldwell, "Memory" 147). Among the effects achieved by the former is the parodic—especially, as Hutcheon (*Canadian Postmodern*) has noted, against the romance and against fairy tales. Besides the story of Peter Pan, the novel directly alludes to the stories of Cinderella, the Wizard of Oz, and the Little Mermaid and notes how, like romances, they present female readers with a view of life that is both idealized and patriarchal. Having jumped from words to discursive forms, the novel jumps and shifts to an even larger discursive practice.

The novel features many epigraphs that deal with this larger discursive practice: exploring and mapping. The essence of the symbolic is naming. Men name things with words; men also name land masses and waterways as they explore them and map them. Thomas frequently alludes to these very male explorers and mappers. Throughout the novel, women also explore—and sometimes name. However, their activity is on a much smaller scale: It is confined to the island. As the novel concludes, however, its words suggest that it is now time for women to explore and map. At this point, as Irvine has noted (289), Alice begins describing the cabin as if it were a ship—as Alice says, "It's funny, since I've been reading all this history about the Spanish and the English and the Pacific I think more and more in maritime images" (170). This is a message Thomas has presented previously—for example, in the story "Natural History" from *Real Mothers*. As Tiger has noted, Thomas seemed to believe that women were at a changing point in their relationships with men, with writing, and with life (121):

> What I mean is that what's happening to men and women today is just as exciting and terrifying as the discovery that the earth was round, not flat, or even that the earth was not the center of the universe but just part of a solar system. But we all need new maps, new instruments to try and fix our positions. (171)

An important assumption in drawing this new map is that, as Alice says "imperialism is over, for nations, for men." She asks Stella, "Do we really want somebody planting a flag in us and claiming us forever?" Alice's answer is obviously "No," for she believes that "Women have *let* men define them, taken their *names* even, with marriage, just like a conquered or newly settled region....I really understand all those African nations taking new names with their independence, names that relate to their racial history" (171).

The call then to explore and map is not just one for Alice to heed. Having gained control over the symbolic realm by deconstructing and reinscribing words and the text, Alice seems ready to gain control over an even larger symbolic realm, where *names*, etc., matter but in larger ways. As Thomas either sees it or wishes it, Alice joins women in general in her readiness, for women are ready to sail, not "to be let out at the nearest port or unceremoniously tossed overboard" (170). Especially the woman artist who, Alice says, "has an even harder time" for "[I]f she is to move forward at all she has to develop a layer of selfishness—self-is-ness—that has been traditionally reserved for men" (173).

Women's lives—and women's bodies—are intermediate between the words that the patriarchy controls and land masses (and the like) that the patriarchy also controls. As Alice moves from words to new continents (even new galaxies, for, "a woman was getting ready to go to the moon" [15], and maybe soon a "FIRST MOM ON THE MOON" [70]), she, of course, regains control of her life and her body, and she does so for women at large. A reflection of her doing so is the extent that the semiotic finds its way into Thomas's novel. Like Laurence's *The Diviners*, the novel deals frankly with Alice's sexuality. Aspects of her body—and thus her embodied life—that do not ordinarily make it into discourse are foregrounded in Thomas's work. They are introduced frankly, proudly—not hidden away without name or, at least, without name that is politely spoken. Alice talks about fellatio, thinking about "curv[ing] her fist around his cock, curl[ing] her tongue around it" and "cunnilingus, thinking about Peter's tongue inside her lapping and licking" (36). Alice talks about how the latter "drove her wild," how "[s]he nearly suffocated him, pushing up against him— Oh Peter I love you don't stop don't stop don't stop" (163). After a reprise in their relationship, Alice talks about "how nice it felt to have him in me" and how she "fell asleep with my hand curled around his balls," which felt like "[l]ittle animals soft and warm in my cupped hand" (153).

Challenging the symbolic and recovering the semiotic represent a dialectical process; thus, as Buckman has noted, "[t]he word games, fragments, and gaps that disrupt the narrative" allows for an interaction between the realms (79). The semiotic "refers to formless energies, rhythms, forces, and instinctual drives necessary for representation. When drive energies are released into symbolic structures, they can disrupt the logic of grammar by privileging repetition, rhythm, alliteration, and other sound effects over syntax" (76-77). We see these disruptions in Thomas's text along with the sexual and—linked as in Laurence's novel—the maternal. The semiotic surges into Thomas's novel.

Intertidal Life then is a liberating novel. Even so, there are limits to this liberation. The semiotic can intrude into discourse but not, at least in a novel as "traditional" as Thomas's, become discourse. As Bachman has observed, the critique of the symbolic is not sustained in Thomas's novel: Alice often finds herself falling back into it as "real life" concerns call for her attention. Rather than being a cause for despair, this falling back is simply an indication that *Intertidal Life* is aware of the patriarchy's power. This particular island, despite the illusion of freedom one has as one explores it, has been charted, just as discourse has been charted. The lands and seas to be explored are beyond the island the novel is set in. As an excerpt from one of the books on exploration Alice is reading states, "We immediately realized the danger which we should be in among these islands, the channels between which we did not know and which we had no interest in exploring" (278–79). The islands offer a great deal, but they are, at best way-stations. Words can be seized, but the seizing does no good unless the mastered words become something, if not fully in this book then in some future discourse or—as the novel suggests in the end—in Flora's generation, where, "it, perhaps, [will] be a little *easier*," where there will be "[n]ot so many games" (276). Thus, at the end of the novel, Alice leaves the island. As Thomas implied in her earlier story "Natural History," the island, although it offers clues, does not hold the ultimate answer (Godard, *Audrey Thomas*; Howells, "Inheritance" 106).

The nature of this departure, however, is at best ambiguous. It is clearly not a triumphant departure—off to explore and claim and name, figuratively of course, like the explorers Thomas brings into the novel through her epigraphs. Rather, it is a tense departure for what is described as "minor surgery." At least one critic has read this ending as ominous, suggesting Alice's almost certain death in the pages that follow the novel's end (Hutcheon, "'Shape-shifters'" 224-25). There certainly is an ominous note struck when we hear, "She wanted to see Flora one more time, Anne, Hannah....There were so many things left unsaid. She had never made her will" (281). However, I prefer to interpret those words as the "normal" jitters one has before any medical procedure and the ending in conjunction with how Alice describes the intertidal pools that have become a metaphor for her existence on Galiano Island. She notes that many of the creatures in a pool are wounded. Without help, washed back into the sea, they are perhaps in real danger. Alice has certainly been wounded by the recent events of her life. Similarly to the wounded sea creatures, she needs help. What she has gained as woman and as writer on the island will, of course, help. However, it does not seem to be enough. However, Alice—now ready to leave the island safety—is going to get that additional help. The wounded crustaceans in the pool cannot have "minor surgery" and thereby become better prepared for the sea again. Alice, however, can. What the island has started, the "minor surgery" has the potential to continue even if is impossible to complete.

Therefore, I see Thomas's novel as having a positive ending, but the ambiguity is certainly there. Why did not Thomas simply have Alice move on? In the world of fiction, characters conventionally conclude their stories by marrying, dying, being sent to Australia, publishing that first book. It is understandable that Thomas wishes to reject these conventions: They are overdone, and most reflect the novel as a male-defined genre. However, why "minor surgery"? One is compelled to read back into the novel for hints, and, to the extent one reads backwards, one reverses Alice's progress. Maybe, as she was liberating herself, she was also growing a cancer within her. Thomas will not let us rest too easily in Alice's triumph. In any event, neither romances nor fairy tales end with minor surgery. Thomas is at least not falling backward into patriarchal writing.

4

The Most Puzzling Island of All

Margaret Atwood's *Surfacing*

The islands discussed in chapter 2, L. M. Montgomery's Prince Edward Island and Marian Engel's Cary Island, offer the central characters redemption. The islands discussed in chapter 3, Margaret Laurence's Britain and Audrey Thomas's Galiano Island, offer way-stations at which something happens to push the central characters onward. Although these latter islands did not offer these characters exactly what they thought they might, the island sojourns were nonetheless successful. The island discussed in this chapter, an unnamed one somewhere in northern Quebec near that province's border with Ontario, might offer redemption, might offer a way-station, might offer both, and might offer neither. That island, the site of the very psychological drama of Margaret Atwood's *Surfacing*, and the events that occur on it have proven to be quite a puzzle for readers and critics.

The critics have written voluminously about *Surfacing*. The novel is clearly one of the most critiqued works of Canadian literature, inviting critics with interests in the psychological and spiritual as well as in gender relations and neocolonial politics. That body of criticism, which I will refer to as I discuss the novel rather than review formally, could be classified based on these several foci. However, there has emerged in the criticism itself a tendency to classify commentary based on how the critics view the novel's ending, ranging from pieces that find the novel wholeheartedly redemptive (Bicanic; Clark; Ewell; Kadrmas; VanSpanckeren) to those that find the novel's ending either a false salvation—in Brydon's terms, a "grim message of entrapment" (395)—because the central character must return to the city and to language (Bartlett) or even a parody of quests that end in redemption (Lecker). The majority of those who've commented on the novel try to place it in some kind of middle- ground between these extremes, several citing Atwood's own assessment of the novel's conclusion as ambiguous (Bouson; James; Klovan; Robinson; Woodcock). As James puts it, "Atwood's solution lies in some middle ground beyond the limited choices suggested in such alternatives as fight or flight, the city or the bush, sane or insane, winning or losing, victor or victim" (180). I will do the same—not because I'm following the majority or heeding Atwood's self-assessment, but because, as Huggan (11-12) suggests, there is inherently a problem moving from the semiotic realm to which the narrator has retreated back into the symbolic realm. That there is a problem does not, however, negate the positive effects of the retreat into the semiotic that the novel depicts. Rather, that there is a problem pinpoints the dilemma women writers face trying to convey what's outside of language in the words, sentences, and larger discursive forms of patriarchically defined symbolic. Atwood's answer is characteristically less radical than that of many feminist writers. That it is less radical does not undermine it, but it does produce an ending fraught with tensions.

Surfacing begins with the central character, her lover, and two friends on the road to the island. They are accompanying her for several reasons: She needed a ride; she needed some emotional support;

and they thought the trip to the woods might be fun. Their motives are not that difficult to discern, although we are not immediately sure as to why the unnamed central character might need support. Her motives, though, are more clouded. Her most superficial reason for the journey is to find out what has happened to her father. After her mother's death of cancer, he lived alone on the island in the lake, having only periodic contact with others who lived on the lake's shore. These others have not seen him recently, and their trips out to the island to check-up on him have proven fruitless. They have notified his daughter that he is "missing." Although she has had minimal contact with him in recent years, she feels duty-bound to come and do what she can to locate him—or, highly likely, his dead body. The unnamed central character, who is also the book's narrator, seems, however, to have other motives for coming to the island. There are hints that something has gone very wrong for her in her life in the city, leaving her almost shell-shocked. She seems to need a retreat, safely away from the city and whatever evils or ills it may represent. There are also hints, perhaps related, that she wants to reconnect with her past on the island. Because we discern hints that the city has become too much for her because it lacks roots in the natural, we guess that it may be the natural, the simple, and the innocent that she wants to find and embrace back in the woods. Perhaps this quest is somehow connected with that for her father, because her departure for the city coincides with her loss of contact with him and her mother as well. We are, however, largely working with hints, hints made plausible, as I will suggest later, by the way they fit into genre patterns with which we are familiar and according to which we try to read to novel.

The novel's plot, once it becomes clear (once it "surfaces"), will prove to be more complicated than these initial guesses of the nameless narrator's motives suggest. However, I want to move away from plot *per se* for a while—both because plot is not the crucial element of this novel and because other patterns begin emerging in *Surfacing* before the plot becomes clear. I want to focus on three (related) patterns that get us to the core of Atwood's very rich novel: the indictment of

the unnatural; the multiple failures to communicate; and the indictment of language (the symbolic) as a medium for communication.

There is much in *Surfacing* that is amusing. Atwood's characteristic
dry humor is not as absent from the book as the bulk of very serious
critical commentary might suggest. En route to the lake and the island, the unnamed narrator and her three companions encounter a
house made of bottles. (I don't know if there literally is one in the On-
tario-Quebec border country the novel is set in, but there is one on
Prince Edward Island that still draws tourists.) Houses, of course,
should be made of lumber, logs, and bricks of clay—elements drawn
from nature, not bottles. Thus, in a sense, the bottle house is unnatural. So is the moose family—father, mother, son, daughter—found
atop a general store. What makes the moose family unnatural is both
that they are dead, stuffed, and posed, and that they are dressed in
human garb. Neither of these examples of the unnatural are, however, particularly disturbing. However these examples do—albeit
comically—initiate an important motif in the novel.

The third and fourth instances of the unnatural are more ominous.
First, the road to the lakeside village has changed. The old road
wound its way through the terrain, hugging the hills: "it followed the
way the land went, up and down the hills and around the cliffs and
boulders" (17). It was imposed on nature, but in such a way that it fit
nature's contours. The new road cuts its way through that natural terrain: dynamiting and bulldozing has carved out a path that violates
nature. The narrator senses how wrong this new route is and even
complains that her father ought to have done something to stop its
construction. Second, the lake itself has changed. American timbering
interests have built a dam, thereby raising the water level significantly. The result is dead trees and other vegetation along the shore.
This blight caused by roots rotting joins the timbering of many, many
tall trees and an unspecified "disease...spreading up from the south"
(9) that is killing the birches to make the once pristine lake seem a
place of death and destruction. Damming the lake, timbering the gi-
ant trees and not "allow[ing them] to grow that tall again, making

"big trees as scarce as whales" (54), and "doom[ing the birches] by the disease, tree cancer" (139) — these are all examples of the unnatural.

One needs to define "the unnatural" rather broadly in the case of *Surfacing* to see how this motif embraces much of the novel. For example, Anna is unnatural in at least two ways. She carefully — neurotically — applies a heavy layer of make-up every day in order to present to husband David a façade that is pleasing. "He doesn't like to see me without it," and then, contradicting herself, "He doesn't know I wear it" (51), Anna tells the narrator. The narrator thinks of the "subterfuge this must involve, " "sneak[ing] out of bed before he's awake every morning and into it at night with the lights out" (51). Anna also has been practicing birth control, denying the natural reproductive processes of her body, stopping when she "got a blood clot in my leg," unlike the narrator who stopped because "I couldn't see...Things were blurry...It was like having Vaseline on my eyes...(95)." As Anna has denied this natural reproductive process, she has masked others — so much so that the narrator comments how both eating and defecating — natural processes — are so covered up by Anna that it seems as if nothing goes in and nothing comes out.

Equally unnatural is the behavior of the supposed American tourists on the lake. They boat in motorized, not paddled, vessels — even committing the absurdity of portaging a heavy metal motorboat from lake to lake to avoid the natural, but tiring rhythm of paddling. They fish and hunt for the thrill of the kill, not for the natural purpose of gaining nourishment. "They're the kind who catch more than they can eat and they'd do it with dynamite if they could get away with it" (76–77). More elaborately, she recalls

Raygun fishing rods, faces impermeable as spacesuit helmets, sniper eyes, they did it; guilt glittered on them like tinfoil. My brain recited the stories I'd been told about them: the ones who stuffed the pontoons of their seaplane with illegal fish, the ones who had a false bottom to their car, two hundred lake trout on dry ice, the game warden caught them by accident. "This is a lousy country," they said when he wouldn't take the bribe, "we ain't never coming back here." They got drunk and chased loons in their powerboats for fun, backtracking on the loon as it dived, not giving it a chance to fly, un-

til it drowned or got chopped up in the propeller blades. Senseless killing, it
was a game; after the war they'd become bored. (144)

After killing, trashing: "...trash was strewn around [their encamp-
ment], orange peelings and tin cans and a rancid bulge of greasy paper" (131). The narrator observes, "It was like dogs pissing on a fence,
as if the endlessness, anonymous water and unclaimed land, compelled them to leave their signature, stake their territory, and garbage
was the only thing they had to do it with" (131).

They even "lynch" a beautiful blue heron from a tree in a pose that
suggests a crucifixion just, according to the narrator, to show that
they can kill, that they have power over nature. She couldn't tell how
they'd killed the bird, whether "bullet, smashed with stone, hit with
stick" (138), but she understood why:

> Why had they strung it up like a lynch victim, why didn't they just throw it
> away like the trash? To prove they could do it, they had the power to kill.
> Otherwise it was valueless; beautiful from a distance but it couldn't be
> tamed or cooked or trained to talk, the only relation they could have to a
> thing like that was to destroy it. Food, slave or corpse, limited choices.
> ...(138)

The novel's original title, *The Transfigured Lake*—which preceded the
very Canadian (because echoing Frye's famous question in *The Literary History of* Canada) title *Where is Here*—seems to point to this envi-
ronmental damage (Wilson, *Margaret Atwood's* 102).

When the narrator thought these particular unnatural victimizers
were American, she was able to distance the problem somewhat, to
locate it in "the South," even farther South than the Toronto she and
her friends had left behind. However, what she thought was an
American flag on their boat was a New York Mets pennant, and, although Mets fans, the men are Canadian. The unnatural is closer than
she had thought: Canadians are becoming "American":

> It doesn't matter what country they're from, my head said, they're still
> Americans, they're what's in store for us, what we are turning into. They
> spread themselves like a virus, they get into the brain and take over cells
> and the cells change from inside and the ones that have the disease can't tell

the difference. Like the Late Show sci-fi movies, creatures from outer space, body snatchers injecting themselves into you, dispossessing your brain, their eyes blank eggshells behind the dark glasses. If you look like them and talk like them and think like them then you are them, I was saying, you speak their language, a language is everything you do. (152–53)

The narrator speaks here of the future. Not long after, she will look around at all her compatriots as well as those who still live by the lake and declare, "they are all Americans now" (199). The virus acts quickly.

Much has been made of the novel's anti-American rhetoric (Lozar). Yes, as *Survival*, which was published in the fall of 1972 along with *Surfacing*, suggest, Atwood was at this point in her career embracing a Canadian literary nationalism (Mackenzie 32). However, the opposition in the novel to the "American" is not a rejection of a country or its people as much as it is an indictment of an attitude, an unnatural attitude. The fact that the men who lynched the heron were Canadian, not American, points to this attitude. As Wilkins notes, Atwood makes the point about "Americans" only to quickly complicate it, rejecting the naïve assumption of Canadian innocence or a Canadian "victim fantasy" (Fiamego, "Post Colonial"). Further complicating the point is the narrator's eventual indictment of David as "American." This indictment is significant because, throughout the book, David had been the most vocal in announcing his dislike for Americans and all that they stand for, calling them "Bloody fascist pig Yanks" (12) and spinning elaborate paranoid scenarios premised on the United States needing fresh water and invading Canada to get it. The U. S. would "hit the big cities and knock out communications and take over, maybe shoot a few kids" (116). Separatist Quebecois would help the Americans; guerilla resistance would develop in the wilderness but be defeated by starvation or American defoliation. His strong words notwithstanding, he is as much an American as those he indicts because, as Ewell notes, he's an oppressor and is, as a result, turning into an unnatural, mechanized being (193):

The power flowed into my eyes, I could see into him, he was an impostor, a pastiche, layers of political handbills, pages from magazines, *affiches*, verbs

and nouns glued on him and shredding away....Secondhand American was
spreading over him in patches, like mange or lichen. He was infested, gar-
bled.... (178–79)

In the world presented by the unnamed narrator, those who act
against the natural eventually become unnatural. Curiously, men
tend to be unnatural; women more often aligned with the natural
(McCombs 116; Rocard, "Margaret Atwood's" 155). In fact, the natural, women, and colonized nations blend together, as the oppressed,
nicely linking Atwood's several themes in the novel together (Gerstenberger; Howells, *Margaret Atwood*; Huggans; Quartermaine 129-
30).

The world that is rapidly becoming unnatural is also a world that is
featuring less and less meaningful communication. Determining
whether the unnatural attitude feeds the lack of communication or
the lack of communication feeds the unnatural attitude is futile. It's
the chicken-and-egg situation. From the narrator's (and, I would suggest, Atwood's) perspective, they're connected, coincident. The novel
highlights both possibilities. As far as communication is concerned,
the four central characters pair-off. The narrator and Joe seem
wounded and pushed into communicating less; Anna and David, on
the other hand, pervert communication, turning something natural
into something unnatural.

Joe is described throughout the novel as taciturn. As David mock-
ingly notes, "You should wire him for sound. Or fix him up with a
plug and a shade, he'd make a great end-table lamp" (132). His silence seems to annoy the narrator occasionally, but, more often, she
finds that silence to be satisfactory, for it permits her to maintain her
distance from him. She chose to live with him almost off-handedly.
She seems to find in him primarily physical satisfaction. She describes
him in physical, animal terms; and she admits that she likes his body.
"Everything I value about him," she says, "seems to be physical: the
rest is either unknown, disagreeable or ridiculous" (65–66). The rest of
him she will not say she "loves." Perhaps she is drawn to him because, he, like she, is a struggling artist (Rigney 43), but she does not,
in the novel, make much of this connection. She does note how his art

is a commercial failure because, evidently to reflect his vision of the world, he makes pots that are grotesquely malformed, pots he "mutilates, cutting holes in them, strangling them, slashing them open" giving them "a disagreeable mutant quality" that doesn't "sell at all in the few handicraft shops that will even stock them" (66). To the extent his art is a form of communication, it seems thwarted by his disturbed view of things. Personally, he can't communicate readily; professionally, he can't communicate successfully.

The narrator herself is much the same. Because she is the narrator and is talking to us for nearly two hundred pages, we readers may be under the illusion that she's very communicative. As several have pointed out, the truth is the opposite (Quartermaine 124-25). She is probably more communicative than Joe, but only because she has to be. After all, this is her island, her cabin, her quest. Her communication is, however, very functional; rarely is she self-disclosive, even to her friend Anna or lover Joe. In fact, she is rarely self-disclosive to us. The result is that we know relatively little about her and what we do know we find out very gradually as the novel progresses. She is to a large extent, as Woodcock notes, "a voice rather than a person" (48). The fact that much of what she does eventually disclose is fabricated further undermines her as a communicator. Her art also suffers from communication problems. She is an illustrator, and her current task is illustrating a volume of Quebec fairy tales. She is having two problems with this task, however. First, her publisher will not permit her to illustrate the text as her imagination dictates; rather, she must do what will sell. Second, she can no longer draw the desired "sanitized" images. Selling out to what's commercially acceptable seems to have finally debilitated her. It would perhaps be "neat" to be able to pin the blame for the dearth of creative, communicative energy on her publisher with his crass commercial orientation, but its roots go deeper. They at least go back to art school, where her teacher (more about him later) gave her Cs, told her that there were no important female artists, and advised her to become an illustrator. Blaming him, though, is also too "neat," for even her earliest artwork suggests problems. That artwork had been preserved by her mother in scrapbooks, and, while on the island, she discovers these books. Her earliest work was "Page after page of eggs and rabbits, grass and trees, normal and green, surrounding them, flowers blooming, sun in the upper right-hand corner of each picture, moon symmetrically in the left. All the rabbits were smiling and some were laughing hilariously; several were shown eating ice-cream cones from the safety of their egg-tops" (109). Unlike her older brother's artwork, which rather violently de-picted the realities of World War II, her artwork reflected the safe fantasy world foisted upon young girls. Her later work, largely cut out of magazines, not even drawn, focused on fashion models and on women performing gender-typed tasks: "They were ladies, all kinds, holding up cans of cleanser, knitting, smiling, modeling toeless high heels and nylons with dark seams and pillbox hats and veils" (109). Her artwork again reflects the safe fantasy world, this time the one foisted upon adolescent girls. The unnamed narrator then seems to have never really been able to communicate *her self* through her art. Finally, as she tries to illustrate the Quebec fairy tales, that failure un-dermines her effort and work.

The world seems to have done something to Joe and the narrator. Perhaps it was over a long period of time; perhaps they were com-plicit in it. David and Anna, on the other hand, seem more in control. They both talk a great deal. Initially, David's talk has a take-charge quality: He knows his politics; he knows what his movie *Random Samples* needs to be; he even knows what they all need to do on the is-land. Initially, both the narrator and we the readers are somewhat taken in by David. He is a tad bombastic, but he seems knowledge-able. As already noted, eventually the narrator discovers how his anti-American politics mask an attitude that is very "American." Just as his political communication proves superficial so does his movie-making. Eventually, the narrator and we readers realize how stupid *Random Samples* is. Whereas David's early pronouncements on film might make some sense, his enactment of them has him—using his "Goofy" or "Woody Woodpecker" voice—stringing together shots that are both random and incoherent. One might fit together the bot-tle house, the clothed moose family, the spilled fish guts, and the crucified heron—as I did earlier—as examples of the unnatural. However, when one gets to the clip of Joe and David carrying the log they "conquered," one sees that David connects the filmed scenes based more on his ego-centric vision of the absurd than on any truly meaningful basis. Then, the film turns from stupid to dangerous. David insists that the film have a nude woman, so he perverts his communication skills to coerce his wife Anna into stripping for the camera. The scene is, as Strobel notes, pornographic; furthermore, it feels like a rape, with Joe "train[ing the camera]" on Anna "like a bazooka or a strange instrument of torture" (160). The camera is, as Wilson notes, entrapping, if not worse. Then, David (with Joe and Anna complicit) decides that the film must have a couple fucking in it and that the narrator must be the woman fucked: "'Where,'" David asks, "'would we fit her in, though? We don't have anyone fucking yet; but I'd have to do it,' he says to Joe, 'we need you running the camera' 'I could run the camera,' Anna says, 'you could both do it,' and everyone laughs" (194). But not the narrator. Fortunately, she cannot be coerced—and, in her case be gang-raped—as Anna was.

These latter scenes for *Random Samples* are both about communication and sex; the two are very much connected because sex is, after all, a very intimate form of communication. These scenes suggest that at least David doesn't see sex in this manner. He demonstrates repeatedly his sexism, telling Joe that Anna's "got a neat ass" (107) and telling the narrator that he likes her body because he "like[s] it round and firm and fully packed" (117). Earlier, the narrator overheard David and Anna making love. The narrator describes the love-making in a disturbing way: There is no communication; rather, Anna is being used, is being conquered. "She was praying to herself, it was as if David wasn't there at all. *Jesus jesus oh yes please jesus.* Then something different, not a word but pure pain, clear as water, an animal's at the moment the trap closes" (99). That scene ought to have alerted the narrator to the fact that the relationship between David and Anna was not as good as it initially seemed. In fact, the relationship has become a power game—fueled much more by mutual hate than mutual love. David's "got this little set of rules" for Anna. "If [she] breaks one of them [she] get[s] punished, except he keeps changing them so [Anna is] never sure" (145). The punishment, it seems, is by being publicly humiliated, like commenting leeringly on other women's bodies in front of her. As Anna says, "He was doing it to me. He always does stuff like that to other women in front of me, he'd screw them with me in the room if he could. Instead he screws them somewhere else and tells me about it afterwards" (118). Anna evidently retaliates by being unfaithful herself. So, they both play games, although Anna does seem the more desperate, more disempowered player: "...Anna was more than sad, she was desperate, her body her only weapon..." (180). The games are largely word games, but, Anna's body is very much the playing field or the battleground (choose your metaphor). David, however, tells the narrator that his infidelities are a response to her infidelities: that he is the aggrieved party. We don't know whether to believe him or not, especially since this statement is part of his strategy to seduce the narrator—to convince her she should avenge Joe's infidelity with Anna by having intercourse then and there with him. I think we are disinclined to believe him, since his sexist words (referring to Anna as "a pair of boobs" (163) or "that cunt on four legs" (177) or suggesting that Canada's national emblem be a "split beaver" (141) join his sexist behavior in undermining his credibility. No matter who is the guiltier, it is clear in all of the coupling—real or proposed—that sex has nothing to do with intimate communication. It has to do with games, with winning.

David and Anna exemplify this perversion of communication, but the novel in general depicts sexuality in such terms. Joe's proposal to the narrator is presented in terms of game-playing. As the narrator deconstructs the game, if the woman wants to marry, the man wants to just fuck; if the woman wants to just fuck, the man wants to marry. The man wants the opposite so that he can declare victory: "As long as there's a victory, some flag I can wave, parade I can have in my head" (104). The narrator perhaps sees male-female relations in this manner because of her personal history with men. In her true past, she was seduced by her married, middle-aged art teacher. When she became pregnant, she was at least partially coerced by him into aborting their child. He arranged the abortion, which she experienced alone, while he was attending a birthday party for his "real" children. The power dynamics in the relationship are such that both their sexual relationship and her abortion can be easily viewed as her disempowerment, even her rape. She has been abused by patriarchal power, with communication being used as the tool of her disempowerment (Prabhakar 70). There was thus no true communication involved: It was a game, and she was a plaything. That relationship scarred her, the result being her no longer trying to bring her full person to sex. She comments on how Joe thought the detached way in which she first removed her clothes for him was so "cool," so sophisticated—as if she was beyond middle-class emotions. She confesses to us that the reality was that she really felt nothing. Sex was no longer a way to communicate feelings; it was now, for her, physical release, no more.

The communication problems that *Surfacing* depicts are oftentimes sexual ones, and these problems do seem to center on the quartet of Joe, the narrator, David, and Anna. It is worth noting that the communication difficulties presented in the novel do extend beyond sex and this group. For example, as Jolly notes, the friends speak in "second hand language and jargon" (311). Moreover, moving from these friends to others, we note that the English-speaking in the community have difficulties, because of language, communicating with the French-speaking. The narrator's father seems to have had difficulties interpreting the Indian rock paintings he has found at various points on the island, and the narrating daughter is now sharing those difficulties. She thinks that there is a secret, special message for her from her father; similarly, she thinks that there ought to be a message from her mother. However, she is having trouble finding and deciphering the messages. She is also experiencing difficulties "reading" nature's messages, simple ones such as "birdsong" for which her "ears are rusty" (47), as well as the complex messages that she feels she's being sent by whatever gods inhabit nature and the complex messages implicit in the visions she has of mother and father near the novel's end.

Finally, there is her communicating to us. She is, as Quartermaine notes, evasive about her past, and, when she does choose to speak of it, she proves to be an unreliable narrator—telling us she was married and divorced, abandoning her child when she did so rather than telling us she had an affair and an abortion (124-25). Of course, she tells her friends and herself these same lies because she comes, for a while, to believe it. She thus has problems with intrapersonal communication as well as that with friends and readers. There is, in fact, very little successful communication in the novel. Even the message relayed to the reader in the end is so ambiguously communicated that, as noted earlier, critics disagree widely about that ending.

The relationship—the communication relationship—between the narrator and the reader should be discussed a bit more. She lies to readers in the beginning; she leaves us uncertain in the end. Neither of these is her fault: She believes what she tells us at the outset, and she only knows so much as the story concludes. She is trapped then within a discourse she believes and within a discourse that is still imperfectly unfolding. She is also—it would seem—trapped in between that beginning and that end. She is trapped within discourse structures that she may believe give definition—and therefore meaning—to what she is doing and telling us about. These discourse structures, not surprisingly, are ones of popular fiction. She sends signals that the story is a detective story: she (and maybe friends) will find out what happened to her father (Bartlett 21; Bouson 41; Rigney 38-39; Staels, "The Social" 23-24). She sends signals that the story is a ghost story—*not* the Henry James variety that Atwood herself links the novel to, but to a plot such as that found in the many *Friday the Thirteenth* movies. In this plot, the young people in the wild are threatened by a menace that lurks just beyond the safe encampment in the lake or in the woods: "What I'm afraid of," the narrator says, "is my father, hidden on the island somewhere and attracted by the light perhaps, looming up at the window like a huge ragged moth" (71). Furthermore, should they have sex, they become especially vulnerable! The narrator gives the story this twist—as opposed to the detective story one—when she talks about how they are endangered by the dead father and whatever else lurks out there. A third structure forgets the father entirely and focuses on the quartet, in the woods alone together. Secrets will be revealed; tensions will surface and explode; partners may well be swapped. In the end, though, all will know themselves better as a result of their time—their therapeutic time—in the wilderness together. There are narrative structures evoked beyond these three: wilderness writing (Bouson 41; Murray); autobiography (Bartlett 21); romance parody (Bouson 43-44); fairy tale, with twists (Wilson, *Margaret Atwood's* 97-119). There is, of course, a shred of truth in each of these discourse structures: that is why we attend to them and believe them—if only temporarily. They are also familiar structures, and that familiarity makes it comfortable for us as readers: we know the kind of story; we know therefore how to read. Unfortunately, the novel really is not any of these stories. The discovery of the father's fate proves anticlimactic; there is no Jason out there; and the quartet's drama proves far less significant than the narrator's drama. Thus, the narrator—insofar as she signals these structures—poorly communicates what her story is. Of course, again, she does not know what her story is herself. Here, it is important to separate the narrator from Atwood: the narrator's being lost in a forest of discourse structures suggests her not knowing (yet) what her story is; Atwood's evoking these structures is her signal that the woman's story, whatever it is, must exist outside of these largely patriarchal structures (Bouson 56), structures Atwood critiques if not parodies (Staels, *Margaret Atwood's Novels* 50, 54-55).

Tied necessarily to this motif of poor communication is the novel's extensive commentary on language itself. This commentary starts at the novel's beginning, when the narrator notes how language is inaccurate and polyphonic. She notes how a particular place is marked by a sign saying "Gateway to Great North"; then she notes how that "at least four towns claim to be that" (11), belying the assumption that there was a single gateway. She notes the words scribbled on a cliff—words in French and English, words reverent and irreverent, and words commercial:

VOTEZ GIDEZ, VOTEZ OBRIEN, along with hearts and initials and words and advertisements, THE SALADA, BLUE MOON COTTAGES 1/2 MILE, QUEBEC LIBRE, FUCK YOU, BUVEZ COCA-COLA GLACE, JESUS SAVES, melange of demands, an X ray of it would be the district's entire history. (18)

Then, she notes, comically, her parents' attempts at communication in French: how her mother knew but five French words and Madame but five English ones, leading her mother to "shout" "'Il fait beau,'... no matter what the weather was like and Madame to scream 'Ow are you'" (24).

Eventually, the nameless narrator will talk specifically about language, offering a critique that sounds like much poststructural commentary. She notes how, when growing up, she "discovered people could say words that would go into my ears and mean nothing" (14). Although she means to be commenting on the dominance of French in the region, she makes a larger point about how the meaning of words is problematic. Sometimes the problem is the word has no meaning; at others the problem is that we naively think the words have meaning and become trapped in "mirages raised by words" (193). The word "love," for instance. It was a "magic word," one that "was supposed to make everything light up" (55), but, having experienced its abuse, she'll "never trust that word again" (55). She won't use it toward Joe and wonders if "'I do give a shit about you,' repeat[ed]...like a skipping rhyme...was the equivalent of saying I loved him" (104). She says more:

It was the language again, I couldn't use it because it wasn't mine. He must have known what he meant but it [love] was an imprecise word; the Eskimos had fifty-two names for snow because it was important to them, there ought to be as many for love. (127)

She objects to separate words for the head and the body: In her mind, the separate words reinforce a troublesome mind-body split in her and society. In general, she feels that, "Language divides us into fragments, but [she] wanted to be whole" (172). She also objects to the language that she associates with being "American." If you start using that language, you can become "American." Thus, she rejects her work as a "caseful of alien words and failed pictures" (193) because that work connects her to the commercial and, thus, the "American." Finally, seeing the problem as broader than "American," seeing rationality as the problem and all language, because it assumes and reflects that rationality, she "burn[s] through all the words" (207), including *Log Cabin Construction*, Boswell, and the Bible. This large indictment—and conflagration—brings her position very much in line with Kristeva's (and other feminists) toward the symbolic.

However, before even beginning this increasing sophisticated critique, her very language indicates problems. As Robert Cluett reveals in a fascinating linguistic study of Atwood's novel, the narrator's language is characterized by simple syntax, very few modifiers, heavy pronominalization, and heavy right-branching. Cluett compares novels by Morley Callaghan, Robertson Davies, Margaret Laurence, and Leonard Cohen with Atwood's *Surfacing* and finds the prose in Atwood's novel to be "unique not only in the Atwood canon but in all twentieth century fiction" (67). What then do these characteristics suggest about the narrator? The simple syntax (i.e., short, sometimes abbreviated clauses) and the absence of modifiers suggest a distrust of language. Coloration, either that provided by embedded syntactic elements or adjectives and adverbs, is lacking; the style is as direct as possible, suggesting an attempt to minimize those verbal elements that might misdirect. The heavy pronominalization may be a reflection of the narrator's distrust of nouns. Nouns fix; nouns freeze; nouns name once and for all. Thus, late in the book, she declares her allegiance to the more semiotic verbs and actually yearns to be transformed so as to become more like a verb: "In one of the languages there are no nouns, only verbs held for a longer moment" (212). Maybe this can be her language, or, maybe she can become like "The animals" in nature which "have no need for speech" because they "are a word" (212). However, should she become a word, she wants not to be bound as a noun but in "verb-ed" and in motion: "I lean against a tree, I am a tree leaning" (212). In addition, rather than nouns, she uses pronouns. This use does keep discourse more fluid by reducing syllables and introducing some ambiguity. That ambiguity, as Shuli Barzalai notes, also allows Atwood to imply hidden meanings—and the hidden truth—in the narrator's words. "He," for example, although intended to refer to the father, may implicitly refer to brother or lover or aborted child. The narrator, of course, is unaware of these language elements in her prose. The other referents are surfacing from her subconscious. That they do is, however, yet another indication of language's slipperiness. Ironically, in trying to avoid the tyranny of nouns, the narrator slips into pronouns that allow the repressed to bubble to the surface. Finally, the right branching suggests an additive style, one with a hesitancy that indicates a discomfort with the syntactic building blocks, a fear that anything more elaborate than a horizontal row will court collapse. This additive style also mirrors the process of exploring or discovering the novel presents, and all of these stylistic elements taken together suggest the narrator's distance from others and, perhaps, reality. Thus, in addition to using the narrator's language to depict her distrust of the medium, Atwood uses the language to mirror the novel's plot and the narrator's state of mind.

Eventually, the narrator's discomfort with words turns more strident. Whereas early in the novel she saw ambiguity, now she sees words as dangerous. David and Anna sling words at each other. Men use words to win their way with women. Men use words to win their way with land—trying to seize it, claiming that Americans of the Detroit branch of the Wildlife Protection Association of America want her father's land to commune with nature—"'a kind of retreat lodge where the members could meditate and observe,' he puffed, 'the beauties of nature'"—when they really want is to "do a little hunting and fishing" (113)—in other words, to kill nature. She "foresaw motels, highrises" lurking beneath his words about the place's "rural charm" (113).

Increasingly as the novel progresses, the narrator offers comments on language that seem right out of Kristeva. The narrator does not use the terms "symbolic" and "semiotic"—although Atwood's critics often do, but she talks of language as that create by the head, by the rational part of the human being. She feels as if this language is not at all connected to the body and to bodily experience. In fact, this language may pervert the body and bodily experience as the disembodied pictures of genitalia on the barge cabin's wall suggest (Ewell 191; Strobel 36). These pictures are so disembodied that the narrator's brother must interpret them for her. That bodily experience, she says, must be in another language, but she only gets glimpses of that other language when she foregoes the rational and focuses on the physical, the animal, the natural. It seems as if this language is there in the vibrations and stirrings of the semiotic chora.

These three motifs—the unnatural, failed communication, suspicious language—can be traced throughout the novel. One must superimpose of these motives the novel's plot to understand what happens to the central character during her island sojourn. The first part of the novel has the characters arriving, settling in, and exploring. Meanwhile, largely on her own, the nameless narrator tries to solve the mystery of her father's disappearance. Her efforts seems rather half-hearted at times. She feels duty-bound to do her—the daughter's—part; however, she seems to wish that she could go through the motions, declare she has done all she can, and head back to Toronto. What hooks her into the search a bit more is her fear that her father has gone mad and is alive. The strange drawings of primitive-looking figures he left behind are what causes her to think he might have become "bushed" by living alone in the wilderness. Oddly, however, the hook is not that he might be alive, but that he might be mad. She wants to disconfirm this possibility, probably because she fears for her own sanity (Barzilai 65). When she discovers correspondence between her father and a professional archaeologist about the drawings, she realizes that they were of cliff or cave paintings he had discovered. Convinced he was sane and convinced that he was, therefore, likely dead, not roaming mad in the woods, she nonetheless stays hooked. She begins to search for these paintings herself at points that he had marked on a map.

This search leads to the novel's first climactic scene. She goes out alone in a canoe to one of the sites. Realizing that the cliff paintings would have to now be under water because the lake was higher than when the Indians lived there, she repeatedly dives into the water to examine the cliff's surface. What she sees is not painted on the wall. Aided perhaps by the oxygen deprivation one suffers if diving repeatedly, she sees a vision that is both that of father's corpse and that of something else: "…a dark oval trailing limbs. It was blurred but it has eyes, they were open, it was something I knew about, a dead thing, it was dead" (167). The something else seems initially to be either her brother (who almost drowned) or the creatures he kept pent-up in jars, for she "sees" it as if "in a bottle curled up, staring out at me like a cat pickled" (168). Eventually, she realizes that the vision was of the fetus she aborted: "…Whatever it is, part of myself or a separate creature, I killed it. It wasn't a child but it could have been one, I didn't allow it" (168). She realizes she's been lying about her past to others and, more importantly, to herself. She also realizes that she has been complicit in the unnatural behavior she has indicted in those around her as well as in the flawed communication that has characterized most interactions in the book thus far.

The fact that this shocking vision occurs to her while immersed in the lake's water is suggestive. It suggests the possibility of redemption. The lake, at first sight, was seen to be "blue and cool as redemption" (18). The shocking vision also suggests that the way to that rebirth will be by attending to the womb—her womb as well as the womb Kristeva associates with the semiotic. The shocking vision then sends the nameless narrator on a quest very different from the way that she and we thought defined the novel. She will spend the rest of her time on the island getting back in touch with the semiotic and, through that, back in touch with her self.

She has much to learn, and she knows—she feels—that she must learn what she needs alone. Thus, she begins distancing herself from the other three. She will eventually put physical distance between herself and the trio, but, for the moment, she puts just psychological distance. Paradoxically, this distancing allows her to see them better, and what she sees mirrors herself in various ways.

In Anna, she sees the logical conclusion of selling out to the image of woman that society reinforces through all of the messages it sends girls as they grow up. Anna has become both painted doll and sex object—as the narrator puts it, an imitation of an imitation of an imitation of nothing that is really there. The narrator realizes that, in her own adolescent fascination with fashionable and stereotypical images of the female, she was pursuing the same path that led Anna to be the sad being that we meet in the novel.

In David, she sees someone who, like her, sees the world through a veil of cynicism. As a result, neither of them can feel or love: "David is like me, I thought, we are the ones that don't know how to love, there is something essential missing in us, we were born that way..." (161). However, But there is an important difference in power between the two. Because of his gender, he has greater power to use his bitterness against others. Her bitterness, on the other hand, has driven both her past and her anger beneath the surface. David is very much what she could have become if she had dealt with the world around her in overt terms.

In Joe, however, she sees someone very different from David. Early in the novel, we tend to merge the two: they are the two buddies working on their bizarre film together. Gradually, they separate for us—and for the narrator. She sees in David someone who has, like her, been wounded by the world. She also sees that he has not become as complicit with that world as David. Whereas David is unnatural, perverts communicate, and uses language as a weapon, Joe is still somewhat animal-like, looking "like the buffalo on the U.S. nickel, shaggy and blunt-snouted, with small clenched eyes and the defiant but insane look of a species once dominant, now threatened with extinction" (10), and withdraws from communication and language rather than abuse them. In some ways, he is less complicit in the problematic human world the novel depicts than she is. After all, he neither killed his unborn child nor has deceived everybody about the past. "For him," the narrator notes, "truth might still be possible, what will preserve him is the absence of words" (186). Thus, she chooses to have a child with Joe, a child that she thinks will partially compensate for the one that she has allowed to be killed.

Anna and David mirror what the narrator might have become— "already turning to metal, skins galvanizing, heads congealing to brass knobs, components and intricate wires ripening inside" (186); Joe mirrors what she in some ways is. The trickier mirrors, however, are her father and her mother. Until she can fully understand the message they convey, she will not be ready to be redeemed. Having a replacement child will not be enough. She comes to the island remembering her childhood as a happy one. She must admit the contrary and then realize that the problem with true communication in her life is partially rooted in both her family's lack of communication and her father's excessively rational communication (Klovan 9-10).

Her father was the epitome of rationalism. His idols were various thinkers and writers from the eighteenth century. He used their rationalism—actually, an exaggerated version of that rationalism—to reject religion and to undergird his scientific explorations of the natural world. Although there is clearly distance between the narrator and her father, she is nonetheless quite like him—more than she is comfortable admitting. She has not only absorbed his rationalism—as evident in how she proceeds as detective, but she has absorbed his tendency to think in binary terms that categorize and separate (Ewell 187-88). For example, she believes he is either mad or dead. On a larger scale, she believes people are either "Americans" or not. This way of thinking not only blinds her to the irrational and the ambiguous, it also may have informed her life. For example, having been told she cannot, because she is female, be a great artist, she opts for the opposite extreme of a sell-out illustrator. For example, having had an adulterous affair and a semi-coerced abortion, she is "bad," not "good," and therefore necessarily distanced from her "innocent" parents who could not possibly understand or deal with either her true life in the city or the fictitious one of marriage, divorce, and abandonment of child that she created.

The dangers of rationality and bipolarity are best illustrated in her brother's life. Thus, she serves as yet another mirror, maybe even, as

Pratt suggests, as her Jungian shadow (144). He was, like her father, scientifically-inclined, maintaining a semi-secret "laboratory" in the woods. In fact, as Klovan notes, he was a demomic version of the father (12). Her brother sorted everything into "good" and "bad." There were good leeches (ones with red dots on the back) and bad ones (mottled gray and yellow); there was Hitler and those opposed to the incarnate evil. The bad and the evil, you attack. His childhood drawings illustrate attacks, as does his throwing of the "bad" leeches onto the fire. He was, however, not alone in acting in this manner. The narrator was complicit in killing the supposedly "bad" leeches. She was also complicit in "killing" one of her least favorite dolls:

> ...one time we were a swarm of bees, we gnawed the fingers, feet and nose off our least favorite doll, ripped her cloth body open and pulled out the stuffing, it was gray and fluffy like the insides of mattresses; then we threw her into the lake. She floated and they found the body and asked us how she got lost, and we lied and said we didn't know. Killing was wrong, we had been told that only enemies and food could be killed. (154)

So, which was the doll? Furthermore, the narrator she was somewhat complicit in the killing her brother did off in his woodland "laboratory" of creatures he had captured and jarred. She wanted to free them; she knew she should free them. However, "Because of [her] fear they were killed" (155): she allowed them to be killed, just as she allowed the fetus within her to be killed. She yielded to her older brother's power, and she yielded to her older lover's power. She realizes, however, that she was nonetheless complicit. Recognizing this complicity, as Tschachler argues, is crucial in her growth (66-67). She could have freed the creatures; she could have said "No."

Exploring her father and her brother's stories more fully makes one thing clear to readers—perhaps more so than to the nameless narrator: the "sin" she needs to be redeemed from is not just the abortion she consented to. She needs to be redeemed from the excessive rationality with words that "confine, fence off, evade, and lie" (Clark 7), and the imprisoning bipolarity that poisoned her father, her brother, and her.

What I have just said about reason may sound to some like an almost stereotypical critique of patriarchal language offered by many
feminist critics during the 1970s and 1980s. Not surprisingly then,
Surfacing has been embraced by feminists in a manner that seems to
have made Atwood uncomfortable. Atwood did not want to be identified with any movement or any ideology. Rather, Atwood saw a
problem facing human beings, and she wanted to encourage readers,
regardless of gender, to address the problem. As the novel says in a
number of ways, the essence of the problem seems to be a separation
of the head from the body—a fragmentation of the human being. The
nameless narrator feels this fragmentation. She complains that the
narrow neck separates head from body, thinking from feeling. Then,
she realizes that "[a]t some point my neck must have closed over,
pond freezing or a wound, shutting me into my head; since then everything had been glancing off me, it was like being in a vase, or the
village where I could see them but not hear them because I couldn't
understand what was being said" (126). Recognizing where the
dominance of the head might lead—indeed, has led—is then only
part of the solution. She must become reconnected to the body.

Her mother provides her with a clue. She feels that her mother's
sprit has led her to one of her childhood drawings. In this drawing,
the narrator has depicted herself as a baby, sitting within her mother's
womb, watching the world. The picture is one of safety for the child
and maternal fulfillment for the mother. Standing beside them is the
narrator's rendition of God, a rendition which refutes the binary God-
devil split by giving God the horns and tail of the devil. Adding God
to the safe, maternal picture suggests that there is a divine harmony
to be found in the fruitful womb. However, this is not the only picture
of the mother that influences the narrator. She remembers on several
occasions how her mother exhibited total harmony with nature: how
she was not frightened by visiting bears; how she could be so still that
bluejays would land on her hands. The narrator's mother then exhibits what the narrator could be: attuned to her body; through that, attuned to nature. Notably, this harmony seems outside language—as

suggested by her mother's quiet and her mother's largely blank diary pages (Staels, *Margaret Atwood's* 56).

Having learned from the mirrors offered by her parents (as well as by her brother), she knows that she must do more than become pregnant to be redeemed. In an important symbolic gesture, she lashes out at all that the film *Random Samples* has come to represent by dumping it in the lake. To her, after Anna's "rape," the film no longer just depicted what "The machine" was doing to "dead things," like the log or the fish or the heron, but about what these mechanized beings were doing "to each other also, without knowing" (195). Thus, she lets the film "spiral into the lake" (195). The very language captures how she is liberating, returning things to nature:

> The film coils onto the sand under the water, weighted down by its containers; the invisible captured images are swimming away into the lake like tadpoles, Joe and David beside their defeated log, axemen, arms folded, Anna with no clothes on jumping off the end of the dock, finger up, hundreds of tiny naked Annas no longer bottled and shelved. (195)

She says no to the unnatural; she says no to oppression, especially that of women (the disempowered) by man (the empowered). The image in the novel of thousand of tiny Anna's floating in the lake free from the film frames they had been imprisoned in as in bottles or jars is a liberating one. The narrator wishes she had acted in a similar manner to free the jarred creatures her brother had collected for his experiments. The narrator wishes she could free the real Anna. The narrator wishes she had said "No" and prevented her unborn child from either being removed from her like a pickle and jarred or swept down the drain into the city's sewers. She was not able to act before; now, symbolically, she acts. Then, she goes off into the woods—in Wilkins' words, into "a retreat into a pre-discursive, pre-rational realm which she identifies with a pure Canada and a unified selfhood" (207)—to enact a redemptive ritual that may bring her back, more fully human, into the world.

She has—she thinks—already prepared herself within for the experience, for she has conceived a life within her womb. She needs now to prepare herself without. This process is one of rejection: she must reject all that might be considered unnatural. She must reject the violent artwork of her brother and the fantasy and sell-out artwork of her youth and adolescence. She must reject all of the ways in which humans have tried to impose boundaries on nature: All enclosures, whether garden fences or cabin walls or cans, must go, as well as anything that might intervene between her body and nature. Thus, bedding goes, and clothes go. She must, furthermore, bring that body more intimately in touch with nature by taking into her body only that foodstuff that is absolutely natural. In an ironic twist of the *loup-garou* story, she must become animal-like to become truly human (Baer). Perhaps more than anything else, she must reject language—that human invention that, by defining, imposes boundaries. Thus, books and all other documents must go. More profoundly, she must find a way to feel—not think--herself out of language. She tries bodily to become a tree so she can discard the label "tree" as irrelevant; she tries bodily to become a place so she can discard any and all place names and live in harmony with "the trees and animals mov[ing] and grow[ing]" in her embrace. As noted earlier, she tries to become more verb-like, using heavily verbs of sensing (Staels, *Margaret Atwood's Novels* 62), so she can reject the more finite nouns in favor of being and moving and acting as nature and bodies attuned to nature are, move, and act.

Several critics have pointed to the nameless narrator's struggling with language and have read that struggling, as I do, in terms derived from Kristeva. Howells suggests that the narrator is on "a gendered quest for a new language which is more responsive to an organic conceptualization of reality" (27). Robinson notes another dimension of this new language. It will be "a language closely tied with the maternal, and thus with women, will allow writers to disrupt traditional structures of discourse and will ultimately lead to transformations in language itself" (107). Staels more explicitly evokes Kristeva, describing where this new language will emerge from. "In the pre-verbal realm, instinctual motility or biological rhythm prevails. The experiencer rhythmically enters the *chora* and repetitively moves again to-

ward the surface, or the thetic realm, which is the realm of significa-
tion" (*Margaret Atwood's Novels* 64). Before surfacing, this "experiencer," according to Ward, is immersed in "a level of language
largely unregarded by man, one which might be said to exist around
or beneath the elaborations of a human dialect—a level which has a
semiotic if not a symbolic force" (99). In so immersing herself and surfacing, the narrator, according to Robinson, "undergoes a fantastic
transformation into a non human being in an attempt to escape from
a language that excludes her and proves repressive of her female experience and desire" (108).

In addition to enacting this ritual of rejection, she enacts a ritual of
purification. She immerses herself in the baptismal water of the lake
once again. This time, the immersion leads to a rebirth: "When I am
clean I come up out of the lake, leaving my false body floated on the
surface, a cloth decoy" (208). She emerges naked, without that false
clothing, from the womb-like water and waits for the fur to grow on
her body and her baby, figured as the first new human on earth, to
grow within her. She also at this point—aided, perhaps, by mushrooms she has eaten, has a last vision of her mother and her father. As
Fiamengo notes, the novel does indeed involve to a large extent her
coming to terms with her parents ("'A Last Time'"). Neither speaks.
They both convey their final messages, appropriately, out of language.

The mother's message is one of affirmation. She is, once again, depicted with the birds. Her harmony with nature is suggested by her
utter simplicity and the birds' taking food from her. It is suggestive
even more by what seems to be her becoming a bird and flying away:
"The jays cry again, then fly up from her, the shadows of their wings
ripple over the ground and she's gone" (213). The narrator's oneness
with nature is being affirmed, maybe even saluted as the mother
"turns her head quietly and looks at me" (213). The father's message
is more complex: It both warns and affirms. He is depicted as a wolf.
He is perhaps the werewolf or *loup-garou* figure from Quebecois folk-
lore. As such, he serves as a warning to her about what over-
rationality can be: how it can transform a thinking and feeling human

into an oppressor (Grace). However, as soon as this warning sinks in, the father transforms himself into a fish and flashes forth with multiple facets—fish as idea, fish as redemptive emblem or iconic "protecting spirit," fish as carved creature mounted on some human wall, fish as natural creature at home in the life-giving water. "How many shapes can he take," the narrator asks as she watches "for an hour or so" (219). The mind can destroy, leaving one with "yellow eyes, wolf's eyes, depthless but lambent as the eyes of animals seen at night in the car headlights" (218), but the mind can be made to cohabit with the body and form a human if she works hard to achieve and maintain this harmony, a human with the variety and the complexity of the metamorphosing fish. She is linked to her mother through the body, but she is also linked to her father through the mind. Her foot, as Ward notes, fits into the wolf's pawprint (117).

These visions occur outside of language—perhaps signaled by breakdowns in normal grammar (Clark 11; Ewell 199; Staels, *Margaret Atwood's Novels* 64). That is doubly appropriate, for they are not as much thought as felt by the narrator, and they must reject language because the symbolic is, as the novel reveals, at the root of so much that has gone wrong. Earlier, the narrator had decided not even to "never teach [her new child] any words" (191). That pledge, though, was, of course, unrealistic. Then, as the visions fade, the narrator makes an uneasy peace with the world that is calling for her return and with Joe. Language will necessarily be part of this world—and the world of that new child, which, as Wilkins notes, she ironically imagines herself delivering onto newspapers, which are full of words (218). However, she will proceed with a full understanding of language's inadequacies and dangers. She says,

> For us it's necessary, the intercession of words; and we will probably fail, sooner or later, more or less painfully. That's normal, it's the way it happens now and I don't know whether it's worth it or even if I can depend on him, he may have been sent as a trick. But he isn't an American, I can see that now; he isn't anything, he is only half formed, and for that reason I can trust him. (224)

Furthermore, there is hope, as Clark puts it, that it will be "the old language, cleansed and reinvented with power by herself" (12).

In the end, she seems to choose to return to the city with Joe. He is, after all, not like Anna and David; he's not an "American." He has enough human potential, she thinks, to be worth risking a life with. Although the narrator leaves the island with Joe in the screenplay Atwood wrote based on the novel, in the book, we never do see this moment. The novel is thus more ambiguous than the screenplay, which also, like earlier drafts of the novel, present Joe in more appealing terms (Stein, *Margaret Atwood* 56). Nonetheless, most readers feel she will, even though that event is not in the language of the novel. There is, however, ambiguity—both in this irresolution and in the forecasted problems ahead for the narrator, Joe, and their child. There is also ambiguity in the fact that the narrator never is given a name in the text. At the end, Joe calls her by name, but we never hear it. Her lack of identity has suggested to some readers that she has not really found herself at the novel's conclusion. An alternate reading would suggest that her lack of a name is an indication that she has managed to stay—healthfully—outside of language. That her namelessness in the end can be read negatively or positively is an indication of Atwood's rather typical ambiguity.

As I indicated earlier, critics have arrayed themselves into camps based on their readings of the conclusion (Kokotailo 155). Like Swift's *Gulliver's Travels*, Atwood's novel seems to have good end-ian interpreters, bad-endian interpreters, and those, such as myself, who tilt one way or the other but admit that there is much deliberate ambiguity. Critics have devoted much time and attention to the novel's rather brief third section, discussing their sense of the ending, as well as the intertextuality of the narrator's various ritualistic experiences. This intertextuality requires a comment.

I do not intend to survey in detail the voluminous criticism devoted to rooting what the narrator experiences in one tradition or another, sometimes playing straight with the tradition, sometimes giving it a feminist twist. Some see her ritualistic actions in terms that Joseph Campbell (Donaldson; Rigney) or Northrop Frye (Berryman) has ex-

tracted from many Western mythologies or simply in those mytho-
logical terms without the mediation of Frye (Grace). Some see her actions in magical (Mendez), Christian (Hinz), alchemical (VanSpanckeren), or either Amerindian terms (Guedon) or terms that blend the
Amerindian with the psychological (James); others find in Jung
(Pratt) or Kristeva or the mystical experiences of Mary Magdalene
and Mary of Egypt (Thomas, "Mythic") clues as to her experiences in
the week alone that the novel chronicles rather rapidly. I, of course,
find that Kristeva's distinction between the semiotic and the symbolic, her emphasis on the thetic boundary between and what crossing it entails, her notion of a semiotic chora that can still pulse
through into the symbolic, and her connection between that chora
and the body, both sexual or maternal, of the female human very use-
ful in understanding *Surfacing* and the other texts considered in this
book. The ending, however, strikes me as containing no one of the
above "systems," but, instead, all of them. If so, the ending sends an
important set of messages.

First, the ending rejects any of these –ism's as both ideologies and
language systems. They are all confining; they are all potentially dangerous. The ending then is quite consonant with the attitude toward
language (paradoxically) communicated throughout the novel. Second, the ending embraces all, not because they are all "correct," but
because they represent multiple voices. The ending then validates
multiplicity. Again, this validation is quite consonant with the novel's
overall position with regards to a rationality that stresses bipolarities
and insists on choices that give us winners and losers and, perhaps,
validate the killing of the latter by the former. Third, the ending un-
dermines language as a system by swirling different myths, different
religions, and different cultures around in a mix that, in the end, suggests that the ritual means something, but we cannot find in language
the words for it. It is all words, but no words. It is something that the
different words dance around but never quite get at—at least to the
point where a phrase or a set of phrases captures it. It happens
within, and is felt within, but the experience, like much in the semiotic, does not have simple expression in the symbolic. Again, this cri-

tique of the symbolic (paradoxically in language) and this affirmation of the semiotic is quite consonant with the way the novel gradually brings it more and more to the fore and allows it to surge across the thetic moment and bubble provocatively (but without sharp resolution) in the symbolic. Perhaps the novel's concluding section is so brief because it is so semiotic and can therefore be captured only inadequately by the symbolic. If so, the brevity should not be read as a limitation of the semiotic, but the other way around, as a limitation of the symbolic. In addition, perhaps all of the pages of criticism that attempt to pin down the drama of the ending are proof. Alternatively, perhaps that critics feel obliged to write and writing is a testimonial to the power of whatever it is that is not in language but nonetheless a felt presence as Atwood's novel concludes.

5

Small-Town Traps

Margaret Laurence's *A Jest of God;*
Alice Munro's *Lives of Girls and Women*

Not all islands are masses of land surrounded by water. Much like the island of Bohemia in Shakespeare's *The Winter's Tale*, some are more states of mind than geographical entities. Shakespeare's Bohemia is an idyllic pastoral island. Despite the fact that death, at the claws and teeth of a bear, marks its shore, the island provides safety. The bear may suggest that the safety is tenuous or even illusory. Be that as it may, the island functions in the play as a safe retreat from Sicily, where much has gone wrong in the play's initial two acts. Not all islands-of-the-mind offer such safety. Some offer the opposite—a sense of entrapment. Such is the case with much of the fiction written by two of Canada's more famous chroniclers of small-town life, Margaret Laurence and Alice Munro. Laurence has created the prairie town of Manawaka; Munro the western Ontario town if Jubilee. Both iso-

lated places entrap their heroines. There is, of course, irony in that entrapment, for, on the surface, the two small towns would seem to offer something idyllic if not exactly pastoral.

   Much has been written on Laurence's Manawaka (Coger). Based on
the small Manitoba town where Laurence grew up, Manawaka is
given a history in *The Stone Angel* (1964). Then, we get more contemporary stories: those of Vanessa MacLeod in *A Bird in the House*
(1970), Morag Gunn in *The Diviners* (1974), and the Cameron sisters
Stacey and Rachel in *The Fire-Dwellers* (1969) and *A Jest of God* (1966).
By the time we have read all of these works, we have a sense of Manawaka's landscape and cityscape; more importantly, we have a
strong sense of the town's social structure. We know who has the
money and the power and who does not; we know where the various
social lines of demarcation are drawn. We also know that these lines
are rarely crossed and that the citizens are kept in their proper places
and that those in the better places are restricted to behavior deemed
"proper" by scrutiny and gossip (Drummond 401, 403). Early in the
novel, Rachel's mother exemplifies how gossip works in Manawaka
when she reports to her daughter, with both relish and moral outrage,
that Cassie Stewart has given birth to twins out of wedlock. Late in
the novel, thinking she is pregnant and unwed, Rachel imagines the
effect on her mother as others in the town report that news with the
same relish and moral outrage:

> She would be—how?—broken up, wounded, ashamed, hysterical, refusing
> to believe it, believing it only too readily, willing to perjure her soul or pawn
> her wedding ring to be rid of it, never able to trust again (she would de-
> clare), not able to hold her head up forever after on Japonica Street, outcast
> and also seeking exile because unable to meet the sympathetic stutterings of
> the world, and worst of all, perhaps, blaming herself (or claiming she was)
> for something unknown and unsuspected in her rearing of me. "What, I ask
> myself, Rachel, could I have done, in bringing you up, that you would do a
> thing like that?" Bringing her grey hairs to sorrow to the etcetera. (166–67)

In her Mother May's imagined reaction, we see the power gossip has
in Manawaka.

Manawaka is surrounded by great expanses of open land. Rarely, though, do we go there (Howells, "Margaret Laurence's" 41). When we do, it is significantly for moments of transgression against the town's strict norms. Rachel's "pet" pupil, James Doherty, plays "hooky" there; Rachel and Nick Kazlik make love there (Stovel, "Rachel's Children" 26).

At age thirty-five, Rachel Cameron very much feels the claustrophobic oppression of the place (Easingwood 255; Hartveit 345; Legendre 67; Relke 35). She is stuck living at home with her aging widowed mother, who manipulates Rachel into not growing up and growing out. So, facing the prospect of providing her mother with care into the foreseeable future, Rachel settles for one of the few tasks a single woman of her generation could take on: She becomes an elementary school teacher. Within the Manawaka world, the maternal role, whether as mother, caretaker, or early elementary school teacher, seems almost destined to take over a young woman's life (Gandesberry 71). Playing this role entails control. At home, she is very much controlled by her mother; at work, she is very much controlled by the patriarchal structure of the school, as embodied in its controlling, condescending principal (Baum, "Self-alienation" 156; Hartveit 345; Martin 61; Stein, "Speaking" 81-82). In both of these cases, the controlling figures may well be more sympathetic characters than narrating Rachel makes them out to be. Sympathetic or not, they are felt by Rachel to be controlling and confining.

Laurence uses both setting and narration to emphasize the confinement Rachel feels. Two aspects of her home are suggestive. First, Rachel's bedroom. It is still the room she occupied as an adolescent girl, replete with furniture appropriate for a maid of fourteen but not a mature woman of thirty-five:

> This bedroom is the same I've always had. I should change the furniture. How girlish it is, how old-fashioned. The white spindly-legged dressing table, the round mirror with white rose-carved frame, the white-painted metal bed with its white-painted metal bow decorating the head like a starched forgotten hair ribbon. (22)

It is in this room that Rachel experiences her masturbatory sexual fantasies, and it makes sense that she would experience them there, for the room is suitable for adolescent sexuality only (Stovel, *Rachel's Children* 24-25):

> —A forest. Tonight it is a forest. Sometimes it is a beach. It has to be right away from everywhere. Otherwise she may be seen. The trees are green walls, high and shielding, boughs of pine and tamarack, branches sweeping to earth, forming a thousand rooms among the fallen leaves. She is in the green-walled room, the boughs opening just enough to let the sun in, the moss hairy and soft on the earth. She cannot see his face clearly. His features are blurred as though his were a face seen through water. She sees only his body distinctly, his shoulders and arms deeply tanned, his belly flat and hard. He is wearing only tight-fitting jeans, and his swelling sex shows. She touches him there and he trembles, absorbing her fingers' presence. Then they are lying along one another, their skins slippery. His hands, his mouth are on the wet warm skin of her inner thighs. Now—(24–25)

This fantasy emphasizes the natural; another, of an Egyptian orgy, emphasizes the animal as the "Egyptian girls and Roman soldiers… copulate as openly as dogs, a sweet hot tangle of the smooth legs around the hard hairy thighs" (65). Both fantasies take her well beyond the walls of the chaste room.

Second, the rooms Rachel and her mother occupy themselves. They are over top the funeral home Niall Cameron operated until he died from the accumulated effect of years of furtively consuming alcohol, in essence embalming himself. Rachel remembers the scent of the actual embalming fluid from her younger days, and it seems to her to still be lurking in their rooms. In a sense, then, Rachel and her mother are embalmed—looking as if alive but really dead in a life filled with stultifying routines (Stovel, "'Sisters'" 70).

Laurence chose to narrate Rachel Cameron's story in the first person. The first person narration, however, is rather complex, rather polyphonic (Davidson; Stovel, *Rachel's Children* 57). I would suggest that we hear at least three different voices—all Rachel's. One is the public voice: She tells us about her life just as she might to a Manawaka acquaintance. This voice has the aura of objectivity. Nonetheless, it is evaluative. The aura of objectivity causes us to accept her evaluations (usually negative) of others. This aura also causes us to accept her self-evaluations, which are also unremittingly negative. A second voice is one she addresses to herself. This voice tells her what to say and how to act, or evaluates her words and actions. When Rachel consents to meet Calla at the Tabernacle, she does so because "I don't want to hurt her feelings. I don't want to argue." Rachel feels very much "trapped into this falseness" (34). When she renews her acquaintance with Nick Kazlik, she finds herself evaluating him as some in the town might: "Who does he think he is? High School or not. Nestor Kazlik's son. The milkman's son" (70). Then, Rachel castigates herself for offering this prejudiced assessment: "I can't be myself thinking like that. I don't believe that way at all. It's as though I've thought in Mother's voice. Nick graduated from university. I didn't" (70). This voice embodies the norms—polite or prejudiced— of Manawaka. It reinforces the town's social and moral expectations. That Rachel uses this voice very much *against* herself suggests the extent to which she has absorbed those norms and expectations and has consented to be governed by them. A third voice is Rachel's rebellious voice (Powell 23-24). She uses it to reject the town and reject her mother, and she feels quite guilty using it. She imagines herself using that voice to defend James Doherty against principal Willard Sidley: "I want to say—*that's not fair*— *you've no right to imply that about James*— *he would never do a thing like* that" (*sic*) (51). She uses it to rebel against her Mother when she says, to herself, "Why can't she die and leave me alone" (120). More comically, when Hector Jonas proudly reports that he has acquired an upright organ for the funeral home, she wants to rebel against the town's expectations for proper young women and crack the off-colored joke, saying, "how splendid for you, and I hope your wife appreciates it" (132).

A fourth voice is related: It is rebellious but it is buried so deeply within Rachel that it only surfaces at those moments when she's on the verge of escaping (Bailey 63; Howells, "Margaret Laurence's" 42; Kertzer; Stovel, *Rachel's Children* 56). We hear it in Calla's church where Rachel is trying to escape her imprisoning island through religion. We hear it during and after sex with Nick when she manages to free herself by focusing only on her body. We hear it at the moment when, coming out of anaesthesia, she decides to leave prairie-bound Manawaka for Vancouver.

Several characters in Laurence's novel serve the function of mirroring her state and suggesting how she might escape from the imprisoning island. Her sister Stacey was similarly trapped in Manawaka, but she escaped by marrying young. She married a man who offered more physical appeal than great prospects (Hartveit 342-43). So, her escape mixed marriage and sexuality. In Rachel's mind at least, the escape to Vancouver, a city with a vista onto the open ocean, was resonant with possibilities. She believes Stacey is reveling in these possibilities, ignoring subtle indications in Stacey's letters home that marriage and sexuality and Vancouver are not necessarily viable escapes.

Her fellow teacher Calla Mackie (Rachel's "shadow," in a Jungian reading of the novel offered by Bailey) is also trapped in Manawaka (63). The caged bird she keeps in her classroom suggests both her and Rachel's situation (Stovel, "'Sisters'"). Calla is perhaps even more trapped than Rachel because Calla's lesbian sexual orientation effectively eliminates marriage and sexuality as escapes for her. The mores of Manawaka would not tolerate an overt lesbian, so Calla keeps that aspect of her being hidden—except from Rachel, whom she, overcome with emotion, kisses one night. Calla is a bit older than Rachel, so she has resigned herself to her solitary existence in Manawaka. What has helped her along has been the enthusiastic religion she has strongly—one might say desperately—embraced. She will, in fact, lead Rachel a few steps down this path.

As Buss (99-100), Hartveit (346) and Waterston ("Double" 83) all suggest, the final mirror is Nick Kazlik—Rachel's "animus" in the Jungian interpretation offered by Bailey and also by Buss. Nick's roots are Ukrainian. In the social order of Manawaka, the Ukrainians are beneath the Scots. Therefore, Rachel and Nick did not interact much during their high school days. In addition, he ran with a wilder crowd than Rachel's mother (and Rachel) felt to be proper for the Cameron girls—as Nick sardonically puts it, "[l]aying girls and doing gay Slavic dances" (94). Nick escaped Manawaka, taking a secondary school teaching job in "the city" after finishing his university degree. However, during the book's summer, he returns to Manawaka—to visit his family. There was still considerable tension in his family, tension born in the death from a polio epidemic of Nick's twin brother, Nick's father's grief, Nick's guilt that he—not his favored brother— survived, and Nick's refusal to remain in Manawaka and take over the family dairy farm. So, to escape the tension, Nick roams the town, looking for "action." He finds Rachel and invites her to join him in escaping the tedium of Manawaka through sex. As they talk, the fact that he really has not escaped Manawaka becomes apparent.

These mirroring characters reflect Rachel's trapped state. They also suggest escape routes—Vancouver, religion, sex. And Rachel will pursue all three of these routes. The stories of Stacey, Calla, and Nick suggest, however, that these escapes may prove just as unsatisfying for Rachel as for these three mirroring characters.

Let's consider those escapes.

Religion was not a significant part of Rachel Cameron's life. She was disconnected from religion because the Manawaka Presbyterian Church, where the Camerons worshipped, was much more a setting for a Sunday social gathering than a place for prayer. The Church was very much enmeshed in Manawaka's social structure. Thus, one's attendance, one's dress, one's behavior, and who one talked to were what mattered, not one's beliefs or one's fervor. Rachel's attitude toward the Church was similar to that toward the town and her mother: She was hostile but guardedly so. Therefore, she never developed much in the way of a personal relationship with God. In fact, as the novel's title suggests, she felt herself and various things that happened to her--to be jests of God, if he did exist. In fact, Rachel often expresses—to herself, of course—her doubts about God's existence

There were, however, other churches in Manawaka than the Presbyterian. For the Ukrainians, there was the Catholic church. That was not an option for Rachel and other people of "her kind." However, the Tabernacle of the Risen and Reborn was an option for Rachel and others who wanted a more emotional religious experience than that offered in the establishment Presbytrerian Church. It was to the Tabernacle that Calla Mackie had turned for fulfillment. Indeed, she wanted to share the uplifting emotional experience with Rachel. Rachel finally consented to go to the Tabernacle with Calla. Rachel was not at all looking forward to the evening, especially when Calla excitedly informed her that members of the congregation had had the ecstatic experience known as "speaking in tongues." However, guilty at having turned Calla down before, Rachel went.

The scene at the Tabernacle is beautifully orchestrated by Laurence to communicate simultaneously Rachel's growing discomfort and Rachel's growing emotional responsiveness. Feelings that might be thought objectively to be contradictory feed on each other and catapult Rachel to the point where she leaves the social reality of the situation—in the church and in Manawaka—behind, speaks in tongues, and then faints dead away. Immediately afterwards, Rachel is mortified, and, literally and figuratively, she runs from the Tabernacle and all that it suggests. Among the things it suggests are escape *and* a specific route to escape. Rachel's having given way to the atmosphere of the place suggests her desire for escape; however, Rachel's flight suggests that this particular escape route is not the one for her. The Tabernacle then may represent a false escape route, as Heinemann implies. However, it might just as easily be read as a route not appropriate for Rachel or a route Rachel is not yet ready for. Stovel's discussion of the Tabernacle's natural, life-affirming coloration in *Rachel's Children* draws one's attention to a positive environment that serves as a counterpoint to the bizarre behavior—a as seen and described by Rachel—of many attending the service. This counterpointing creates a richly ambiguous picture of the place.

Sex was a part of Rachel's life, but it was furtive, masturbatory sex—accompanied with wildly romantic fantasies. When Nick Kazlik turned to her for some "action," she was a thirty-five year-old virgin. She was, however, more than willing to experience sex with another person. Initially, she was nervous, self-conscious, and, therefore, uncomfortable. Gradually, her comfort increased, and sex became increasingly pleasurable and increasingly intimate. Laurence reflects the growing intimacy linguistically. In early scenes, words fail Rachel. When initial intercourse proves less than satisfying for the couple, Nick says that sex is never especially good the first time. Rachel is mortified, for Nick has, she thinks, discovered how embarrassingly inexperienced she is. What Nick meant, however, was not what Rachel understood him to mean. He meant that sex is never especially good a couple's first time, for they do not yet know the other's body and sexual rhythms. Rachel and Nick share words, but the words misfire. In later scenes, words are more successful, as the two share thoughts about their lives thus far. Both express their true feelings with an openness that Manawaka usually suppresses. They achieve an intimacy. Words, however, are not yet a perfect tool for Rachel. After she begins to dream aloud of a future with Nick, he shows her a photograph of a young boy. When he says "Mine," she interprets his comment as meaning the boy is his child and he has a wife to go along with the child back in "the city." What Nick meant was that the picture was of himself as a child. He was responding to Rachel's voiced desire to have Nick's baby by showing her—with a dose of typical self-deprecating humor—what the child might unfortunately look like. The word "mine" misfires.

Laurence is indeed commenting on the limitations of language, and she is indeed noting how problematic human communication is here and elsewhere in the novel. However, she is also using language metonymically for sexual intimacy. To the extent language works, sexual intimacy is possible for Nick and Rachel. However, to the extent language fails, sexual intimacy and a genuine escape through sexuality are beyond their grasp. The ultimate failure of words then suggests that sex is not to be a viable escape route for Rachel just as religion had not proven to be in the aftermath of the Tabernacle debacle. As several critics have noted, the setting Laurence uses for Nick and Rachel's sexual experiences mirrors both sex's potential as an escape and its ultimate failure as such. They often make love in the open air, a natural setting removed from the oppressive atmosphere of Manawaka. This characteristic of the setting is hopeful. However, as Nick notes, "Look up there....Along the ridge. I never realized you could see the cemetery so well from here, did you" (155). Rather disturbingly, the couple make love within sight of the Manawaka cemetery (Bird 271; Stein, "Speaking" 84). Death is present here as it is in the rooms Rachel and her mother reside in. The intrusion of death into the scene suggests, from the very beginning of their sexual relationship, that it is doomed to failure.

The ultimate escape to Vancouver perhaps has its origin in Rachel and Nick's love affair. Rachel's naivete extended to birth control. She fumbles with old wives' tales and old douching contraptions; nonetheless, she ends up presumptively pregnant. Rachel had avoided Calla after the evening at the Tabernacle on which Calla revealed her sexual orientation to Rachel by kissing her. However, pregnant and in a town that would not tolerate her condition, Rachel, on the verge of suicide, turns to Calla. Calla suggests she'll help Rachel raise the child, or she'll help Rachel get an abortion. A visit to see the doctor is the first step. There, Rachel discovers that she is not pregnant after all. Instead, she has a tumor growing in her womb. Rachel is relieved, and she's not relieved. After surgery, she could quietly return to her previous life in Manawaka. No scandal. No ostracism. Or so she thinks, not knowing that her departure from Manawaka for "surgery" elsewhere would raise gossipy eyebrows. However, she had begun to take some pride in "the fact" that she had done something as profound as create a child within her. The rebelliousness of the act delighted her, but what really delighted her was that she had acted and there had been living consequences of her action. When the supposed fetus becomes a tumor, she felt that, once again, she had failed to act in a manner that gave life to an otherwise deadly existence. She felt that, once again, she was acted upon by forces she could not control.

When coming out of the cloud of anaesthesia, she utters the phrase "I am the mother now." This phrase suggests that Rachel will assume the controlling role in her relationship with her elderly mother (Stovel, *Rachel's Children* 68). The phrase, however, means more. In conjunction with her failure to act independently—to mother a child, the phrase is Rachel's assertion, offered by the rebellious voice deep within her, to so act, to be the creative force behind all that henceforth happens to her. Accordingly, she decides to leave Manawaka. She decides to escape.

A few matters cloud the escape. First, she will take her mother with her to Vancouver. The fact that she tells her mother that she is taking her to Vancouver and will tolerate no discussion or debate about the matter is a positive sign that Rachel is now controlling her own destiny. Nonetheless, her mother has very much been her nemesis throughout the novel, keeping Rachel in line through transparent but nonetheless effective manipulation. Are we to read her mother's presence on Rachel's escape from the imprisoning island of Manawaka as a sign of Rachel's total triumph? Conversely, are we to read her mother's presence as an indication that she has not yet achieved total freedom?

Second, Rachel is following in sister Stacey footsteps. To the extent we intuit that Stacey's escape has not been as fulfilling as envious Rachel might think, we find Rachel's imitation of Stacey to be less than a fully optimistic note. Third, Rachel has no great expectations for herself upon her arrival on the Pacific coast. She spends the concluding pages of the novel reflecting on what her life there will be like:

> Where I'm going, anything might happen. Nothing may happen. Maybe I will marry a middle-aged widower, or a longshoreman, or a cattle-hoff-trimmer, or a barrister or a thief. And have my children in time. Or maybe not. Most of the chances are against it. But not, I think, quite all. What will happen? What will happen. It may be that my children will always be temporary, never to be held. But so are everybody's.

> I may become, in time, slightly more eccentric all the time. I may begin to wear outlandish hats, feathered and sequined and rosetted, and dangling necklaces made from coy and tiny seashells which I've gathered myself along the beach and painted coral-pink with nailpolish. And all the kids will laugh, and I'll laugh, too, in time. I will be light and straight as a feather. The wind will bear me, and I will drift and settle, and drift and settle. Anything may happen, where I'm going.

> I will be different. I will remain the same. I will still go parchment-faced with embarrassment, and clench my pencil between fingers like pencils. I will quite frequently push the doors marked *Pull* and pull the ones marked

Push. I will be lonely, almost certainly. I will get annoyed at my sister. Her children will call me Aunt Rachel, and I will resent it and find then that I've grown attached to them after all. I will walk by myself on the shore of the sea and look at the freegulls flying. I will grow too orderly, plumping up the chesterfield cushions just-so before I go to bed. I will rage in my insomnia like a prophetess. I will take care to remember a vitamin pill each morning with my breakfast. I will be afraid. Sometimes I will feel light-hearted, sometimes light-headed. I may sing aloud, even in the dark. I will ask myself if I am going mad, but if I do, I won't know it. (208–09)

She imagines that it is more likely she will end up a spinster school teacher than a wife and mother; she imagines she may become increasingly "eccentric"; she imagines she may eventually go mad but, of course, not know it. She is open to other possibilities: that is a positive note. However, these are the ones she chooses to mention. That she will choose them rather than have them dictated to her is indeed a positive note; nonetheless, that positive note is qualified by how limiting her realistic prospects are. One wonders — with more than a tad of irony — whether Rachel is bound for Vancouver the city or Vancouver the island, for her "new" life there does seem still bounded.

No such irony exists at the end of Alice Munro's *Lives of Girls and Women*. Del Jordan is headed for Toronto. We believe she will become a successful writer, and, if we closely read the novel's last chapter, "Epilogue: The Photographer," we have a sense of what her writing will be like. It will fall into the traps of neither the writing tradition gendered "male" nor the writing tradition gendered "female." Rather, it will escape from these traps, taking the cold reality of the one and the romantic magic of the other. And Munro's work of fiction — usually but not always termed a "novel" — is partially about how Del Jordan as a writer escapes from traditions that would limit her (Meindl; Warwick, "Growing"). In fact, the way Munro plays with the novel genre may well be, as Gilbert suggests, a post-colonial way of signaling the rejection of "metropolitan" traditions in general (138). The novel, however, at a more fundamental level is also about how Del Jordan as a young girl escapes from a small town that would limit her.

Munro's small town is, ironically, named Jubilee. It is not as large a place as Laurence's Manawaka. It is, however, quite similar in having its clearly delineated social groups and its enforced norms of behavior. From the very beginning, Del is outside these norms because her mother refuses to conform to Jubilee's picture of domestic bliss. She lives largely apart from her husband, who prefers life in the country to that in town; and, rather than do the domestic and civic work women are "supposed" to do, she makes money by going door-to-door selling encyclopedias.

The early chapter of *Lives of Girls and Women* are strikingly episodic. Based on these chapters alone, one is hard pressed to demonstrate that Del is the work's central character. These early chapters focus on other women. Del is very much an observer of these women's lives. Given Del's age, however, this observing role is quite appropriate. Very young girls rarely act much; rather, they tag along, looking and listening. What Del sees and hears begins her education as both a woman and a writer. With reference to the former, what she observes are stereotypes—woman as sex object; woman as pillar of the family—and what seems to be an inevitable choice between irresponsible passion or passionless responsibility (Baum, "Artist" 204, 207; Perrakis). On the latter, what she observes are stereotyped gendered traditions of writing, the male being tied to fact and boring and the female being tied to romantic fantasy and inconsequential. She is not necessarily confined to the female. Her aunts make her the heir of Uncle Craig's tediously factual regional history. She may continue it. Or she may tell tales, orally, as her aunts do, or continue writing her secret "Gothic" novel. She has a choice, but, like her choice between irresponsible passion and passionless irresponsibility, her choice as a budding writer seems to be bimodal—either *a* or *b*, either her uncle's historical fact-based way of writing or women's sensationalistic tale-telling.

The early episodic chapters yield to ones that focus more on Del and have her acting not just observing. Munro—I would suggest—is altering the nature of the first person narration as Del matures in a way that mirrors her maturation. Early, the voice is that of an observing young girl — taking things in and then putting them down on the page without much by way of judgment. Later, the voice is that of a young girl who is recording the actions of herself and others. The voice is more engaged, and it is intent on explaining and defending; sometimes, the voice seems committed to using writing to figure life out.

As this second voice emerges, the mirroring characters that Del might look at to figure her life out shrink to two — her mother and her best friend Naomi. A third mirroring character is important as well, Del's friend and (arguably) first boyfriend Jerry Storey.

Del's mother comes into her own as a character in the novel's third chapter, "Princess Ida." Before that chapter, narrating Del — it seems — so closely identified herself with her mother that Ida was not one to be observed the ways the aunts and uncles were. However, in the third chapter, there is separation between daughter and mother, fueled to some extent by Del's embarrassment by her mother's "work," selling encyclopedias door-to-door. Del also may have felt that her mother, as already noted, was outside the norms of Jubilee. What only becomes slowly apparent is the extent to which Del's mother is a proto-feminist, espousing ideas of gender equality and how the world *should* provide equal opportunities for male and female. Ida, one might argue, was compelled by her particular circumstances to embrace this proto-feminism. Regardless, she embraced it and shared it with her daughter as Del grew up. Ida also shared innate intelligence and iconoclastic outspokenness with her growing daughter.

Del might be like her mother, but she certainly had no intention of modeling her life on her mother's. Encouraged by her mother and others, Del had grander ideas. Del was a bit of a snob in looking down upon the peddling of encyclopedias. However, it was not just snobbery that caused her to want an independent life different from her mother's independent life. It was also what Del perceived as the cost her mother paid for her proto-feminism. As Ida sees matters, Del's life could well be different, for she foresees

. . . a change coming . . . in the lives of girls and women. . . . All women have had up till now has been their connection with men. No more lives of our own, really, than domestic animals. *He shall hold thee, when his passion shall have spent its novel force, a little closer than his dog, a little dearer than his horse* [sic]. Tennyson wrote that. It's true. *Was* true. (146–47)

She warns Del, however, to "[u]se your brains. Don't be distracted. Once you make that mistake, of being—distracted, over a man, your life will never be your own. You will get the burden, a woman always does" (147). Ida very clearly sees a woman's sexuality as a problem. One can try to steer an equal and independent course; however, sexuality will distract one from that course. Once boys enter the picture, she tells Del, dreams of an equal, independent course will be lost. At a time before contraception was within a woman's purview, a pregnancy could, of course, throw a young woman off course—permanently. However, it was not just unplanned pregnancy and, perhaps, a forced marriage that Ida had in mind. It was also sexual passion. Once that was discovered, Ida suggests, a young woman's course would be altered. Therefore, within Ida's proto-feminism, if a woman wanted equality, she had to forego sexual passion (Thomas, "Reading" 111).

Del is a passionate girl. She turns to everything with a passion, and she is not about to deny that passion. Therefore, Ida was not a model Del could easily follow. It was a too stoic model; it was a too limited model. Del wanted the equality and the independence but not at the cost of passion, sexual or otherwise.

Her friend Naomi shares Del's interest in sexuality. She is as interested in boys as Del is, and she is much more adventurous in seeking them out and in pursuing pleasure with them. She and Del together pour over a sex manual they found in Naomi's mother's room. However, Naomi is much quicker to act on what they read. Del seems bothered by two things. First, the manual inscribes sexuality totally from the male point of view: Male arousal, male action, and male climax are foregrounded; the female's role seems to be either incidental to or nothing more than the site of this male-focused activity (Kambourelli 35-36). Del's early sexual experiences with the older Mr. Chamberlain and with Jerry Storey reinforce this view of the female role. Mr. Chamberlain has Del passively witness a masturbatory performance of which he is quite proud; Jerry has Del submit to a clinical and a comical examination of her naked anatomy. Neither engages her in any meaningful way. Second, as the society of Jubilee has structured the sexual activity of its youth, young women who allow themselves to become the site of such activity must surrender their mind as well as their body. The latter, they surrender to the men who caress and penetrate them; the former, they surrender, period, for the ideal young woman is largely mindless. Del is not mindless and wants neither to be such nor play such in order to attract boyfriends, one of whom might be "the one" to marry her and make her mindless forever.

Naomi, who lacked the intellectual gifts Del has, plays the assigned role. She ends up pregnant; she ends up married at a very young age. Del feels Naomi has trapped herself permanently in Jubilee. Del also feels that Naomi has confirmed what Ida has said about sexuality being the ruin of independence. However, Naomi is quite happy with the life she has stumbled into. From that moment on, a gap develops between the two girlhood friends. Naomi settles comfortably into Jubilee; Del increasingly sees the town as a trap to be escaped from.

Del intuits that her escape will necessarily be by using her mind. The fact that she is one of the best students at the local high school suggests to her—and others—that she should go to university and she has the "smarts" to earn the scholarship that will be necessary for her to do so. Her academic ambition further distances her from the more sexual route Naomi has taken: The boys of Jubilee seem scared away by Del's intelligence. That ambition—and that lack of boyfriends—links Del with Jerry Storey. Jerry is the other top student, the other scholarship aspirant. They are rivals, yes, but, because they clearly have different strengths, the rivalry does not become unduly intense. Del's strength is, as one might expect for an aspiring writer, the language arts; Jerry's is the sciences. In fact, they end up helping each other along in preparation for the competitive entrance and scholarship examination.

Jerry Storey mirrors Del in more than just intelligence. Just as Del is being pushed onward by her mother, so is Jerry. Jerry will earn a scholarship; Jerry will go to university; Jerry will become a famous scientist or a rich doctor. As Mrs. Storey sees it, no girl will get in Jerry's way. She thus sees Del as a threat, not because Del will defeat Jerry in the competition, but, rather, because Del will lead Jerry into sexual experimentation that will result in her pregnancy, their forced marriage, and the end to her dreams for her son. She thus tells Del that she "musn't get into trouble" because "Jerry couldn't get married. I wouldn't allow it." She doesn't "agree that it's the boy's responsibility and he should have to sacrifice his career should the girl become pregnant." She asks Del, "Do you have a diaphragm?" and then "Well why don't you get one?" (167-68)

This scenario is somewhat plausible because their being together all the time has caused Jubilee society—both adult society and youth society—to declare them boyfriend and girlfriend. Somewhat accepting this label, they begin to act as such. The culmination is Jerry's request to see and explore Del's naked body. Wanting to feel a modicum of sexual passion, Del consents. However, Jerry's caresses prove more clinical than either romantic or lustful:

> He stood by the bed looking down on me, making faint comical faces of astonishment.—We both giggled. He put a finger against one of my nipples as if he was testing a thorn. Sometimes we talked a dialect based roughly on the comic strip *Pogo*. "Yo' is shore a handsome figger of a woman." "Has I got all the appurtances on in the right places does yo' think." "As jes' has to git out my lil ole manual an' check up on that." (169–70)

Then, ruining any chance at romance or lust, he, in the Pogo-like voice, jokes with Del about her supposed third breast (Besner, "The Bodies" 140-41). Then, when Mrs. Storey suddenly returns home unexpectedly, he shoves Del, nude, into the basement of the Storey house.

Del concludes that she has no sexual future *with* Jerry. She might also be wondering about having a suppressed future *like* Jerry. Like Jerry, Del is bright; like Jerry, Del is yearning to escape Jubilee; and like Jerry, Del is being told to suppress her sexuality if she wants to escape. Jerry has seemingly managed to suppress his, and Del seems to think that's fine and good for Jerry, but not for her. She wants to discover her sexuality and make it a part of her being.

In Laurence's *A Jest of God*, Rachel's two nonliteral escape routes out of the trap of Manwaka are religion and sex. At times, in fact, the two merge a bit as, for example, when Laurence describes the religious enthusiasm Rachel becomes overwhelmed by in sexual terms (Van Herk). In Munro's *Lives of Girls and Women*, Del tries the same two escape routes, keeping the more literal one of going to university off in her future a bit. In Munro's novel, religion and sex also blur at times.

Del is passionate, and she turns to religion seeking a venue for expressing this passion (Robson 77). She tries out the various churches of Jubilee, trying to find one that might allow the passion within her to surface. Her choices are reminiscent of Rachel's in Manawaka. The socially dominant United Methodist church "was the most modern, the largest, [and] the most prosperous" (78). Del finds it too "cold" a place; she also sees it as less a church and more a social gathering place for the town's elite and would-be elite. The Presbyterian church caters to an elderly congregation that wants to fight Puritanical battles against such unlikely to be defeated practices as playing ice hockey on Sunday, and the Catholic church was strongly ethnic Irish and highly secretive and seemed "bizarre" and "exotic." Rumors about "babies' skeletons" and "strangled nuns" abounded, but the place itself struck Del as "too bare and plain and straightforward-looking to be connected with such voluptuousness and scandal" (78–79). The Baptist Church was attended by people Del felt were socially beneath her. She also found their Puritanical behavior in contrast to the "loud, rollicking, and optimistic" hymns that gave them a "vulgar cheerfulness" (79). The contrast puzzled her, and their church building itself she found "hideous" (79). None of these are viable options for Del. The Anglican church, however, temporarily meets Del's needs, for it offers beauty in the bell atop its undistinguished looking building and in its services (Lamont-Stewart 117). Del finds aesthetic delight in what she terms "the theatrical in religion," but she doesn't find passion (83). So, she drifts to the tent revival co-sponsored by Manwaka's

Protestant demoninations. There, she finds some passion. More importantly, she finds Garnet French.

As a Baptist, Garnet perhaps embodies passionate religious experience. Garnet also embodies another kind of passionate experience, that of sexuality. Evidently not at all a novice in such matters, Garnet seduces Del into increasingly intense sexual pleasures. He takes her virginity; he brings her to her first climax and, after the first, many others. Eventually, sex, in his pick-up truck or in the open air, becomes a daily ritual. Del immerses herself in the sexual passion she is experiencing — so much so that she neglects her studies and enters the wordless world of bodily pleasure. Neglecting her studies proved to be a negative consequence of her love affair with Garnet, for she did not do well on the university entrance and scholarship examination. She would not be able to take the university escape route she (and her mother) had counted on. Entering what I termed a "wordless world," however, was a positive experience.

One needs to understand who controls words in Del Jordan's Jubilee. As the text of the sex manual Del and Naomi read suggests, words are controlled by men. They inscribe their gendered experience in words. They do not completely deny words to women; however, they create a hierarchy that vests greater value in the words of men than in the words of women. This hierarchy can be seen in the ways of writing Del was considering as she plotted her course as a budding writing. The male tradition, represented by authors such as Dickens and Tennyson, was valorized. Even Uncle Craig's history writing, although patently boring, was valorized and was dominant (Prentice 31). The female tradition, whether the gothic tradition of the Brontë sisters or the oral one of Del's aunts, was trivialized. *If* women's experience finds its ways into this female writing — and that's a big *if* since the very words are male-created and male-defined — then it quickly becomes marginalized within the patriarchal hierarchy that views the female tradition as inferior. Del, through her sexual experiences with Garnet, discovers dimensions of her body that are not yet inscribed in the language (Besner, "The Bodies" 141; Gold 6-7). Her sexual experiences thus are to be applauded as liberating, and they

constitute a positive retreat on her part from the symbolic to the semiotic. Furthermore, they make her mother's insistence that sexual
passion must be suppressed in favor of independence seem flat and
sour. They also have what one might argue is the negative effect of
causing Del to retreat from the male-defined academic world of
words she had to gain control over to win her scholarship-funded escape: "Astronomy, Greek, Slavonic languages, Philosophy of the
Enlightenment—she bounced them at me as I stood in the doorway.
Such words would not stay in my head" (192). Instead, she focused
on the tangible, not verbal reality of her sexual relationship with Garnet. She focused on the body—hers and his.

The crucial question to ask of Del's love affair with Garnet is does
this discovered sexual passion have a place within that relationship.
This may seem, at first, to be a peculiar question to ask, for, after all,
that passion is something their shared activity had given rise to.
However, it is perhaps *the* crucial question in Munro's novel.

Initially, Del would answer the question affirmatively. She feels that
she and Garnet have together entered a realm for which there aren't
words. When she feels this way, she is oblivious to signals the reader
picks up on—for example, the notches Garnet makes on the wood
post supporting his family home's porch that signify his conquests
and the way Garnet has perverted his little sisters into cheerleaders in
support of his sexual victories over several deflowered young girls.
Del finally begins to realize that there is a gap between how she experiences sexuality and how Garnet does:

> Garnet and I went to Third Bridge to swim, after supper. We made love first,
> in the long grass, after scouting around for a while to find a place free of
> thistles, then walked awkwardly holding on to each other down a path
> meant for one person, stopping and kissing along the way. The quality of
> kisses changed a good deal, from before to after; at least Garnet's did, going
> from passionate to consolatory, pleading to indulgent. How quickly he came
> back, after crying out the way he did, and turning his eyes up and throbbing
> all over and sinking into me like a shot gull! Sometimes when he had barely
> got his breath back I would ask him what he was thinking and he would
> say, "I was just figuring out how I could fix that muffler—...." (196)

She experiences profound bodily pleasures for which she has no name; he experiences physical release after which his mind turns to auto mechanics or other similarly unromantic matters. As Garnet sees things, she is a site for his fleeting pleasure; as Del sees things, she is a site of nameless bodily passions, which she is experiencing largely alone. Thus, although Garnet certainly plays a role in her passion, he increasingly becomes largely irrelevant to it. She is experiencing the *jouissance* of the semiotic and is experiencing it separately.

The gap between Del and Garnet climaxes in the chapter "Baptizing." Within Garnet's lower-class Jubilee social structure, it is evidently time for him to marry. He has chosen Del to be "the one." She had never really given much thought to marrying or not marrying Garnet. She was so lost in her immediate sexual passion that their immediate situation was all she had focused on. Before Del has much of a chance to think about and respond to Garnet's "proposal" that they marry, he announces the condition—she must be baptized into his religion. Then, before she has much of a chance to think about and respond to this condition, Garnet proceeds to forcibly baptize her in the river where they have been swimming after making love.

This scene is both the most powerful and the richest scene in Munro's novel. Garnet's action is an attempt to control Del. Should he succeed, her aspirations will be for nought. Del will be trapped in Jubilee. As the scene proceeds and it becomes increasingly violent, it becomes very clear that Garnet is using the cloak of religion to exert male power. Moreover, as power emerges as *the* issue in the scene, it becomes for all intents and purposes a rape to which Del will either submit or die. Water, which begins the scene as literally refreshing and then becomes for a second spiritually refreshing, becomes the site where Del's being might well be drowned. One should link to this scene Del's long-imagined novel. In it and in the Jubilee story of Marion Sheriff upon which the novel will be based, the heroines drown. Del almost suffers the very same fate.

However, Del successfully fights Garnet off. When she wins, she conceives of the matter not as avoiding baptism or marriage but as achieving power, control:

> He pushed me down again but this time I was expecting it. I held my breath
> and fought him. I fought strongly and naturally, as anybody does, held
> down in the water, and without thinking much about who was holding me.
> But when he let me come up just long enough to hear him say, "Now say
> you'll do it," I saw his face streaming with water I had splashed over him
> and I felt amazement, not that I was fighting with Garnet but that anybody
> could have made such a mistake, to think he had real power over me. I was
> too amazed to be angry, I forgot to be frightened, it seemed to me impossible
> that he should not understand that all the powers I granted him were in
> play, that he himself was—in play....(197)

She even says that Garnet was foolish to think that he had ever
gained power over her, for whatever power he had was power she
had granted him—temporarily. Now, she was taking it back. As she
declares this victory, she retransforms the water from threatening to
spiritually refreshing once more. Her spirit is very much refreshed in
that water. She is baptized, not in Garnet's religion and not in sex but
in self-determination.

Del leaves the river and walks by herself back into town. Along the
way, she passes through the Jubilee cemetery. She notes that this is
the place where the town's young lovers come to dally:

> I cut through the cemetery. It was getting dark....I saw a boy and girl—I
> could not make out who they were—lying on the clipped grass over by the
> Mundy mausoleum....I looked at these lovers lying on the graveyard grass
> without envy or curiosity. (199)

The proximity of loving and dying, just as in Laurence's *A Jest of God*,
is ironic. The young lovers think they are embarking on a course of
joy. The reality, Del knows, is that they are trapping themselves in Jubilee. She passes by them on her route out. Yes, she is saddened by
the loss of Garnet. She even, much as a passive Tennyson heroine,
waits for his call. She does not let very much time at all pass before
she explicitly rejects that Tennysonian vision, a vision which renders
her—and women—passive, and leaves on the bus for Toronto (Harris; York, "Lives"; York, "The Rival"):

> I was watching, I was suffering. I said into the mirror a line from Tennyson, from my mother's *Complete Tennyson* that was a present from her old teacher, Miss Rush. I said it with absolute sincerity, absolute irony. *He cometh not, she said.* From "Mariana," one of the silliest poems I had ever read. It made my tears flow harder. Watching myself still, I went back to the kitchen and made a cup of coffee and brought it into the dining room where the city paper was still lying on the table....I opened it at the want ads, and got a pencil, so I could circle any job that seemed possible....Cities existed; telephone operators were wanted; the future could be furnished without love or scholarships. (200)

I questioned Rachel Cameron's escape from "the island" of Manawaka. How positive an ending does it provide Laurence's novel? The same question might well be asked of Del Jordan's escape from "the island" of Jubilee. If the novel ended with "Baptizing," one might feel compelled to at least qualify what "feels" like a positive conclusion. Del has no prospects in Toronto. She will turn to the "want ads" and find some menial job, but she won't find fulfilling work and she therefore won't be fulfilled. Furthermore, she may not ever again find the sexual passion she allowed her body to feel and express with Garnet. Given how Garnet, whom she trusted, tried violently to force his way on her, she may never trust another man sufficiently to allow him a role in co-creating this nameless passion within her.

Munro does not, however, end the novel with "Baptizing." She almost did. The last chapter, "Epilogue: The Photographer," was in and out of the novel a few times before Munro determined that it had to be the book's end. This chapter complicates the novel but, ultimately, causes it to end on a more positive note. It complicates the novel because it brings back to the fore the fact that *Lives* is a *künstleroman* as much as a *bildungsroman*. If the *bildungsroman* ends with Del's fate as a young adult woman in Toronto in doubt, the *künstleroman* ends with Del's fate as an artist more settled (Bowen; Eldredge; Tausky).

Munro's novel is intensely intertextual (Besner, "The Bodies"; Godard, "'Heirs'"). The voices that reverberate through the text represent writing traditions that Del might choose to participate in. As noted earlier, these traditions seem gendered. The male tradition is dominant and seems tied to the facts of life. Uncle Craig's compilation of the area's history is an extreme example, "full of newspaper clippings, letters, containing descriptions of the weather, an account of a runaway horse, lists of those present at funerals, a great accumulation of the most ordinary facts" (27). The female tradition is marginalized, sometimes right out of print in orality. However, even in its oral form, as practiced by Del's Aunts Elspeth and Grace, it was embellished "for their own pleasure." Whether spoken or written, this tradition is often tied to fantasies, often fantasies of escape. Del's imagined novel would be in the latter tradition. The real events it was based on had receded way into the background, and the version Del was going to offer was sensationalistic, very much in the Gothic tradition dominated by women (and marginalized by men). The simple-minded younger brother would be "gentle and loving" and "happy once a year, when he was allowed to ride round and round on the merry-go-round" from which he smiles "beatifically" (204). Caroline, "wayward and light as a leaf," would bestow "her gifts capriciously on men," the beaten-down men and, sometimes, "the deformed and mildly deranged" men. Caroline would be "a sacrifice, spread for sex on moldy uncomfortable tombstones, pushed against the cruel bark of trees, her frail body squashed into the mud and hen dirt of barnyards, supporting the killing weight of men" (204–05). She became enamored with a stranger, an itinerant photographer. She "tramped the hot roads" pursuing him; she "offered herself to him . . . with straining eagerness and hopes and cries. Then, he left, his car mysteriously overturned in a ditch, and she, pregnant, "walked into to Wawanash River" (205). Del changed Jubilee as well—making it more Gothic; she had its residents' words teeter on the brink of madness as the "white, brutal heat" (206) pushed them closer and closer to the edge.

"Epilogue" takes place before the events of "Baptizing." Some of the events go back to when Del and Jerry Storey were friends, but the crucial event takes place just a short time before the August dusk when she runs away from Garnet. One day she visited with Bobby Sheriff, the brother of Marion, the girl upon whom the tragic Caroline of her novel was based. Through her conversation with Bobby, Del learned two important lessons about the writing career she was going to embark upon soon. First, she learned that real life, although lacking excitement, was so daunting in its flesh-and-blood reality that writing the kind of novel she had long imagined was silly:

> Bobby Sheriff talked about rats and white flour. His sister's photographed face hung in the hall of the high school, close to the persistent hiss of the drinking fountain. Her face was stubborn, unrevealing, lowered so that shadows had settled in her eyes. People's lives, in Jubilee as elsewhere, were dull, simple, amazing and unfathomable—deep caves paved with kitchen linoleum. (210)

Worse than silly, doing so was almost blasphemous because it turned its back on aspects of real life that should not be ignored. Del became "greedy for Jubilee" and, like her Uncle Craig, began making lists—of businesses, of families, of movies that played the Lyceum, of those who died in the world wars, and of "every smell, pothole, pain, crack, delusion" (210). Second, she learned that this real life could be made exciting by an artist who saw the magic in it and was able through his or her art to convey that magic to readers. Bobby showed her this possibility when he punctuated the clearing away of the plate he had served her cake on with an unexpected and unexpectedly graceful ballet movement:

> Then he did the only special thing he ever did for me. With those things in his hands, he rose on his toes like a dancer, like a plump ballerina. The action, accompanied by his delicate smile, appeared to be a joke not shared with me so much as displayed for me....(211)

The action is described by Del as being "a letter, or a whole word, in an alphabet I did not know" (211). It suggests a kind of writing, not in the male tradition and not in the female tradition, but in a tradition as much out-of-words as the sexual passion her body had felt. At the novel's end, she commits herself, as a writer, to finding those words. With those words may well come passion as well as independence and allow her to be a whole woman, whereas her proto-feminist mother could only be half. In the novel's last line, Del affirms these roles, saying "Yes" to Bobby's cryptic message. So, as she escapes from "the island" of Jubilee, she leaves with prospects far brighter than initially seemed to be the case. The precise job she will get in Toronto does not matter, for that job will simply be her way of providing herself with food and shelter. What matters is what she has said "Yes" to a month or so before she strongly said "No" to Garnet French when he tried to push and then hold her under the water.

6

Trapped in Fantasy

L. M. Montgomery's "Pat Books"; L. M. Montgomery's *Magic for Marigold*

Manawaka is island-like, but much more of a trap for Rachel Cameron than either a redemptive spot or a waiting place; similarly, Jubilee is island-like, but much more of a trap for Del Jordan than anything positive. The traps in both cases have much to do with the gender roles the two women are expected to assume, gender roles others in the two towns subtly enforce. The traps in L. M. Montgomery two "Pat Books," *Pat of Silver Bush* (1933) and *Mistress Pat* (1935), and in her *Magic for Marigold* (1929) are different. In both books, the enemy is change. Furthermore, in both books, the central characters escape into fantasy worlds to avoid change. These fantasy worlds become traps.

Before looking at these three relatively late Montgomery novels closely, I need to address my choice in this chapter (as in chapter 2) to discuss Montgomery alongside more venerated writers such as Margaret Laurence and Margaret Atwood. I also need to address my decision to treat in this chapter three of Montgomery's lesser known and less successful novels.

Atwood once commented that L. M. Montgomery's most famous creation, Anne Shirley of *Anne of Green Gables* and its several sequels, was "subcutaneous in all Canadian women writers." Atwood's comment suggests Montgomery's importance insofar as she has exerted a powerful influence on Canadian women writers at a formative moment in their lives. Atwood's comment, however, may relegate Montgomery to the ranks of "juvenile fiction" writers. Others have gone a bit farther than Atwood and have decided to, first, obliterate the boundary line between "juvenile" and "adult" as artificial and, second, discern what messages Montgomery's fiction offers to its multiple audiences. Elizabeth Epperly, author of *The Fragrance of Sweet-Grass*, is probably most noteworthy among these critics. One would also list Swedish scholar Gabriella Ahmansson, the scholarly team of Mary Rubio and Elizabeth Waterston, and a good number of Canadian and American literary critics including Helen M. Buss, Frank Davey, Susan Drain, Carole Gerson, Judith Miller, Laura Robinson, Catherine Sheldrick Ross, and myself. Although there is still some resistance among many in the Canadian literature "establishment" (particularly among the males in it) to admit Montgomery, there are quite a few critics—joining many, many fans—who take Montgomery's fiction quite seriously. Probably the foremost reason she is taken seriously is that her fiction speaks so well to the emotional situations girls and women found themselves in at the time the novels were set or written and still find themselves in today.

Most of the scholarly attention has been focused on *Anne of Green Gables* and, to some extent, its sequels. Some has been devoted to Montgomery's three "Emily books," which are very well-crafted and tell—much more so than the "Anne books"—the story of a female writer in a patriarchal world. Very little attention has been devoted to the other heroines Montgomery created, Jane of *Jane of Lantern Hill* (discussed in chapter 2) or Pat or Marigold; and very little attention has been devoted to Montgomery's two attempts to write more "adult" books. There are two reasons I would posit for this neglect. First, although *Jane of Lantern Hill* is a very well-crafted novel, the "Pat books," *Magic for Marigold*, and the two "adult" novels are not. They are interesting, but artistically less accomplished than *Jane*, some of the "Anne books," and the three "Emily books." Second, most of these less discussed books offer a disturbing vision, one very much at odds with the exuberance of Anne Shirley and Emily Bird Starr. The prevailing "larger" view of Montgomery's work foregrounded this exuberance and an optimism rooted in the central female character's success. As a result, the books that offered a different view faded into the background. Those who have chosen to comment on either the "Pat" books or *Magic for Marigold* have noted how the central heroines do indeed recall Anne Shirley in many ways (Whitaker 55). However, they are quick to note how they are different. Whitaker terms Pat a "bore" and a "snob" as well as "queer to the point of being dim-witted" (55). Fredeman goes beyond labeling and outlines how Pat (and Valancy, the central character in Montgomery's "adult" *The Blue Castle*) are different (62). According to her analysis, they are domi-nated by relatives, are emotionally ignored, are essentially friendless, and "possess neither the beauty nor the charm and manner" of Mont-gomery's more successful heroines (62). Epperly calls the "Pat" books a "depressing study" because Pat, who is "ungifted and determinedly unambitious," becomes very sadly self-imprisoned (212). Epperly also very curiously notes how Montgomery put more of herself into the "Pat" books than into the more famous ones focused on Anne Shirley or Emily Bird Starr (219).

As Epperly's comment suggests, to understand this mixture of exu-berance and optimism with entrapment and pessimism in Montgom-ery's fiction, one must understand a bit about her life. Fortunately, Montgomery compiled a journal, which has been carefully edited in five volumes by Rubio and Waterston. This journal, although not without problems because some of it was written retrospectively, of-fers considerable insight into Montgomery's life, both her personal life and her writing life. One needs to be careful in saying that Montgomery felt as she said she did on the particular day in question because the comments may have been revised long afterwards; however, one can safely conclude that Montgomery felt as she said she did later in her life if not on the day in question.

Her personal life was not, in general, a happy one. She married without feeling much in the way of either love or passion for her husband. Then, he took her from her beloved Prince Edward Island to Ontario. There, she performed the necessary duties of a minister's wife, and she bore two sons. However, she never seems happy in the role of either spouse or mother. On October 12, 1906, she wrote, "The life of a country minister's wife has always appeared to me as a synonym for respectable slavery—a life in which a woman of any independence in belief or character, must either be a failure, from an 'official' point of view, or must cloak her real self under an assumed orthodoxy and conventionalism that must prove very stifling at times" (I, 321). Several years layer, on May 23, 1911, she wrote,

> I found myself sitting there by my husband's side—*my husband!*—I felt a sudden horrible inrush of *rebellion* and *despair*. I *wanted to be free!* I felt like a prisoner—a hopeless prisoner. Something in me—something wild and free and untamed—something that Ewan had not tamed—could never tame— something that did not acknowledge him as master—rose up in one frantic protest against the fetters which bound me. (II, 68)

There is much that is quite sad in the pages of Montgomery's journals, as she repeatedly offers comments such as these lamenting her state and desiring freedom.

Her writing life was also troubled. She was, of course, pleased with the publication of *Anne of Green Gables* in 1908. However, the contract she somewhat naively signed with a Boston publishing house soured matters rather quickly. The contract kept her from enjoying the fruits of the initial book's success, and the publishing house—as she saw matters—"compelled" her to write sequel after sequel (Waterston, "Lucy Maud"). Sometimes, she wrote sequels with a measure of enthusiasm, but, more often, she wrote under duress. As she notes on August 6, 1913, "I began work on a third 'Anne' book. I did not want to do it—I have fought against it! But Page gave me no peace and every week brought a letter from some reader pleading for 'another Anne book'" (II, 133). This duress shows up in the sequels' very unevenness as far as quality is concerned; and this duress shows up in her having an emotional breakdown along the way of generating "more stuff" about Anne. In her journals, she talks about killing off Anne—so much was her desire *not* to churn out more and more words about "that red-haired girl." Montgomery had other characters in her mind, most notably the more autobiographical Emily Bird Starr, whom Montgomery had held "in embryo in my mind...christened for years" (II, 390). Furthermore, Montgomery wanted to write "adult books." On December 26, 1918, she evaluated *Anne's House of Dreams* as "pretty well of its kind," but she added, "I'm tired of the kind. I've outgrown it. I want to do something different" (II, 278). On August 24, 1920, she evaluated *Rilla of Ingleside* as "fairly good," but noted it was "the last of the *Anne* series. I am done with *Anne* forever—I swear it as a dark and deadly vow" (II, 290). When Canadian publisher Charles McLennan took up her cause and freed her from the American contract, the burden on Montgomery lifted a bit. Even so, it didn't lift entirely, for readers had come to see Montgomery almost irrevocably as a "juvenile fiction" writer and the creator of the beloved Anne Shirley. As Montgomery put it in late 1920, "I am becoming classed as a 'writer for young people' and that only. I want to write a book dealing with grown-up creatures—a psychological study of one human being's life" (II, 390). Thus, bouts of frustration and depression marked Montgomery's career even after she was a McClelland and Stewart author. As Epperly suggests, the "Pat books" and *Magic for Marigold* reflect this mood, making the books very sad ones, despite some of the innocent goings-on one would expect in a novel with an adolescent audience (219).

Patricia Gardiner is an island resident: She does not escape to one. Like other Montgomery heroines, Pat is devoted to Prince Edward Island. In a letter to housekeeper Judy, Pat comically tells how a deceased islander went to heaven but "couldn't find any Islanders" there. As Pat tells the tale, "after a while he found out there were lots of them, only they had to be kept locked up for fear they would try to get back to the Island" (*Pat of,* 165). Pat is still more devoted to "Silver Bush," her stately childhood home that becomes, very much, an island on the island. To it she increasingly escapes. Its name associated it with the "green world" that Frye finds characters retreating to, as does Pat's last name, which links her to the garden. Her descriptions of "Silver Bush" ooze the same kind of passion that Anne Shirley and Jane Stuart feel about Prince Edward Island. She describes the grounds with this passion:

> The old farm lay before her in the golden light of the mellow September evening. She knew every kink and curve of it. Every field was an intimate friend. The Pool glimmered mysteriously. The round window winked at her. The trees she had grown up with waved to her. The garden was afoam with starry white cosmos backed by the stately phalanx of the Prince's Feather. Dear Silver Bush! Never had she felt so close to it...so one with it. (*Pat of,* 234)

She also describes the house itself with this passion:

> Every window was loved for some special bit of beauty to be seen from it. She loved her own because she could see Hill of the Mist...she loved the Poet's window because there was a far-away glimpse of the bay...she loved the round window because it looked right into the silver bush...she loved the front hall window because it looked squarely on the garden. As for its attic windows, one saw everything in the world worth seeing from them and sometimes Pat would go up to the attic for no earthly reason except to look out of them. (*Pat of,* 254)

It is clear that "Silver Bush" is a very special place in Pat's mind. There, she can delight. A curious scene very early in *Pat of Silver Bush* depicts this delight in terms that are childish and incipiently semiotic:

> Pat disrobed. There was not much to do...she was already bare legged. Her pale-blue cotton frock and two small undies were cast aside and she stood among the shadows, a small, unashamed dryad, quivering with a strange, hitherto unknown ecstasy as the moon's pale fingers touched her through the trees. (122)

Many storms punctuate the two "Pat books." Because of the proximity of the house to the waters that surround the island, these storms remind us of Pat's insularity. They also suggest, metaphorically, from what Pat is seeking safety:

> They [the windows] shut out the rain and the cold wind. Never had the old kitchen held a more contented, more congenial bunch of people. Grief and loneliness had gone where old moons go....Outside it might be a dank and streaming November night but here it was the eternal summer of the heart. (*Mistress,* 148-49)

Storms threaten, but, as Pat's story unfolds, it becomes increasingly clear that Pat is seeking safety from change (Epperly 213, 217):

> It's another change...and Rae is gone...and Judy is going. Oh, Hilary, life seems to be just change...change...change. Everything changes but Silver Bush. It is always the same and I love it more every day of my life. (*Mistress,* 143–44)

Change threatens her, and, to the extent that she can pretend that Silver Bush is immutable, she can emotionally avoid the threat. "Silver Bush made everything bearable" for Pat. "Always when she came home to Silver Bush its peace and dignity seemed to envelope her like a charm." She felt protected—that "Nothing very terrible could happen there" (*Mistress,* 161). Even the weather seemed different at Silver Bush: "'Really,' said Rae, 'the weather at Silver Bush isn't like the weather anywhere else, even over at Swallowfield. I've teased you so often, Pat, for thinking things here were different from anywhere else...but in my heart I've always known it, too'" (*Mistress,* 248) Elsewhere, the wind is roaring—storms, change, but not so within the womb-like safety of Silver Bush.

Pat is, for the most part, a static character in *Pat of Silver Bush* and *Mistress Pat* (Whitaker 55). Therefore, if we followed just her story, we'd see little change. Montgomery, however, uses the stories of other characters to depict change. The change she depicts is positive. However, she also makes it clear that the effect of these positive changes to others' lives is negative on Pat. We see the negative effect in Pat's reaction to her sister's marriage and Hillary's departure for university. Perhaps we see the negative effect most dramatically in Pat's reaction to the felling of an "ancient" tree. Pat reflects that, if a tree that seemed immutable could fall, so might Silver Bush.

Pat is not (despite Fredeman's declaration above that she lacked beauty) an unattractive girl and young woman. Thus, several men court her during the two novels. They lead her, repeatedly, to the brink of leaving Silver Bush and changing. However, they can lead her only as far as the brink. Repeatedly, she rejects their suits and chooses to stay entrenched at Silver Bush. Eventually, the interest of young men in her declines: One imagines that the word is "out" that she's not likely to be responsive to anyone's attentions. Pat seems destined to assume the role of "old maid." However, she is not entirely uncomfortable with that role because it would allow her to remain at her beloved Silver Bush.

Montgomery, as an artist, seems torn among several possible ways to portray Patricia Gardiner's situation. There is a long tradition of novels centering on courtship beginning in the eighteenth century and blossoming in the nineteenth. This tradition is a comic one. Montgomery's novel sometimes seems to fit this genre and assume the expected comic tone. There are also touches of the psychological whenever we witness the extent of Pat's devotion to "Silver Bush" and the extent of her fear of change. These touches give the comic a disturbing edge. Furthermore, there are also touches of what one might term the gothic that turn Pat into a paranoid caricature. These touches give us a fiction that anticipates Eudora Welty and Flannery O'Connor, a fiction that even offers glimpses of Faulkner's Miss Emily Grierson, whose fear of and resistance to change is not *that* unlike what we see in Montgomery's two books. This mixture of ways of portraying Pat make *Pat of Silver Bush* and *Mistress Pat* uncomfortable books to read. Something "dark" keeps coming through as we sense, increasingly, that Pat has entrapped herself, but that "dark" feeling jars with the comic courtship genre. The result of this contrast—I would suggest—is not only to make readers ill-at-ease but to offer a parodic commentary on the comic genre. That parodic comment undermines a male-defined form as well as the male-defined social conventions embodied within that form. This double-voiced discourse then makes a protofeminist comment. If one thinks that reading the contrast in this manner represents a forcing of feminism on an earlier text, one should note how Pat does change in one way as the novel progresses. Pat does speak more and more words that suggest that she is acquiring a proto-feminist awareness of how a woman's choices in life are limited by society and how marriage can be a trap—a spirit-souring trap as it was for Montgomery herself. As Judy tells Pat at a rather young age, "Oh, oh, it's a man's world, so it is, and we women must just be putting up wid [*sic*] it" (*Pat of*, 128). Pat seems to have absorbed this lesson.

However, as the "Pat books" move the central character toward proto-feminism, they also move the central character increasingly into an isolation that is depressing for both her and readers. The novels then enact a different kind of double-voiced discourse, positing social conventions, undermining them by parody, and, then, calling into question the liberation the parody had offered. Proto-feminist Pat and novel might well be, but, if so, it's a very sad proto-feminism. In fact, it is much like the proto-feminism one finds throuhout Montgomery's journals. Both in her journals and in her fiction, Montgomery expresses a desire for independence and an awareness of how the patriarchy entraps women; however, she seems at times either resigned to the situation or even supportive of it. This position, which seems to us inconsistent, is not all that surprising if one remembers when Montgomery was writing and what society was like then.

Stories, of course, have to end. If Montgomery had ended Pat's story with the heroine entrapped and growing older and older, fiercely resisting any and all changes, she would have created an ending consonant with the bulk of the two books. This ending, however, would not have satisfied most of her readers or her publisher who were, after all, reading the two "Pat books" as primarily "juvenile fiction." Thus, Montgomery offers a quick, very contrived ending. Silver Bush burns to the ground, Hilary returns from points West, he proposes marriage and a life together in the little house by another sea that he has already built for Pat. There, he says, "we'll build up a new life and the old will become just a treasury of dear and sacred memories...of things time cannot destroy'" (273). Pat realizes that her true reason for rejecting a string of suitors was not her attachment to Silver Bush but her attachment to childhood friend Hilary. This ending perhaps satisfies adolescent readers, for they expect the twists and the happy-ever-after resolution of books written for young people. More sophisticated readers, however, can see not only how contrived the ending is, but also how Montgomery, through its rapidity if nothing else, signals its contrivance. One is reminded of the ending of Shakespeare's *Pericles* where the numerous problems within the plot are resolved, rapidly, one after another, in what Shakespeare must have known was hilariously parodic of traditional stage comedy. I am not suggesting that Montgomery's ending is entirely parodic. Montgomery conforms to the genre and she gives all readers hope for Pat insofar as they recall that Hilary's "dream was of building beautiful homes for love to dwell in...houses to keep people from the biting wind and the fierce sun and the loneliness of dark night" (*Pat of,* 247). His dream is to provide for Pat (and others) what Silver Bush had. This hope, however, seems as staged as the rapid-fire, multiple resolutions of Shakespeare's romance. One also must note, as Epperly does, that Pat had to be rescued: Her powerlessness, exhibited throughout the book in her ability to do little more than say "no," is still evident in the end.

Epperly terms *Mistress Pat* "one of the saddest books Montgomery ever wrote" (217). This assessment reflects Epperly's refusal to see the ending as anything but transparent contrivance required by conventions Montgomery was herself trapped in as a writer of "juvenile fiction." The ending then is sadly ironic insofar as Montgomery could find a way to write her character out of her trap, but she could not find a way to write herself out of the trap she was in as writer and as woman. There was not even a Hilary to rescue her.

Even sadder, I think, is Montgomery's *Magic for Marigold*. In it, there is similar entrapment. And, at the end of it, there is no similar illusion of escape. In this novel, Montgomery explicitly addresses "place."

This had, of course, been a motif in her writing ever since *Anne of Green Gables*. For Anne, the treasured place was Green Gables. Although none of the other places in Montgomery's fiction rise quite to the mythic level of Green Gables, *Anne's House of Dreams, Rainbow Valley, Rilla of Ingleside, Chronicles of Avonlea, Pat of Silver Bush,* and *Jane of Lantern Hill* all focus on places that are or become special. Some of these places, in line with the conventions of nineteenth-century fiction, reflect the central character's traits (Epperly). According to Marigold's "Old Grandmother," places are human with human needs and human feelings. I would go one step farther than Old Grandmother and suggest that Montgomery's places are human and gendered. They are female, with the needs and feelings of the female lives contained within. Marigold's ostensible place, the house where she lives, is strikingly female as the young girl resides there with her mother, her Young Grandmother, and her Old Grandmother. Given how feminine this place is, one is tempted to associate it with the semiotic. In fact, one is tempted to go back to the "Pat Books" and try to read Silver Bush as place in semiotic terms and go to other Montgomery novels and try to read all the treasured places in semiotic terms. Such an attempt both succeeds and fails. It succeeds insofar as one finds much in these places—and these novels—that occurs outside of language, quite frequently in the nonverbal communication between mother and child. However, the attempt fails because none of these places is stable. The suggestion might be that the semiotic has already been compromised to the symbolic in these places. Although the female characters within them engage in a struggle with words in an attempt (often successfully) to make those symbolic bits work for them, there is a nagging sense of ultimate failure. The "story girl" Sara Stanley grows up, Emily Bird Starr settles for domestic bliss, and Anne Shirley sees Green Gables sold and, after a bit and marriage and children, seems to write very little. Moreover, of course, Pat Gardiner sees her special place, Silver Bush, burn to the ground and then quickly loses her "green world" name and takes Hilary's name as his wife. Perhaps the fate of these semiotic places was long ago sealed when they were themselves named, rather than allowed to just be.

Marigold seems very aware of the limitations of her place as semi-otic retreat. It is as maternal as possible, with multiple generations of women living there. Nonetheless, it's very much in language. Thus, Marigold finds another special place, another island within the island. Marigold spends a fair amount of time searching for this place. She felt that it was within the harbor, "a great gleaming mirror, all faint, prismatic colors like the world in a soap bubble" (31). She felt that it was across the bay. She felt that it was over the hill, where the grass "would be ever so much greener—'living green,' as one of Salome's hymns said" (33). Marigold eventually finds the island within an is-land close by, on her own property, in the grove called "Cloud of Spruce," its very name suggesting its connection to nature and its ethereal (i.e., not bounded here on earth) quality. "Cloud of Spruce" literally exists, but the place Marigold retreats to is special—through "The Magic Door" and through "The Green Gate." One can only reach this special place if one recites "The Rhyme." There, Marigold has not only safety but her special imaginary playmate Sylvia. Mari-gold, the novel suggests, needs such a place because, like Pat Gar-diner, she fears change. This fear surfaces when she thinks her mother will remarry and leave their home—also called "Cloud of Spruce," af-ter the grove. "Would she have to leave dear Cloud of Spruce?" (185). Marigold "tortured herself" (185) with this question. Would she and her mother "soon be living" in "an ugly square house, with not even a tree about it. And no real garden" (187)? Pat's fear of change, the novel suggests, might be tied to her father's death of pneumonia, an event that Pat has to be reassured was not—somehow—her fault.

"Cloud of Spruce" is the name the house and the grove are known by. However, Marigold, of course, has named Sylvia, just as she has named the Magic Door, and so forth. Much like Anne Shirley, but without quite as much imagination, she delights in the words she can bestow. Like many of Montgomery's heroines, Marigold delights in naming (Fredeman 65). In so doing, Marigold enacts the dilemma fac-ing women as Kristeva sees it: retreating into the semiotic but ironi-cally insisting upon expressing what it is in symbolic terms. The irony, however, will not catch up with Marigold until the end of her story. In the meantime, she delights in "Cloud of Spruce."

Having a special place and having an imaginary playmate are not unusual for a child. However, Marigold's Young Grandmother and her reticent mother believe that, in Marigold's case, these behaviors are symptomatic of something wrong with the child. Thus, they try to deny Marigold her retreat. In response, she falls seriously ill. When she's allowed back through the Magic Door and the Green Gate into her imaginary green world, she is restored:

> Marigold stood still for a moment, transfigured. Her face was as blithe as the day. It was as if a little shower of joy had rained down upon her out of the sky. She flew through the orchard room—through the Magic Door— through the blue-eye grass of the orchard as if there were some Atlanta wizardry in her feet. Through the Green Gate. For another moment she stood, almost afraid. Suppose Sylvia—Then she shut her eyes and said her Rhyme....There was a pale moon-glow behind the cloud of spruce. There was a dance of great plumy boughs in the western wind. And there was a sound not heard in the orchard for a long time—the sound of Marigold's laughter as she waved goodnight to Sylvia over the Green Gate. (98)

The place does then seem to exert a powerful influence on the girl's physical and psychological health. So, rather than forbid her the place, her Young Grandmother and her mother try to find Marigold a real playmate to replace Sylvia. Each mirrors Marigold's joyous being only for a short while: Each eventually shows a dark, if not evil, side, ceasing to be a mirror to Marigold *or* becoming a mirror of a part of Marigold that the girl defiantly suppresses as she grows increasingly isolated. For example, there is Princess Vavara, who was visiting the island. She proves to be not "a bit like a Princess" (130) with her wild behavior and bad table manners and egotistical selfishness. Even the adults recognize that troubled side: Lord Percy calling her "An incorrigible little demon" (130) and Lucifer noting that "princesses aren't what they used to be in the good old days" (131). Although there is a comic edge to the portraits the novel offers of these others, children as well as adults, they, in sum, offer a negative picture of the world be-

yond "Cloud of Spruce." As Epperly notes, "The world around Marigold is full of hidden ugliness" (241).

The reader certainly sees the duplicity of these "real" playmates.
However, the reader also realizes that these playmates are simply enacting the behavior they see all around them in the adult world. Their
duplicity then would normally be a way—perhaps a traumatic way—
for the young Marigold to learn about the adult world she must one
day enter. Marigold, however, does not want to enter that world; she
wants to stay in "Cloud of Spruce" with her nonduplicitous imaginary friend Sylvia. Revulsion and fear entrap her into her imaginary
world. Although she chooses to stay there in the island within the island, the choice begins to seem increasingly pathological as Montgomery's novel progresses, and the place begins to be less an idyllic
retreat and more a trap.

Montgomery does not burn down or cut down "Cloud of Spruce."
Her way of putting an end to the once idyllic, now entrapping place is
more subtle but just as sad. Montgomery has Marigold grow up just
enough to become enamored of a boy playmate named Budge. Budge,
however, is more interested in playing with Tad than with Marigold.
So, to woo Budge away from Tad, she reveals to him the secrets of the
Magic Door, the Green Gate, the Rhyme, and Sylvia. She had already
put what suggested the semiotic into words. Those words, however,
were protected because they were spoken only to herself or within the
confines of her very female household. Now, Marigold chooses to
speak these words to the male, who regulates the symbolic realm the
words very fragilely exist in. As she did, "She had a curious unpleas-
ant sense of loss and disloyalty...as if she were losing something that
was very precious" (163). Budge's response to her verbalization is
devastating. "Aw, that sounds awful silly," (169), he replies.

Marigold, hurt by Budge's words, tries to retreat to the safety of
"Cloud of Spruce." She finds, however, that she cannot. She finds
that, "Her lovely dream was gone" (269–70); that, "The old magic was
gone forever—gone with Sylvia and the Hidden Land and all the
dear, sweet fading dreams of childhood" (273). The reader is tempted
to interpret what has happened as simply Marigold's growing up.

However, such a reading, although attentive to how the author describes Marigold's state in the novel before revealing all to Budge—i.e., the state of being at the edge of childhood--does not pay adequate attention to what pushed Marigold in this direction. What pushed her was her trying to make the semiotic retreat that she could only understand in words a place that might exist in those very words in the full light of the symbolic.

What Montgomery then does in *Magic for Marigold* is present the core mythos that defines a woman's life in Kristeva's terms. We see, in something close to fable terms, the retreat into the semiotic and its restorative power. We see how the retreat ultimately must end, how the retreat, if prolonged, becomes a trap. We see how the semiotic proves ultimately incompatible with the symbolic: How Budge, in just a few words, can destroy all of the magic. Retreating then is possible in the world Montgomery depicts, but only temporarily so. Beyond a certain point, retreating becomes self-entrapping. However, moving out of the retreat brings one into collision with the duplicitous world; trying to accommodate the retreat to a world defined by the male-controlled symbolic destroys the semiotic retreat. No matter which of these three ways a female child moves, she is lost.

What does that loss entail? In a passage fraught with both Wordsworthian echoes and bitter irony, Montgomery answers that "there were compensations" (173), for now Marigold knew her true place. It wasn't "Cloud of Spruce," it was to "'be here for him to come back to'" (274). The words are spoken so quickly that their impact is probably lost on most readers. In addition, the words have a faint romantic flavor, suggesting the loving women wandering men or working men or warring men return to. In addition these romantic words are accompanied by her discovery of "her own ground" (274), a discovery that at first (quick) hearing sounds positive. However, all of these words, if examined closely, offer women nothing but statis: They wait; they wait on ground that seems quite confined. If "Cloud of Spruce" were to become a trap because devoid of reality, then the ultimate alternative was equally a trap because devoid of mobility,

mobility in senses real and metaphorical. And at least "Cloud of Spruce" had its magic.

The ending I have posited for *Magic for Marigold* is probably a more feminist one than Montgomery herself would have voiced had she been asked to describe it. I am suggesting that, in the text, there is evidence for a reading of Marigold's situation—and, by extension, many girls' and women's—that goes beyond what Montgomery could have articulated in her time and in her society. Epperly's reading of the ending similarly picks up on the feminist notes. As Epperly reads it, Montgomery either exposes the female plight *or* exposes and endorses the female plight. Epperly expresses her fear that it is the latter and notes that in Montgomery's journals there is a similar pattern of exposing and, then, acceding to, sometimes resignedly and sometimes supportively. What we might see as a fundamental contradiction is, then, simply something the author and, by extension, her characters lived. The result is a book whose tone is, overall, uneasy. As Epperly puts it, "sorrow, cruelty, madness, and unimaginativeness alongside dancing, joy, imaginative ecstasy, and loving kindness" (243). What one might add to Epperly's description is the note that such is, in Montgomery's vision, the female condition.

7

Dangerous Idylls

Gabrielle Roy's *The Tin Flute*; Margaret Atwood's *Bodily Harm*; Marie-Claire Blais's *These Festive Nights*

We ordinarily associate L. M. Montgomery with *Anne of Green Gables* and, thus, with a very positive view of the island. However, as the readings of later, lesser known Montgomery novels indicate, the author's view was not always this positive. Sometimes, the island could be a trap: initially positive, but eventually not so. Similar to the late Montgomery novels discussed in chapter 6 are the three novels analyzed in this chapter. Gabrielle Roy's *The Tin Flute* (1945), Margaret Atwood's *Bodily Harm* (1981), and Marie-Claire Blais's *These Festive Nights* (1995) all present a seemingly positive retreat to an island. The retreat offers, respectively, prosperity, safety, and recovery. However, the retreat, in the end, offers none of these things. Rather, the illusion of retreat drops away, like a curtain, to reveal bleak prospects—for the main characters, for women, and for humankind. These three novels, then, are like Montgomery's later books, but far bleaker, for their ominous message extends far beyond young girls named Pat or Marigold.

Roy's *The Tin Flute* is an important work in French Canadian literary history. As noted in chapter 1, it is the first urban novel. As such, it marks a departure from a rural myth, one which celebrated the land and established, very firmly, gender-based roles for those who lived that myth (Smart). What happened in French Canadian literary history rather accurately paralleled what was occurring in social history. Just as Roy's novel rejected the rural myth, so were many in Quebec. They were leaving the lands along the St. Lawrence and moving to the island of Montreal—seeking what they thought would be a better life.

The Tin Flute deals with two women, mother and daughter. The mother, Rose-Anna, married Azarius Lacasse in the countryside and moved with him to the city. She literally escaped the ennui and the borderline poverty of the habitants; she tried to follow "the secret path of her dreams" (168) to the glamorous island city of Montreal. The daughter, Florentine, was born in the city—more specifically, in the poor St. Henri district of the city.

Roy rather accurately depicts Montreal as a city of neighborhoods, neighborhoods clearly marked off, one from another. Thus, St. Henri, even though it is in the heart of the city, is set-off—by railroad tracks, a canal, and industrial development—from other sections, "[f]or no part of Montreal has kept its well-defined limits or its special, narrow, characteristic village life as St. Henri has done" (284). It is island-like, although, as Lewis notes, it at times seems more like a concentration camp or even hell. Other areas in the city such as the Jewish district along Rue St. Urbain or the affluent English district of Westmount are similarly insular but not in the claustrophobic way Roy describes St. Henri as being.

Looking at St. Henri, Florentine has realized how futile her mother's escape was. "She now perceived her mother's life as a long, grey voy-

age which she, Florentine, would never make" (116). Thinking specifically of how Rose-Anna suffered through repeated pregnancies,
"She saw her mother, heavy and moving with difficulty. A vision of
herself as victim of the same deformity was vivid in her mind" (242).
So, Florentine wants to escape the trap of St. Henri for one of the
more prosperous islands within the island, most notably to the area
flanking Rue St. Catherine where the posh shops and restaurants are:

> She could see St. Catherine Street, the department-store windows, the ele-
> gant Saturday-night crowd, the florists' displays, the restaurants with their
> revolving doors and tables set almost on the sidewalk behind gleaming bay
> windows, the brightly lit movie theatres, their aisles disappearing into the
> dark behind the cashier's glass cage amid tall, glittering mirrors, polished
> banisters and potted plants, rising toward the screen that brought the most
> beautiful visions in the world. Everything she desired, admired and envied
> floated there before her eyes. (17)

Florentine's attraction to Jean Levesque is tied to her association of
Jean with "the city 'downtown,'" for he made "the lights shine
brighter, the crowd seem gay" (18). With Jean, "everything turned to
a dream, and bravely she entered the dream to play her part in it"
(78).

The mother serves as a mirror for the daughter; the daughter serves
as a mirror for the mother. There is also the grandmother in Roy's
novel. She remained for her entire life in rural Quebec. She mirrors
mother and daughter, revealing what they might have become if their
lives had not taken them off to an island. The grandmother is presented nobly—as someone who worked hard, suffered life bravely.
However, the effect of the rural life on her is telling. She has become
cold, bitter—in Smart's words, "the icon of maternal negativity" (170),
seeing life, especially that of women, in "hard" terms. Her bitterness
is reflected in the comments she makes to Rose-Anna both on Rose-
Anna's wedding day and on the day Rose-Anna and Azarius return
to the country for a visit. On the wedding day, Madame Laplante
said, "You may think you're running away from poverty, that you're
going to play the fine lady in town, but you mark my words: poverty
finds us out. You'll have your miseries too" (195). Upon Rose-Anna's

return, the grandmother said. "'My poor Rose-Anna! I thought as much. I was sure you'd had a bad time. Of course I knew it. Why should it be better for you than for anybody else? And now you see, my girl, you can't just make things happen as you like in your life'" (192–93).

"Hard" would be an apt description of the life Rose-Anna lives on the island of Montreal. Repeatedly pregnant, she must bear and then raise multiple children in the poverty of St. Henri. Since her husband proves incapable of dealing with most of the demands of the family's daily life, she must shoulder those responsibilities as well. As a result, she looks much older than her forty-some years, and she is more often than not on the brink of exhaustion. Nearing childbirth again during the novel's few months, Rose-Anna is "longing for rest and death" (358), feels "herself sink into an infinite abyss, then rise, then sink again" (359), and feels "such a need to go gently to her death and escape her suffering" (360). Within the novel's brief chronological framework, she must deal with a dying child as well as with the child she will very soon bear. At the same time, she must participate in what seems to be an annual ritual in St. Henri—relocation. The majority in the community, it seems, every spring, abandon where they have been living because the rent has been raised and is now too high and move to a new house they can afford. This ritual of renewal is enacted with some enthusiasm by Rose-Anna and the others in St. Henri: They all act as if the move will be a move for the better:

> It seemed that once a year the neighbourhood gave into a folly of escape stimulated by the passage of trains and the blowing of locomotive whistles, but, unable to afford a real voyage, settled for a move next door. Two houses out of five had their much-used signs up: "To Let, To Let, To Let!" (95)

What they do not see is that they are on a downward spiral, relocating each spring to drearier and drearier lodgings. The move we see, into a dusty set of rooms too close to the railroad tracks, is treated in an upbeat manner by Azarius and Rose-Anna; however, we see how bleak their new house really is.

Rose-Anna maintains this upbeat façade, but the reader sees how beaten a woman she is—so beaten that she can no longer truly function as mother. Yes, she does give birth. However, she fails to comfort her dying son, and she fails to deal in a constructive manner with what she knows is Florentine's pregnancy and Florentine's marriage to a man other than the baby's father. She simply stares at her first-born daughter:

> When she [Florentine] stood straight again, her face pale and humiliated, her mother was looking at her. Looking as if she had never seen her before, Rose-Anna stared wide-eyed, with an expression of mute horror. Without pity, without affection, without kindness. (261)

Rose-Anna addressed her daughter "violently" (161) but "stopped short" (262) of articulating her fears. "[T]he two women stared at each other like enemies." Florentine broke that stare, replacing it an expression that was "a call for help, the call of a hunted creature. But Rose-Anna had turned away" (262). The silence is not the out-of-language silence of female communication; rather, it's the silence of indifference and despair.

Roy's novel departs from the French-Canadian literary tradition in a way other than being urban. *The Tin Flute* also is a departure insofar as it centers on female protagonists. In the traditional Quebecois novel, female characters played stereotyped roles until they married; then, they virtually disappeared (Smart 160, 173). The characters in Roy's novel who are on the verge of disappearing are the male ones. Azarious Lacasse dreams of abandoning his family and their poverty and escaping to the West, where youthful adventures are to be had, he thinks. He does not do so; instead, recognizing his failure as husband and father, he enlists in the Canadian military and goes off to fight in World War II. "Free, free, unbelievably free, he was starting a new life!" (371) Azarius thinks. His salary will provide better for them than any of the jobs he has drifted among. He so drifted because, early-on on this island, he yielded to failure. Unwilling to admit his failure and, therefore, unable to enact a mature response to it, he lost himself in his words. These words he spoke in the male-defined world of The Two Records café. Although his listeners there did not pay much heed to these words, they tolerated them. Azarius, in this world of empty words, felt like a man. As a result, he did not see how he had failed to be a man in any of the realms of life that truly mattered.

Florentine seems determined to avoid her mother's fate. A determinism, however, colors the novel: There is a strong sense of St. Henri almost being a character and playing a role in the characters' fates that they cannot totally control (Lewis 73). So, from the very beginning, the reader doubts Florentine's ability to escape. Her job as a waitress behind the counter at a St. Henri drug store does not especially lift the reader's hopes for Florentine; neither does the content or the caliber of the young girl's conversations. She seems very materialistic and rather shallow.

Her relationship with Jean Levesque, who has been frequenting the counter, is a peculiar one. She flirts, but she does not flirt. She is attracted, but she also acts as if she is—for some reason—superior to him, although the reader cannot discern anyway in which she might be. There is, in any event, an awkwardness to her flirting. Perhaps, realizing what marriage to Azarius did to her mother, Florentine does not want to be similarly trapped. There is an awkwardness to Jean's flirting as well. It is as if he sees her as a trap as well, a trap that could keep him in St. Henri and not allow him to fulfill his more expansive ambitions. Their first date, a date that never really occurs, is symptomatic of their shared hesitancy: She almost does not go to meet him; he lurks in shadows to see if she will show up; he waits too long to join her in front of the cinema and she, saddened, goes in with her girlfriends.

What Florentine and Jean enact is an awkward dance. He moves, relying primarily on his words; she moves, relying primarily on her body. He is motivated because of a pity he feels for her, for her poverty, which is also his. She is motivated because Jean, who is working to escape that poverty, has money and can expose her to the fancy goods and services of Rue St. Catherine. "[s]he was no longer Florentine the waitress who was angered and humiliated by her menial job.

Let them call for her with rough words, plague her with vulgar approaches, that didn't bother her now....She was a new Florentine..." (114). Their different "tools" in this dance are worth noting: Jean, embraced within the symbolic, uses words; Florentine, still attuned to the semiotic, uses the body. What is also worth noting is how neither is especially good with the "tool" he or she has chosen. Jean's socialist ideas are uttered with a fervor, but without much sophistication. Florentine's body is far too thin to be attractive, and her inability to put bodily adornments such as clothing and make-up to particularly good use to enhance her appearance is sadly comic. After she excuses herself at a posh restaurant Jean had taken her to, "He was furious when he saw her coming back [from the restroom], her lips smeared red, and preceded by a perfume so harsh that people on both sides of her path looked up and smiled" (80). Her body, which yearns for involvement, arguably, proves more powerful than Jean's words, which counsel disengagement: She seduces him in a scene that reads at times, as Smart has suggested, like her rape as "his dark eyes stared down at her with a kind of madness" and "his fingers ripped one of the thin straps of her apron" and "[s]he fell back, her knees bent, one foot kicking feebly" (206). Roy's suggestion might well be that, although she arguably initiates the intimacy, the situation, not Jean *per se*, rapes her—disempowers her. She shortly finds herself pregnant— disempowered more completely, for she is now trapped by her body and by the social stigma attached to her condition. Jean meanwhile, knowing he is becoming trapped in a relationship but not knowing that he is a father, flees Montreal.

Florentine now sees a path before her that is worse than the one Rose-Anna followed. Rose-Anna became trapped by her body, experiencing pregnancy after pregnancy. However, at least Rose-Anna had the protection of marriage. Florentine initially is unable to deal with her predicament: She cannot locate Jean for he has fled; she cannot accept the help of a girlfriend named Marguerite for she would have to admit her "sin." She roams the street "seeking only a ray of hope to alleviate her terror" (249). She nearly commits suicide. She feels that she has fallen into "the trap that had been set for her weak-

ness," a trap that was "coarse and brutal" (252). This trap is, in her
eyes, related to her gender, so she expresses "an unspeakable contempt for her fate as a woman, and a self-hatred that left her amazed"
(252).

She finally sees a way out of her trap when Emmanuel Letourneau
returns on leave from the military base he is stationed at prior to
shipping off to the European war. Emmanuel had earlier in the novel
expressed an interest in Florentine, inviting her to his birthday party
at his comparatively posh home outside of St. Henri. She went to the
party hoping to see Jean there. Although she and Emmanuel had a
fun evening together, she makes it clear to the reader that she is far
more attracted to Jean. Emmanuel is, in her eyes, a warm, generous
young man; however, he does not excite her the way Jean does.

Pregnant and abandoned by Jean, she takes advantage of Emmanuel's warmth and generosity. They spend a great deal of time together during his leave and decide to marry before he heads off to the
war. She does not love him; rather, she trades her body for a few
nights for the financial security she will have during his time overseas
and—she presumes—after his death in the war. She coldly calculates
a way to avoid both the trap Rose-Anna fell into and the somewhat
different trap that she was on the verge of falling into. If we chronicle
this relationship, we learn a great deal about Florentine. She turned to
Emmanuel with hope: "More than her safety and salvation were at
stake. It seemed to her that Emmanuel might succeed in restoring her
lust for life, her pride, her joy in being well-dressed and irresistible"
(352). As their courtship began, "she saw herself reborn, loved, pret-
tier than ever, saved..." (336). However, she saw the good of this relationship almost exclusively in materialistic terms: "For him, [the days]
would be days of jealously protected intimacy, an escape into a land
of sweet daydreams, of exquisite laziness; for her, the flashing lights
of the cinema, the department stores, and Florentine there, radiant"
(338). This materialistic joy was not enough for Florentine, for she did
not love Emmanuel, and "She knew he couldn't see her eyes, and was
glad of it, for she felt she would not herself have wanted to see what
was in them then" (339–40). Realizing there was no love in the rela-

tionship, she describes her future: "No more tempests. No more ecstasy, no more despair in her life. Just a long, flat road on which she was no longer surprised to be, since it meant salvation" (340).

However, does Florentine mean salvation from her "problem" or something grander? The former would seem to be the case: "Her life was settled now, once and for all. It wouldn't be what she had imagined, but it would be a thousand times better than what could have happened" (343). Rose-Anna, at this point, describes her daughter's "mouth" as being "hard" and "her eyes determined, almost insolent. This Florentine with the rigid mask, the dark frown, was a stranger to her" (344). On her wedding day, "there had been no sign of emotion, not even a lingering look" (349-50) as she left her family's poor home. Similarly, on the day her groom left for the war, she felt "a vague sense of relief" (378). Realizing what her financial state now was, "[s]he felt an intense satisfaction. Then she grew ashamed of herself…"(379). Just a few minutes later, after Emmanuel's train has left the station, "…she was surprised to notice that she was pleased with herself. A satisfaction she had never experienced—self-esteem—astonished her. She felt she was starting a new life" (381). She walked away calculating how rich she and her child were. "She saw their troubles fly away" (283). She told herself, "Oh, yes, it was a new life they were beginning" (283). "It bothered her somewhat to think" that they were gaining this money at the expense of Emmanuel's life—and presumably death—in war, "but these scruples were dismissed, and her calculations began again" (283).

Those who have read and commented on Roy's novel do not agree on how to read the novel's end. Some have suggested that the relationship between Florentine and Emmanuel is a positive one, positive insofar as it allows Florentine to escape the poverty of St. Henri and it allies her with a man who, unlike the sexist males that dominate the book, seems androgynous and much more likely than others to see her as free and equal within their marriage (Smart 186). I would argue, to the contrary, that Florentine's escape is illusory, and one of the reasons it is so is that the marriage, which might in theory have offered an atypically good, equal relationship, is clearly a charade.

There is no mutual love; the child who will be born in eight months is not Emmanuel's; and Florentine enters it on the assumption that the war will end it. Emmanuel's parents are not especially fond of Florentine. How will they react to the premature birth? How will they deal with Florentine's claims on "their" money after Emmanuel is dead, especially if they doubt the baby's paternity? And, even if, on the material level, Florentine's plan succeeds, how must she feel, knowing that she has abused both Emmanuel and his parents. Is her escape one to praise, to emulate?

In addition, one should recall Emmanuel Letourneau's comments on the riches of Westmount. He resents the concentration of wealth he finds there; he is angered by it. Just as Emmanuel's neighborhood within Montreal is a material paradise to escape to in the eyes of those of St. Henri, Westmount is a material paradise to escape to in the eyes of Emmanuel. Climbing a rung higher does not eliminate what one feels when one realizes that there are some who are so very rich. Despite his having more money than the Lacasse family, he, with working-class roots, feels "he has no right to enter this citadel of calm and order with the stink of poverty clinging to him like the odour of a sickroom" (319). Escape, it would seem, if it is premised solely or largely on the material is illusory. A genuine escape must be premised on something deeper than the material. Florentine's escape is premised entirely on the material. Thus, it seems quite empty. Lewis puts the matter well:

> Although Florentine will eventually raise her economic and social status by her marriage to Emmanuel, she will remain tied to her mother, Rose-Anna, and to the other women of Saint-Henri. Caught in the road, female structures of motherhood, crowds, and hereditary misery, therefore—created by men—these female protagonists will be forced to remain, as well, within the ironically female urban sphere of Montreal. (75)

Before condemning Florentine, one must contextualize her situation. *The Tin Flute*, although quite realistic, does embody a political message, one that—fortunately—does not turn the novel's characters into stereotypes. That message is decidedly Marxist, on the side of the exploited workers of St. Henri. In keeping with Roy's early journalistic writing in Montreal, her sympathy is clearly on the side of this class. Although Roy's presentation of these ideas is not without its ironies, she clearly seems on the workers' side and feels that they are, by some force beyond their control, trapped in poverty. Given then that Florentine necessarily sees the life in St. Henri that she wants to escape in material terms, her constructing a material escape is understandable—understandable, although regrettable. Each of the Lacasse children was "far away in his own dream" (165)—joined there by all of the children in St. Henri. The only successful escape is young Daniel, who, dying of leukemia, finds peace in the hospital ward where, "No one whispered at night, and he never woke suddenly to hear people talking about money, about rent, about expenses, words vast and cruel that came to his ears in the darkness" (226).

Florentine's vision then may be obscured by the material circumstances of her life. Florentine's sense of what alternatives she has may also be blurred, blurred by the patriarchy that dominates her society. Men, although not especially effectual in this society, still dominate. They signal to girls and women that they are primarily valued to the extent that they are physically attractive. They thus encourage women to use their bodies as a means of attracting and securing male protection. They then use women's bodies against women, imprisoning them in marriages featuring recurring pregnancy and maternity. They thereby shut-off avenues of escape, while keeping their escape routes open. The semiotic is, as noted many times in this study, rooted in the body's experiences. To the extent then that the patriarchy regulates women's bodies, the patriarchy is denying women access to the semiotic and to any kind of *jouissance*. Dancing may well serve in the novel as a metaphor for the regulation of the body. Florentine, it is worth noting, initially delights in dancing. She "showed an astonishing docility when she danced, her slim, supple figure submitting to the rhythm and her partner's movements, abandoned, passionate, childlike, almost primitive" (130). Initially, she liked dancing because it made her "the center of attention" and she felt that, through dance, "she was defying her life, burning her life" (131). Later, however, perhaps because she realized that dancing was less her "defying" and more her "submitting," "Dancing had lost its charm" (135). It didn't free the body to experience defiance or *jouissance*; rather it conformed the body to pattern and rhythm set by the male-defined culture.

The men in the novel also maintain networks through which they build a gendered solidarity based largely on empty swaggering, while essentially denying women any equivalent sense of community by keeping women too busy, too tired, to form community. Furthermore, rivalry over men separates girl from girl; fear of social approbation deters sharing experiences and feelings openly in search of support. Even mother and daughter, who ought to share and support, are left distanced in such a society. The sharing and support, between mother and daughter and among women in general, will occur to some extent outside language—through touch, through gesture, through facial expression. However, as the novel points out in one of its most poignant scenes, this very kind of communication seems thwarted. As already noted, Florentine and Rose-Anna stare at each other when confronted by the possibility of the young girl's pregnancy, and both run away from any kind of meaningful nonverbal or verbal sharing and supporting. Just as words seem to be a very awkward tool for them in the scene where Rose-Anna comes to Florentine's counter and the girl buys her mother a good lunch and a nice dessert, nonverbal expression seems awkward to the point of not working in the scene where the two of them should have dealt as fellow women with Florentine's plight. In the restaurant scene, they made communication work, making Rose-Anna "relaxed and almost happy" and giving Florentine "desire" and "joy" and a "rhythm to her body" that "lightened her heavy chores" (118–19). In the later scene, they allow fear and pride to thwart communication. Just before this failing moment, we see how much potential there was, even then, for a strong mother-daughter bond. Seeing her mother through the dining room curtain, Florentine feels "an infinite, poignant affinity" for her family and realizes that the family had been long "made beautiful from start to finish by Rose-Anna's courage," a courage that "shone out like a lighthouse beam before" (257) the young girl. However, just moments later, we are told "an arctic wind chilled her frail efforts to make a fresh beginning" (257). Rose-Anna is described as trapped in an "abyss" so deep that "you could scream for days and hear no response but the echo of your own despair" (259), and Florentine is described as "sinking into a suffocating darkness in which no help, no counsel, came from any side, wherever she might turn" (261). The possible moment of connection is not to be. Smart describes both the attraction among women and their separation in Roy's novel well:

> ...Roy shows how the feminine role as defined by patriarchal society separates women from each other, thus perpetuating the status-quo of a culture founded on their subjection....Roy's narrative technique reveals with remarkable finesse and subtlety a deep-seated love between mother and daughter, but a love frustrated by the constraints imposed by language and culture. (173)

The failed moment of connection is suggested by the way mirrors are brought into the novel. Mirrors can be used to signal those female characters from whom the central character not only learns from but with whom she also forms a powerful connection. Mirrors become a sign as to how the relationship between the characters should be read. Mirrors, however, are used quite differently in *The Tin Flute*. Mirrors are ubiquitous in the novel, but they are always something Florentine is looking into and seeing herself in. This use suggests how self-absorbed the girl is. It also suggests that there are no others out there serving as helpful mirror images. She seems disconnected from female friends, siblings, and her mother; she seems alone, checking her hair or her makeup in a mirror. Mirrors then, rather than signaling those who might form a community, emphasize Florentine's shallow isolation.

The Quebecois novel, prior to Roy, embodied a patriarchal mythos. Roy's novel, as noted several times, is a startling departure from that tradition: It is urban; it features central female characters. Despite these departures, the novel's story is still trapped in the patriarchy. Showing that very trap seems to have been one of Roy's intentions, for the novel very much depicts how girls and women are trapped, not just in a place but in a set of patriarchal norms from which escape is either impossible or illusory.

Roy's novel is set in pre-World War II Montreal, more than sixty years earlier. One would think that by the 1980s or the 1990s, the world might have changed dramatically. Atwood's *Bodily Harm* and Blais's *These Festive Days* suggest that little has changed since the time Roy wrote.

Atwood's central character, lifestyles journalist Rennie Wilford, finds living in Toronto increasingly oppressive. She finds herself repeatedly threatened with bodily harm. One day, someone breaks into her apartment, leaving a rope, coiled like a snake, on her bed. A threat of sexual violence is implicit in this act. She feels violated by it, and she feels violated again when the police sent to investigate the break-in seem to leer at her and whatever sexual proclivities the rope suggests she might have. "He wanted it to be my fault, just a little, some indiscretion, some provocation" (15). The rope may have been left by a genuine intruder, or it may have been left by her current boyfriend Jake. Jake's sexual tastes run to the kinky, a favorite being the enactment of his rape fantasies. He would jump out of closets, come through windows. He could be rough too: "Jake liked to pin her hands down, he liked to hold her so she couldn't move. He liked that, he liked thinking of sex as something he could win at. Sometimes he really hurt her, once he put his arm across her throat and she really did stop breathing" (207). His behavior makes Rennie very uncomfortable. She is also troubled by the way Jake seems only interested in her body, an impression validated when he rejects her as lover after her partial mastectomy.

Threatened by real rape and troubled by fantasized rape, Rennie feels "bodily harm," even though she has not literally experienced it. An assignment given to her by the editor of *Visor* magazine furthers this feeling. She is asked to write a feature piece on a pornography exhibit. Believing that she is sufficiently liberated to handle the charge, she visits the exhibit. Much there is the expected — nudity, explicit sexual activity, but there is also a level of violence directed against the female body and a degree of degradation:

> This is our grand finale....The picture showed a woman's pelvis, just the pelvis and the tops of the thighs. The woman was black. The legs were slightly apart; the usual hair, the usual swollen pinkish purple showed between them; nothing was moving. Then something small and grey and wet appeared, poking out from between the legs. It was the head of a rat. (210)

Her response to the exhibit is visceral: "She threw up on the policeman's shoes" (211). He tells her many women respond that way and dismisses the exhibit by saying, "at least it's not for queers" (211).

Rennie's body is not literally harmed, but she feels violated nonetheless. Somewhat ironically, the real harm to her body is experienced at the hands of surgeon Daniel, who excises a cancerous growth from her breast. The cancer itself was, of course, doing "bodily harm," but implicit in Atwood's novel is the possibility that the male doctor goes beyond what is medically necessary in excising her flesh. Although alternate, less invasive responses to the cancer, he is very quick to cut. In doing so, the doctor, like many in a patriarchal medical establishment, is insufficiently sensitive to what the excision might mean to Rennie's identity as a woman and sense of self-worth. Throughout the novel, Rennie refers to the operation and to the scar. Until very near the novel's end, she cannot forget this "bodily harm." Exacerbating that harm is the fact that Rennie became enamored of the surgeon Daniel, thinking him her "savior." Rather than keeping his professional distance, he succumbed to her flirtation, and they had a brief affair. He proves, however, to be far different from what Rennie had imagined: rather than the strong "savior," he proves to be a weak man with many insecurities of his own: "The fact was that he had needed something from her, which she could neither believe nor forgive. She'd been counting on him not to: she was supposed to be the needy one, but it was the other way around....She felt like a straw that had been clutched, she felt he'd been drowning. She felt raped" (238).

Given all that she has experienced in Toronto, it is no wonder that Rennie wants to escape from the city. So, she arranges for herself to do a "light" travel piece on the twin Caribbean islands of St. Antoine and St. Agathe, whose new postcolonial government is interested in attracting more tourists. She views the trip as a respite. In an environment in which she will not be threatened by any "bodily harm," she can recover from the damage that has been done to her psyche and her body. As several have noted, her full name, Renata, suggests "rebirth" (Jones 92; Kirtz 125). It is a kind of rebirth she is seeking on the island.

I have referred to Rennie a couple of times as a journalist. She is, but she has always positioned herself on the "light" side on journalism. "'I just don't do that kind of thing," she tells Dr. Minnow when he tries to interest her in writing about the Caribbean nation's problems. "I do lifestyles" (136), she tells him. She has also always maintained her objectivity as she should as a journalist, but she seems to have maintained that objectivity less to preserve the integrity of her writing and more to maintain her personal lack of engagement. She backs away from such engagement, even though the matters she is covering, "life styles," are not serious ones (Irvine, "The Here" 89). In fact, her choice to do "life styles," not harder news further reflects her retreat from engagement. "Massive involvement, said Rennie. It's never been my thing" (34). Style aside, she may not be what many would consider a "true" journalist. Her writing just is not substantive enough.

Of course, as a writer, Rennie deals with words, with the symbolic. She uses the symbolic uncritically, without questioning its patriarchal definition or finding herself in the awkward position of having to use the patriarchally defined symbolic against the patriarchy — what she might have been in had she chosen to write the article on pornography. Her problem with words as a writer then is her uncritical attitude toward them. She also must deal with words as a reader — not so much as a reader of literal texts but as a reader of the broader texts in which she is living. Her problem with "words" as a reader is her inability to read them correctly (Irvine, "The Here" 88, 90; Smith 258-60).

In Toronto, she seems to misread men. She does not accurately read Jake — not seeing him to be as superficial and as dangerous as he probably is. She also does not accurately read Daniel — not seeing him as weak as he proves to be. These misreadings, however, are not fatal in the largely safe environment of Canada. On the Caribbean island, misreading is more dangerous. "Rennie feels very suddenly as if she's stepped across a line and found herself on Mars" (74). There, she quickly realizes that there is some political tension and instability, but, upon hearing a political speaker, "Rennie can't understand a word he's saying" (78). Part of her problem may be due to poor acoustics, but the problem goes beyond mere hearing. However, intent upon staying out of it, she does not listen carefully, and she deflects those who try to interest her, as a journalist, in investigating and writing about the political situation. She tells Dr. Minnow, for example, that, as a "lifestyles" writer, she looks at what people eat and what people wear. He exposes her to the poverty of the islands:

> Even outside there's a smell of bodies, of latrines and lime and decaying food. There are mattresses under the canvas roofs, most without sheets. Clothing is piled on the beds and hangs from ropes running from pole to pole. Between the tents are cooking fires; the ground around them is littered with utensils, pots, tin plates, pans. The people here are mostly women and young children. (125)

When Minnow tries to get her to understand that food and clothing are precisely the issues in a poverty-defined land, she turns the conversation off. She is in this scene very careful to preserve her neutrality. She cannot see—or will not see—what we see: that the "bodily harm" she and other women have experienced is analogous to the "bodily harm" the residents of the islands have suffered (Goodwin 114). She cannot or will not see the connection and is careful not to make a commitment. Given that care, it is difficult to understand why she agrees to pick up a package at the airport for Lora and Paul. Does she inadvertently become complicit in arms smuggling because she is attracted to Paul? Because she identifies with fellow Canadian Lora? Because she truly believes Lora's "story" about the package's contents and destination? Because she does not know how to say "No" when she is pushed? Regardless of the answer, Rennie very clearly misreads the situation and seems to misread Paul and Lora. She ends up, as a result, gradually sucked more and more into the political maelstrom, which, on election night, explodes into civil war when the defeated incumbent "moves" against his victorious opponents and anyone associated with them. She ends up, in Paul's words, "too involved"; in her words, experiencing "*Massive involvement*" (234). Rennie, however, never really understood what the sides were in the battle, and she clearly did not consciously ally herself with either Dr. Minnow or "The Prince." However, in the chaos, her conversations with Minnow, her association with "The Prince"'s lover Lora, and her involvement with the shadowy Paul made her suspicious. As a result, she finds herself imprisoned in a Third-World jail. There, she witnesses the torture and execution of men who had opposed the postcolonial government. She sees "butchery," "kicks...in the stomach," and "one of the policemen jam[ming] the cattle prod in between [a prisoner's] legs" (289–90). There, she and Lora must prostitute themselves to the prison guards to get any "favors," such as edible food and nonfetid water. One "favor" Lora wants is a word sent to "The Prince," who she is told is alive. She paid for the "favor" by fellating the guards. When they later laugh and tell her "The Prince" is dead, she turns on them. They, in turn, laugh and beat her to the point where her face is unrecognizable:

> Morton knees her in the belly, he's knocked the air out of her. Now nobody needs to hold her arms....They go for the breasts and the buttocks, the stomach, the crotch, the head, jumping, *My God*, Morton's got the gun out and he's hitting her with it, he'll break her so that she'll never make another sound. Lora twists on the floor of the corridor, surely she can't feel it any more but she's still twisting, like a worm that's been cut in half....(292-93)

> Dead end. She [Rennie] hauls Lora over to the dryest corner of the room and sits with her, pulling Lora's head and shoulders onto her lap. She moves the sticky hair away from the face, which isn't a face any more, It's a bruise, blood is still oozing from the cuts, there's one on the forehead and another across the cheek, the mouth looks like a piece of fruit that's been run over by a car, pulp, Rennie wants to throw up, it's no one she recognizes, she has no connection with this, there's nothing she can do, it's the face of a stranger, someone without a name, the word *Lora* has come unhooked and is hovering in the air, apart from this ruin, mess....(298)

Another problem "reading" that Rennie has concerns her relationship with Paul. From her first meeting with him in the hotel restaurant, she seems to script the relationship in the terms of popular romance plots. Paul may be a nice guy, but romance hero he is not. He is a profiteer, looking out for his own personal gain. He may care enough about Rennie to lend her a hand when chaos strikes the island; however, he is primarily interested in preserving himself. He is neither martyr who will sacrifice himself for her nor powerful savior who can rescue her. Rennie has read the relationship in terms of the popular romance script, but it fails to materialize (Howells, *Margaret* 130-31). This is certainly a sad misreading, for the consequence of it is that Rennie finds herself suffering in prison. It is also a very revealing misreading, for that romance script, as Radway argues in *Reading the Romance*, is ultimately a patriarchal one, not the woman's script that it might seem to be. Rennie has read in accordance with the generic lines defined by the symbolic realm, and this misreading has proven tragic, perhaps fatal.

Set against the symbolic is the semiotic, with its rootedness in bodily experience and expression. The semiotic has, throughout the book, been presented as perverted. Sexual experience has been perverted by the coiled rope, Jake's rape games, and violent pornography. The female body has been abused by perhaps unnecessary or unnecessarily invasive surgery back in Toronto and by torture on the island where men punish insufficiently subservient women by tying them naked to a tree and letting the ants attack their flesh. Although Paul is without the power to save Rennie from the political chaos sweeping the island, he does have the power to give Rennie's body back to her and revive its potential as a source of semiotic energy. Sex with Paul does not save Rennie: that cliché of the popular romance is exploded, but sex with Paul—the way he touches her as if her scar does not matter—does, as Rubenstein notes, attune her once more to a body that she had, in essence, turned off because she was numbed by instance after instance of envisioned or experienced "bodily harm" ("Pandora's"). As he undresses her, "He notes the scar, the missing piece, the place where death kissed her lightly, a preliminary kiss." "He doesn't look away or down." His not flinching affects Rennie: "...she enters her body again and there's a moment of pain, incarnation, this may be only the body's desperation, a flareup, a last clutch at the world...but meanwhile she's solid after all, she's still here on earth, she's grateful, he's touching her, she can still be touched" (204). Their lovemaking is "luxurious, indulgent, gleeful as rolling around in warm mud." "He pauses, goes on, pauses, goes on until she comes again. He's skilled and attentive, he's good at it" (222).

The semiotic is often associated with the *jouissance* of sexuality, but sex is not the only way in which body can turn to body outside of language. We see other ways in the prison cell that Rennie shares with Lora at the novel's conclusion. We should preface a return to this powerful, disturbing scene by noting how Rennie viewed Lora up to this point. Although both are Canadians and although both are involved, either through love or through naiveté, in the Caribbean island's politics, there has been a definite divide between the two women. This divide has existed because Rennie found Lora to be too loud, too outgoing, and too promiscuous to be "acceptable." Put another way, it was Lora's excesses of the body that put Rennie off. Even late in the story, Rennie is "thinking that she doesn't really like Lora very much; she never has liked her very much; in fact she dislikes her" (271). We, of course, see Lora through Rennie, even though the bulk of the novel is narrated from the third-person perspective. As a result, we may have shared Rennie's opinion of Lora, just as we may have been trapped in any number of Rennie's misreadings. However, if we try to look at Lora neutrally, we see someone who is very comfortable with her bodily presence. We eventually will discover her history of sexual abuse and rape—her being, in Rubenstein's terms, a "continuous victim" ("Pandora's" 129). We either, like Rennie, see in this history an explanation for her pathology or, without Rennie's prejudices, someone who is amazingly at ease with her body and with the semiotic despite having herself experienced so much "bodily harm."

This latter view, I wish to suggest, is probably the "correct" one. That it is—and that she has been misreading Lora—is something

Rennie learns in prison. First, Rennie learns that Lora has been prosti-
tuting herself with the guards for the sake of both of them. Protec-
tively, maternally, Lora has been accepting the sexual degradation instead of Rennie. Initially, Rennie is angry when she discovers what
Lora has been doing. "You're worth more than a pack of gum" (286),
Rennie tells Lora. However, the anger recedes, and when the guards
say "'Her turn today,'…pointing at Rennie" and Lora "steps in front
of her," Rennie says "I'll go" (291). Interestingly, when Rennie says
that it is her turn to satisfy the guards' sexual demands, Lora does not
let her. Paul, as we noted earlier, does not play the role of savior except insofar as he treats Rennie's body as "undamaged goods." Lora,
although she cannot ultimately save Rennie, comes much closer to
playing that noble role. Lora does give her body for Rennie's sake.

Rennie's recognition of Lora's gift changes Rennie's view of her.
Then, when Lora's has been severely beaten—perhaps to her death,
Rennie rushes to her aid. Weakened by the prison ordeal, Rennie
finds a way to drag Lora's battered body back into their shared cell.
There, she stares at the pulp of Lora's beaten face. Lacking the sani-
tary water to clean Lora's wounds, Rennie turns to the only source of
somewhat pure water, her tongue: "[s]he could lick this face, clean it
off with her tongue, that would be the best, that's what animals did"
(298–99). She turns maternal, and, much like a mother cat, she at least
considers if not actually proceeds to lick Lora's face clean. Meanwhile,
she embraces Lora's body as she might a child's.

The body-to-body connection depicted in this very powerful scene
is rich in semiotic energy. Out of language, body-to-body, like a
mother and her newborn daughter, Rennie and Lora connect. Rennie
realizes that Lora, whom she has scorned, is her "darker double"
(Rubenstein, "Pandora's" 133). Rennie realizes that, "The female body
is captive territory, and in prison she is forced to recognize how much
she shares in common with Lora whom she has previously regarded
with distaste and mild contempt" (Jones 94). The scene is, of course, a
tragic one, especially because we are fairly sure Lora is dead and
Rennie will soon be, but the scene is also one of female community,
female solidarity. The way Rennie extends her hand to Lora in assis-

tance echoes a hand motif throughout the novel, with the extending of a hand suggesting a connection beyond language (Kirtz 120-21; Rubenstein, "Pandora's" 133-34). Several have also commented on how the entire scene—beginning with Rennie's attempt to pull Lora back into life—suggests birth. If it does, it is not Lora's birth but Rennie's rebirth that is being depicted by Atwood, for, as Stovel puts it, "In resurrecting Lora, Rennie has achieved her own rebirth" ("Reflections" 65). It is a rebirth into the semiotic that is there in the body and out of language, into the semiotic that is there despite a patriarchal world characterized by its infliction of "bodily harm."

Bodily Harm's conclusion is, in rather typical Atwood style, ambiguous. As a result, different critics have read it differently. The crux of the debate are the words, suddenly delivered in the future tense, that tell us of Rennie's rescue from prison by a Canadian government official. I read the future tense as Atwood's signal that this rescue has not happened—that Rennie is still imprisoned. Coupled with the novel's opening words, "This is how I got here" (11), the novel seems to be her recapitulation of events told from that cell (Howells, *Margaret* 134). As Irvine has noted, the novel's rambling quality may suggest the loss of clear bearings in time one might experience trapped, maybe dying, in prison ("The Here" 91-92). In that cell, Rennie has learned that, "the ability to identify oneself with another woman, to connect to another person in empathetic touch, is the only real antidote to what she has seen and experienced: the deadening objectification that allows one person to see others as mere bodies to which violence may be done" (Rubenstein, "Pandora's" 134)

Atwood, besides ending novels without stark clarity, also often builds multiple readings into them. The reading I just offered is bleak, even though the ultimate message in this, "Atwood's most politically feminist novel" (Rubenstein, "Pandora's" 120), can give others some hope. Also bleak is an alternative that accepts that Rennie has indeed been rescued. This alternative notes the conditions of her rescue: She must agree not to write about her experiences on the island. In other words, she must agree to remain as disengaged from issues that matter as she was when she arrived, "lifestyles" reporter, on the island.

Much has been presented in the novel that cries out for reporting: people need to know how women are demeaned, objectified, raped, tortured, and beaten to death—in supposedly safe places such as Canada and in less safe places such as a Caribbean island in the throes of political unrest. Rennie has, however, been asked to back away from reporting such matters—to, in essence, lose the voice that might cry against the patriarchy. Read this way, the novel ends with her lost voice. Her life is lost; her voice is lost. You choose, Atwood seems to be saying. Either way, there is tragic loss. Redeemed for those very few moments in the prison cell, Rennie falls into a trap that either literally kills by ending her life or figuratively kills by silencing her newly discovered voice.

Rennie's full name, Renata, links her to redemption. This is the reason she goes to the island and what she, for just a brief time, gains. Very similar is the story of another Renata, the central character in Marie-Claire Blais's *These Festive Nights*. This recent novel's plot ought to sound familiar. Renata, a successful lawyer married to a strict judge in either Canada or the United States, is troubled. Many things that have and are going on in the world are troubling her, ranging from capital punishment in Texas to war crimes in Serbia, from the United States' dropping of atomic bombs on Hiroshima and Nagasaki to the nation's 1991 "Desert Storm" campaign against Iraq. She is also more personally troubled by the surgery she just had. She had lung cancer, and a surgeon had removed one of her lungs, leaving her with "the long, pale scar where her lung had been removed" (36) and a "decline in her life forces" (145). She escaped to an unnamed Caribbean island to hide from the world's problems and to recover from her physical ones, to win "this battle against matter that can only conquer you from below, through the degeneration of your cells" (12). There are no allusions in Blais's novel to Atwood's *Bodily Harm*, nothing to link the two books together definitively. Nonetheless, one cannot help but wonder if Blais has not written a Quebecois version of Atwood's book given how strikingly similar the stories of the two Renatas are. The fact that Blais's novel was published by Anansi

Press, which Atwood played a major role in founding and managing, adds to one's puzzling over a link between the two books.

Blais's style, however, is very different from Atwood's. Atwood's book, although not linearly plotted, nonetheless offers a story that is easy to assemble. It also, for the most part, follows the conventions of formal realism. Although a few characters are types, most are fully developed, and, most certainly, the descriptions of places are vividly real. Toronto looks like Toronto, and the island Rennie Wilford travels to is so fully realized that many have tried—without luck—to pinpoint exactly what island nation Atwood was talking about. Conversely, Blais' book bounces from one cluster of characters to another, sometimes mid-sentence. The book has no chapters, no paragraphs; instead, it moves forward in long, very poetic sentences. These sentences are so long that, at points, one has to search through pages of text before finding a period. The novel offers starkly realistic details, but these details shoot out at the reader amidst prose that seems to be more than characters' thoughts than anything else.

Given the novel's poetic fabric, one might expect words to recur and motives to develop much as in a poem. Two words do repeat, thereby establishing two connected motifs. One word is "thirst." Renata is constantly described as thirsty, as are other characters. Renata "often experienced the hollow sensation of thirst that was gripping her chest" (49), an "unquenchable thirst" (98); others were "delirious from thirst" (107) or experienced an "insatiable thirst" (117) or a "hollow sensation of thirst" (125) or an "eternal thirst" (206) or an "appalling thirst" (229) or an "aching thirst" (229). The other word is "limbo." Renata is described as being in that neither-here-nor-there state, a "limbo [that] clung to her life like the climbing plants around her rented house" (98); others are as well in a limbo sadly termed "futureless" (256). The two motifs are connected insofar as, together, they define Renata's—and others'—unredeemed state. A third motif presented in the novel's verbal fabric is rebirth. It is presented as the antidote—seemingly unattainable—to the thirst of Renata and others trapped in limbo. Very early in the novel Renata felt "she was being reborn" (8), that "the unfailing vitality of youth was being restored" (10), but time will call her early optimism into question.

When "thirst" and "limbo" appear early in the novel, the reader associates them with the condition Renata (and others) have brought to the island. The reader waits for the island to quench that thirst and move the characters onward to heaven. The word "paradise" also appears frequently in the novel: the island is described as "this paradise that was as ordered and harmonious as heaven must be" (189). However, although the island's flora and fauna cause people to say it is a "paradise," it does not function in the novel as a spiritual refuge or goal. The island, in fact, proves to be just as dangerous a place as the world outside the island. The texts notes that "what bad been a paradise was...now becoming a purgatory" (180). Worse was ahead, for the word *inferno* is found just as frequently in the novel's poem-like narrative as the word *paradise* . Furthermore, the words *thirst* and *limbo* continue until the end, suggesting that these words are just as connected with the island retreat as with the world from which Renata and others have come.

Against a lush tropical backdrop, Blais reveals all that is wrong with the world, all that has the world of the edge of the apocalypse. There is poverty. It is found on the island. It is noticeable in "the stench of their pathetic hovels" (149) where one finds "their cadaverous forms melt[ing] in the sun, among the stones, the garbage cans of shanty-towns" (208). It is also found in the United States, where homeless young become "the rigid corpses of children in their fine clothes in a bunker" (208). There is also racism. The novel talks about current racism on the island. Like the young black girl Venus, who sings at a tourist bar, all with dark skin must endure "the racist remarks of those who...strolled arrogantly by the pool" (182). It also glances back into history and offers many glimpses at the slavery Africans experienced on the islands and in the United States. The novels recalls "the African cargo" (250) and, how when slave ships wrecked, "those men, those women whose feet were still encircled with iron had been devoured by barracuda, by sharks" (252). It also recalls the era of plantations when "the sheriff, the awe-inspiring shadows of his friends, of the sailors, the hunters, the hooded phantoms who used to haunt the swamps in the woods, decimating black men, hanging them from trees, a muddy corpse bleeding in the sun amid a cloud of mosquitoes" (134). The novel, however, does not neglect the North American present. For example, one of the novel's many writer characters tells his wife and us that "there is still so much racism in North America that the living conditions in our ghettos can only be compared with those of the Third World" (287).

There is also a great deal of incipient violence in Blais's novel. Gangs seem to lurk in both the Caribbean and the North American contexts, ready to ensnare the young. On the island, it is "the gang of Bad Niggers," described as "depraved, shifty" with "fangs that gleamed under disdainful lips" (58); in North America, "on Street of Warm Breezes in Chicago they were being cut down by bullets" (100), while other cities were seeing "the inexorable resurgence in urban crimes committed by gangs of juveniles, attacking the elderly at night" (278) and attacking the homes of judges, such as Renata's husband Claude, who dared to sentence them severely. These gangs, no matter which location, to some extent seem to be expressing the pent-up rage of those who are on the receiving end of racism.

Activism on the part of the oppressed is very much a part of the novel's fabric. Sometimes that activism has a violent guise; sometimes, as in the case of the liberal household maintained by Melanie and Daniel, a welcoming face. Both sorts of activism, however, inspire a white supremacist backlash. "[I]n his writing Daniel aroused the anger of reactionaries"; he and Melanie were told they "entertain too many black activists in [their] house" (115). This backlash, presented in the visual dressing of the Ku Klux Klan, is oftentimes just a rumored threat or a shadowy threat. There are times, however, when the threat is depicted as a very real one. Sometimes described as a shadow, sometimes as "the White Horsemen of the Apocalypse," who "marched through the city, flinging their torches into the ramshackle framework of houses, of schools, of colleges, setting ablaze those flat shacks like huts on Bahama Street, on Esmerelda Steet" (83), "burning houses of the black community of Bois-des-Rosiers, for a delegate, whom no witness had seen get out of his car during the fire, had given the order to wipe out this town" (178). They, wearing hoods like the Knights of the Ku Klux Klan, would burn the black areas of the city, and they would assault those who supported the blacks. These "neophytes of hatred, of racism,...their hands hungry for stones, for blows with a stick, to rape, to kill these children of Melanie" (228), some of whom were white, some of whom were black and adopted.

Not all of the violence that provides a backdrop to Renata's redemptive quest can be analyzed in racial terms. The novel refers to violence in Colombia and in Haiti: in Bogota, we see children "sleeping in the streets at night on sheets of plastic or cardboard, smoking their pipes of basuco during the day, before bullets pierced their throats in the evening" (284); in Haiti, we hear "the burst of machine-gun fire," see "all of those who didn't leave...succumb[ed] to the machetes, the sabers," and smell "the putrid smell of the corpses dug up by half-starved dogs" (168). The novel refers frequently to the refugees who have fled Cuba in flimsy craft, very few of which made it to safety on the island. It tells the story of Julio, "who had watched...his mother Edna, his brother Oreste, his sister Nina drown before his eyes" (107); and it talks about how "piled up in the harbour, near beaches caressed by the waves, between two mounds of filth, streams of raw sewage, there were the corpses nobody had had time to collect and bury" (140). The novel also goes beyond racism and political oppression in the developing world by referring to the mass suicide at "Jonestown" in Guyana, which involved Americans who had been led there by a charismatic "prophet." And the novel goes beyond "the real" by referring to the violence that on a festive night "swallowed up" (240) the mythical island nation of Atlantis.

The violent political turmoil that provides the novel's backdrop is not confined to the Caribbean. Blais's novel glances at the plight of present-day Palestinians and places in the world where "child soldiers...kidnapped from their families...perpetuate the atrocities of their elders" (221), and the novel takes us back to World War II. It evokes the experiences of Polish Jews who were shipped off to death camps, "towards their butchers, their murderers, in an ultimate and panic-stricken movement of surrender" (102), as well as the experiences of the citizens of Hiroshima and Nagasaki whose lives were extinguished in an atomic flash. "[N]o act of destruction," the novel's words say, "could be compared to that genocide" (248). Nazis are indicted, but so are Americans—not only for Hiroshima and Nagasaki but for both Vietnam, where "a hapless soldier who was also guilty of great massacres had sliced open the bellies of little girls and their mothers" (128), and the January 1991 "Desert Storm" campaign against Iraq.

"Desert Storm," in fact, provides a part of what we might term the most immediate of the apocalyptic "signs" the novel presents. "[T]he bombed communication towers, bridges, and oil refineries of Baghdad" (195) are described, but "a president's declaration of war on a dark night in January" is imagined to be a prelude to something larger: "[T]hat fire in the sky, the smell of charred dust that people inhaled in the streets" (63). The fear that the war will "go nuclear" leads four-year-old Augustino to ask "if today was the day when they were all going to die" (64) because "a very old man…had said on television not to get ready for school or nursery school, it was pointless now, because a cloud of smoke was coming loose from the sky" (154). Although American readers might find the novel's presentation of this military campaign sensationalistic and paranoid, the sense communicated by the novel is that this campaign could well have "gone nuclear" and destroyed all—resulting in a world plagued by radiation as were parts of the Ukraine after the nuclear reactor accident in Chernobyl where "the cloud had transformed [children] into multitudes of hairless youngsters with leukemia, on the edge of the grave" (172).

Nuclear annihilation is very much a threat in the novel, so is the AIDS epidemic, which, in the novel, is taking the lives of many men, old and young, who "now at the age of twenty, without warning, without realizing it,…had fallen into a leprous old age" (159), and face being "turned…out by the hundreds into the streets" (69) by their families or being sent to "camps filled with people with AIDS from which no one returns" (237). So also is capital punishment in the

United States, which is mentioned frequently. In fact, one of the first thoughts in the novel is Renata's of "an event that had seemingly occurred some distance from them, from their lives, in a room or a cell where the cold vapours of hell would prevail for a long time, namely the execution in a Texas prison of an unknown black man" (3-4). Renata's mind "was always wandering in the direction of unfathomable twists and turns [to] the condemned man in Texas [whom] she would not stop talking about" (26). She further thought that "it would soon be legal to be taken to the electric chair, hanged, or killed by lethal injection, long before the legal age," a development that would take us toward "a massive extermination of youth" (279). She perhaps has these thoughts because she becomes aware of experimentation on prisoners also in the United States, which is mentioned, prominently, at the novel's end: "...every day so many condemned men, repeat offenders, were the subject of experiments in the prisons, their testicles exposed to radiation that caused tumours, cancers, but what could you do with those men, those women, who had no future, guinea pigs, subjects of experimentation..." (291). This experimentation is perhaps a thematic extension of the Satanic violence against animals depicted earlier in the book, with its "macabre ritual[s] celebrated in a graveyard" (168) and its horrible aftermath where the "worshipper" "now was grinding the birds' hearts between his incisors, their tender flesh, the fibres of the rabbits and piglets he had sacrificed" (168).

Renata has come to the island to escape the world's problems. Obviously, though, there are also many problems on the island. It turns out not to be the paradise she anticipated it would be. To some extent, the free-floating narrative should be read as the sea of thoughts Renata is trapped within. Read in this manner, she is further assaulted in her desire for retreat by the range of non-island problems that the novel evokes.

The list of such problems that has already been produced in this discussion may seem long enough; however, it must be noted that, beyond these, there are issues raised in the novel that are very particular to women. On several occasions, the novel discusses, in general terms, the situation of women. According to the novel, "the status of women...was constantly under attack" (8), and her condition was "a curse" characterized by "so many injustices" (29) and was "woven" from "sorrows" (91). Women therefore dreamt "about establishing a relationship of power with a man, as men had done with women from time immemorial, a relationship of power with no dependency or servitude" (282). Unfortunately, women are more like "a parrot in its cage," "merely a clump of threadbare feathers forgotten by its master and not the splendid bird it had once been in its jungle paradise" (126).

The two issues the novel seems to focus on are rape and oblivion. Numerous instances of rape are brought into the text. On the island, young girls are abducted "from the bed where they were napping, they had scarcely been deflowered, then returned to their beds where their mothers would discover them and dress their wounds" (214). Jenny, now a servant in Melanie and Daniel's household, was raped by the sheriff and still has nightmares. On another island, "little girls [were] raped by a father, a brother, blindfolded by their assailants, and their souls, their spirits had evaporated" (200). Presumably in the Middle East, eleven young men "entered a kibbutz dormitory and for several nights, with no remorse, no dismay over their acts, they would rape a young girl, for seven days, seven nights, she was fifteen years old" (105). In former Yugoslavia, soldiers committed "rapes of women between the ages of five and eighty," "five thousand murders and rapes" (198). In the United States, specifically the University of Florida campus, a deranged man "with sadistic pleasure" "rap[ed] five young girls, and kill[ed] them all," "took his knife and planted it right in their hearts, backbones shattered, necks, already long and reedlike, snapped, necks that for a long time would be bent over books whose pages were covered with blood" (128). Rape then seems to be a universal problem.

The problem of oblivion Blais associates more specifically with the woman artist. She cites several examples, notably Anna Amelia Mendelssohn, whose music was suppressed by her father and "appropriated" by her brother Felix, an unknown woman writer who had fled Berlin for Sweden just ahead of the Holocaust and "left only a few legible words" before she was dragged back, and a slightly better known woman writer ho had written her books on the island "and then disappeared in Brazil," leaving "no tangible sign of her presence" (90), unlike venerated male writers whose days on the island are reverently noted. Renata has, in fact, chosen to occupy this latter woman writer's lodgings on the island in her personal attempt to bring this marginalized woman writer back from oblivion.

These Festive Nights sounds a somewhat optimistic note insofar as these women artists, who were once forgotten, are being rediscovered. In fact, forgotten women are being rediscovered in many realms. The novel explicitly mentions many: black woman journalist Mary Ann Shadd Cary; black Philadelphia Democratic Party leader from the 1930's Crystal Bird Fauset; black newspaper publisher Ida B. Wells Barnett; black New York actress Nina Mae McKinney; black Cincinnati dental surgeon Ida Gray; black Florida educator Mary McLeod Bethune; black Boston private nursing pioneer Mary Eliza Mahoney. That these rediscovered women are all of color suggests that the oppression based on race mentioned earlier and the oppression based on gender mentioned here are often linked. These names provide a counterpoint to the terrorizing threads that run throughout the book. This counterpoint perhaps energizes Renata, perhaps redeems her. She, in the end, "insisted to all of them that she was cured, hoping it was the truth" (196), hoping "little by little, the hollow sensation of thirst would be dulled" (245). She decided to continue her work as a jurist crusading for the oppressed.

Like Atwood, however, Blais offers us a very ambiguous ending. Yes, Renata does return to her work. However, the island she leaves behind seems very much in danger. The atmosphere of the book is at times festive. However, in the shadows, trouble seems to be lurking, ready to destroy the joy: in fact, the word *shadow* is as prevalent in the novel as *thirst* or *limbo* or *paradise* or *inferno*. One of the novel's final images is that of two young people joyfully singing. It is undercut by Blais when she talks about how their faces and, in general, "the faces of the innocent children seemed to her suddenly to harden" (284).

Another motif that undercuts an optimistic ending is the critique that the novel offers on words. Renata is a lawyer, who must use words to achieve her goals. The more striking users of words are the numerous writers who are minor characters in the novel. Some are dying of AIDS, their words dying with them. Others have either become bored or have just given up. They were young radicals once, they tell each other; now, they have settled into indifference.

Renata, of course, must work within the symbolic realm if she is to be successful crusading for the oppressed people the novel forces on the reader's attention. This symbolic realm, however, seems weak. Perhaps that means that words are less likely to be used as weapons against the oppressed, but it also means that words cannot be appropriated and reinscribed and used on their behalf. The semiotic does not in *These Festive Nights* seem to provide a positive alternative. Yes, there is sensuous joy during the nights' celebrations, but danger, disease, and aging counterpoint this joy. The young who are attuned to their bodies will be killed; some artists who were attuned to their bodies will die of AIDS; Renata who wishes to be so attuned may die of cancer if she cannot finally forego the cigarettes she longs for throughout the novel; and other artists who were once attuned to at least what governments and other entities were doing to bodies will fade from their "fetid boredom," their "insidious boredom" (18), and indifference into death.

8

Once More to the Island

The experience of reading fiction by Canadian women takes the reader (to play with the title of E. B. White's famous essay) "once more to the island." I am, of course, not arguing that the motif characterizes all such fiction. Such a claim would be absurd for there is such richness in this body of fiction that such an argument would be reductive. What I am claiming is that an island motif recurs in this literature to the point where it can at least be said to be a major if not a dominant one.

The motif, of course, does not appear in the same form in even the fourteen works of fiction discussed in this study. One difference is apparent in this study's chapter titles, which take one from the island as redemptive retreat to the island as dangerous idyll, stopping, at some length, at Margaret Atwood's *Surfacing*, which is ambiguously both positive and negative. Another difference is the result of such dynamics as time, plot, and the author's creative inclinations. L. M. Montgomery, writing largely for adolescent girls in the earlier decades of the twentieth century, is not going to produce anything like Marie-Claire Blais, writing for a rather sophisticated international au-

dience of literary connoisseurs in the last years of that century. Both
Montgomery and Blais will, however, take us "once more to the island," despite these differences. Still another difference is tied to how
literal the island in question is. Montgomery's Prince Edward Island
and Thomas's Vancouver Island exist. The islands in Atwood's *Surfacing* and *Bodily Harm*, Blais's *These Festive Nights*, and Engel's *Bear*
we imagine as being based on real islands. All are literally islands. So
is Britain in Laurence's *The Diviners* and Montreal in Roy's *The Tin
Flute*, although the insularity would likely be overlook by many. Not
literal at all, but still very island-like are the entrapping small towns
in Laurence's *A Jest of God* and Munro's *Lives of Girls and Women*.
Whether the place is literal or figurative, these authors take us "once
more to the island."

Noting differences is crucial, for no study should obliterate them in
an attempt to defend a thesis. However, noting similarities is also crucial if the contours of the motif are to be understood. In this concluding chapter, rather than summarize book-by-book what the previous
chapters present, I want to focus on these similarities. As Frye offered
an "anatomy" of literature in his landmark critical study, I want to offer an anatomy of the island motif in twentieth-century Canadian
women's fiction in this conclusion. I would suggest that the novels
studied in detail in the previous chapters exhibit ten interesting similarities.

The islands in these novels are associated with problems. Usually,
the island offers an escape from the problem, but, occasionally, the island *is* the problem. The problem ranges in these novels from the personal to the political. For Anne Shirley in Montgomery's *Anne of Green
Gables*, the problem is that she is an orphan; for Jane Stuart in Montgomery's *Jane of Lantern Hill* and Alice Hoyle in Thomas's *Intertidal
Life*, the problem is separation and divorce—Jane's parents' and Alice's own. For both of Laurence's heroines, Rachel Cameron in *A Jest
of* God and Morag Gunn in *The Diviners*, the problem is being trapped
in a claustrophobic small town. That is also the problem is Alice
Munro's *Lives of Girls and Women*. In this novel, as well as in *Intertidal
Life* and *The Diviners*, a related problem is the inability to write—or

write well. All three women wrestle with words, finding—to varying degrees—that the words in the established lexicon seem alien from their experiences.

Morag Gunn also faces a poverty that embarrasses her. More profound is the poverty that plagues the mother Rose-Anna and daughter Florentine in Roy's *The Tin Flute*. It is joined by pregnancy, Rose-Anna's many and Florentine's unmarried first. Economic forces as well as their bodies trap these women.

Perhaps more psychologically "trapped" are the heroines of Engel's *Bear* and Atwood's *Surfacing*. Engel's Lou is caught in a life of dimly lit library rooms and meaningless sex. Lurking in her past seems to be either childhood sexual abuse or rape. Atwood's unnamed narrator is caught in a life of lies, lies she has told others and herself to cover-up what she feels was the crime of aborting the child she adulterously conceived with her art teacher.

Atwood's *Surfacing*, however, does not restrict its focus to the unnamed narrator's affairs. In its pages, other problems surface, most strikingly poor communication and the many ways humans are violating nature. One can sense in *Surfacing* the beginning of Atwood's strong political engagement. That engagement perhaps peaks in *Bodily Harm*, which shows us political oppression on a fictitious Caribbean island and links that oppression to the more personal abuse Rennie Wilford has either experienced or witnessed in her lover's rape fantasies, unnecessary breast cancer surgery, and violent pornography. Personal and political problems merge in *Bodily Harm*, perhaps Atwood's most overtly feminist novel.

Whereas *Bodily Harm* glances at global problems, Blais's *These Festive Nights* focuses on them. Poverty, violence, disease, torture, war, and genocide are all on the canvas Blais paints. Although the problems affect all, Blais and her character Renata seem especially concerned with how women are the victims of these abuses.

The solution to these many problems often involves either escape to or immersion in a "green world." For Anne Shirley and Jane Stuart, it is Prince Edward Island. For Montgomery's Patricia Gardiner and Marigold Leslie, it is particular sites on that island: "Silver Bush" for

Pat and "Cloud of Spruce" for Marigold. For Lou in Engel's *Bear*, it is an island somewhere in remote Ontario, and for the unnamed narrator in Atwood's *Surfacing*, it is an island somewhere in remote Quebec. For Alice Hoyle, the "green world" is Vancouver Island, where she and her husband had purchased a cottage to which they could escape the city and its pressures. Similar vacation "green worlds" are sought by Rennie in *Bodily Harm* and Renata in *These Festive Nights*: they go off to Caribbean islands. Green, these particular islands might well be, but they, of course, do not at all correspond to the "green world" Northrop Frye often evokes in his theorizing about comedy and romance, for these islands prove to places of oppression, not relaxation.

There is at least an expectation that the island will prove to be magical, transformative. It seems to be for Lou in *Bear* as well as for two of Montgomery's heroines, Anne and Jane, as well as for Laurence's Morag. The transformative power of the island is, however, much more questionable in *Intertidal Life* and *Surfacing*. We simply do not know how positively—or how negatively—to read the endings of either of these novels. In the cases of Montgomery's Pat and Marigold, the island's power to transform seems limited in time. In fact, time and the changes that time brings about are very much "the enemy" in these novels. Finally, in the cases of Roy's Florentine and Blais's Renata, the island's power is not transformative at all. The island has given Florentine the financial wherewithal to live a better life in Montreal than her parents, but at the price of early maternity, loneliness, and (we hope) guilt. The island—it seems--has given Renata the will to return to the United States and resume her legal career but not the spirit. She is too aware of all the horrors of the world to feel that she can do much good.

Whether the island has a great deal of power or little, it seems a place where something happens to the central characters. The mirror images these characters see play an important role in what the island does. Characters—for good or for ill—learn from these mirror images. Montgomery's Anne is pushed forward by her "kindred spirits" Diana Barry and Gilbert Blythe. Diana mirrors Anne's warmth and

Gilbert her intelligence and drive. They inspire her as do the older "strong," intelligent women Muriel Stacey and Josephine Barry. Montgomery's Jane and Marigold see frightening mirror images in their playmates and are pushed in an opposite direction. Munro's Del Jordan is similarly pushed in an opposite direction by the mirror images of Jubilee school friends Naomi and Jerry. Laurence's Rachel sees fellow strugglers in sister Stacey, friend Calla, and lover Nick, and Laurence's Morag sees similar fellows in lovers Jules and Dan. Roy's Florentine sees fellow strugglers in the men in her life, lover Jean and husband Emmanuel, but she cannot identify with them because they have freedoms she does not. So, she constantly—almost obsessively—looks at her own image in the mirror. Atwood's unnamed narrator in *Surfacing* finds the possible mirror images of her victimized state in Anna and her still-natural state in Joe, but neither really helps her. She must wrestle with her guilt and—maybe—win salvation on her own. Finally, Atwood's Rennie find her mirror image in Lora after they are both incarcerated, and, unless you believe Rennie is rescued, this image only forecasts her own future of rape, brutal beatings, and death.

Another mirror-like image is striking in many of these works: that between mother and daughter. In fact, the mother-daughter dynamic plays a crucial role as the central characters try to address their problems. Anne Shirley's case is perhaps the simplest: an orphan, she acquires a surrogate mother in Marilla Cuthbert. Others, such as Laurence's Rachel and Morag and Atwood's nameless narrator in *Surfacing*, have to deal with mothers they've become physically or psychologically separated from. Rachel has to in essence become her mother's mother, as does, in a sense, Montgomery's Jane, who uses the spirit she has acquired on Prince Edward Island to rescue her oppressed mother back in Toronto. The central characters in these novels are not solely the daughters in the relationships, however. Morag, as she comes to terms with stepmother Prin, must also come to terms with daughter Pique, who is much like her. Thomas's Alice must find a way to steer but not over-steer daughter Flora on a path that, she hopes, will be less perilous than the one she has traveled. Sometimes, however, this daughter-mother or mother-daughter reconciliation never occurs. Roy's Florentine remains sadly distanced from her mother Rose-Anna at the end of *The Tin Flute*. Rennie in Atwood's *Bodily Harm* only becomes a symbolic mother to her prison-mate Lora at the moment of Lora's death.

The importance of these female-female relationships on the islands in these novels is connected to the broader emphasis on the community of women found in some of these works. That community is depicted very positively in Montgomery's Avonlea. In other cases, the depiction is not without its qualifications. The women whose stories we are told in Laurence's *The Diviners* form a community, but one that has been wounded by its interactions with men. The women in Montgomery's *Magic for Marigold* seem withdrawn, whereas those in Thomas's *Intertidal Life* seem quite ready to be seduced away from solidarity with Alice by the charismatic Peter. If these are qualified female communities, that in Roy's *The Tin Flute* is non-existent. Florentine hardly associates with her fellow lunch counter workers, shuns the one who tries to help her in her hour of need, and, as noted earlier, tragically fails to find solidarity with her mother just as Rose-Anna failed to find solidarity with either the women of her generation or her lecturing mother in-law. The community of women then seems an important dimension of "island life" to the extent that it is positive. The presence of this community may mark these novels as "feminist." So does the critique that many of them offer of the patriarchy. This critique is implicit in Anne Shirley's breaking a slate over Gilbert Blythe's head and her refusal to yield in academic competition with Gil; it is also implicit in Morag Gunn's walking out on her imperious husband and Del Jordan's walking away from the river where her lover was trying to forcibly baptize her into a circumscribed life. The critique is even voiced in works as "light" such as *Pat of Silver Bush*, *Mistress Pat*, and *Magic for Marigold*. For example, before *Mistress Pat* reaches its conventional happy ending, Patricia Gardiner turns down suitor after suitor and laments the fact that she must marry to be considered socially acceptable.

The critique of the patriarchy broadens out in Atwood's *Surfacing* to include violations of nature. The unnamed narrator's complicity in these violations, however, weakens her ability to engage in social protest. Still broader are the critiques in Atwood's *Bodily Harm* and Blais's *These Festive Nights*. Rennie and Renata, although not complicit, run from responsibility for acting against the crimes of the patriarchy. Rennie wants to be safe; Renata is fatigued. Their disengagement—until the novels' ends—weakens their ability to engage in social protest. The inability of these women, however, does not diminish the force of either novel's critique.

One dimension of the critique not yet mentioned has a special resonance in these novels: that against language. The island often becomes the site of struggle with the male-defined symbolic. In the course of this struggle, a critique of the symbolic's power to inscribe certain experiences, but not others, and of its power to regulate is offered. Anne Shirley is not surprisingly the most successful struggler, but also successful are Morag Gunn and Del Jordan. Less successful is one of the more overt strugglers, Thomas's Alice Hoyle. We simply do not know at the end of *Intertidal Life* whether she has wrestled with words enough to become once again creative as a writer.

Other strugglers choose to act rather than wrestle. Rachel Cameron leaves Manawaka behind rather than deal with the communication problems there; Atwood's unnamed narrator in *Surfacing* chooses to leave civilization behind—at least for her brief, perhaps redemptive time naked in the woods. Not all who feel threatened by the symbolic, however, achieve even the tentative successes of these two who avoid the problem. Florentine Lacasse, who very much sees the world of words to be the world of men, turns to her body and uses it to get the best deal she can to survive in a hostile world. Rennie Wilford tries to avoid the seriousness of words by claiming to be a "light" journalist. When she finally realizes that the symbolic can imprison and torture and kill, it is too late for her to struggle. Her fate is frightening. Perhaps sadder is that of Marigold Leslie, who allows the words spoken to her by her male playmate to crush all that was meaningful to her in the world.

Submerged beneath layers of verbiage created by the symbolic is the semiotic. Most of the island experiences connect the central female characters with the semiotic, with a preverbal realm very much of the body and often characterized by *jouissance*. *Jouissance* is a tricky term: it refers to a pleasure rooted in the body that takes one in some way beyond the symbolic realm and all of the rational constructs that emerge out of the symbolic to regulate life. *Jouissance* can be as innocent as the joy expressed by Montgomery's characters Anne Shirley, Jane Stewart, and Patricia Gardiner, when a child. However, it is more often associated with a sexual joy, and we see such an exhilaration in the love-making of Morag Gunn, Alice Hoyle, and even Rachel Cameron, although she is far more repressed than the first two. This sexual exhilaration, however, is not necessarily liberation from the symbolic, for the symbolic can exert control over sexuality. We very much see how sexuality so-controlled can be a threat in Munro's *Lives of Girls and* Women and Atwood's *Surfacing*. *Jouissance* then is not sexual pleasure; rather, it is a more general and purer bodily pleasure. We see it potentially there in Florentine Lacasse's exhilaration while dancing. Unfortunately, she loses this joy. Jouissance also is not always pleasurable, if one defines that term in too narrow a manner. There is, for example, *jouissance* to be found in the body-to-body embrace of Rennie and Lora in prison at the end of Atwood's *Bodily Harm*. Lora is dying; Rennie sees in Lora's fate her own. The scene is far from a happy one. At this nightmarish moment, however, the two women are driven back to their bodies and the physical comfort they can provide each other, not by words, but by a bodily embrace that exhibits the *jouissance* one can experience by immersing one's self in the semiotic.

Going off "once more to the island" is not always a positive experience for the central character, but it often is. In those cases the island experience could be labeled a success. A characteristic of this success is the central characters' defining and accepting roles for their lives. Anne Shirley becomes "daughter" to Marilla Cuthbert in Anne of Green Gables; Jane Stuart becomes daughter to her estranged parents. Del Jordan becomes a writer, even if doing so entails loneliness.

Morag Gunn becomes daughter to her deceased step-parents and mother to her daughter Pique as well as a writer. Rachel Cameron becomes mother to her mother, reversing power in a relationship that had oppressed her for thirty-some years. Less successful are Blais's Renata and Atwood's Rennie. Renata accepts her role as a jurist in a dangerous, corrupt society, but she seems to do so with a great deal of existential fatigue. Rennie accepts the role she should have adopted—crusading journalist; however, she adopts it in her mind at a point in her life at which career choice is totally irrelevant. She is in prison, facing brutal rape and probable death. Unsuccessful in a different way are Alice Hoyle and the unnamed narrator in Surfacing, for we just do not know how positively to read their stories' endings. Less successful than other of these women, I would argue, is Montgomery's Pat Gardiner, whose happy ending assuming the role of Hilary's lover and wife seems extremely contrived, so much so that we cannot accept it. Just as unsuccessful as Pat of Silver Bush, but more obviously so, is Montgomery's Marigold Leslie. She is left with her childhood dreams burst and no new role to assume in view. Just as pessimistic is Florentine Lacasse's ending. She has assumed a role, that of mother and wife. However, the former role is forced on her prematurely when she becomes pregnant but unwed, and the latter role is engineered by her in order to save face. She will soon be a widow, separated from the joys of youth and despised by her in-laws.

When reading fiction by Canadian women, we are taken to many islands. The experience is different—for the novels' central characters and for us. However, there is enough that is common to argue that the experience represents a motif. The very different theoretical perspectives offered by Northrop Frye and Julia Kristeva offer us lenses through which we can see the motif and helps to extract commonalties resonant with meaning. That meaning is, not surprisingly, very particular to the experience of women. The meaning deals very much with the ways in which the empowered can oppress others and the ways in which the disempowered can gain power.

Thus, the island experience begins with the recognition of a problem. The problem prompts a kind of escape to a place that seems to offer a kind of salvation, for the place is symbolically green and the place has magic. The "salvation," however, is not quickly available: one must deal with mirror images, come to terms with the mother-daughter role, take heart in female community, protest what needs to be protested against, struggle with the symbolic, and find jouissance in the semiotic. Then, at the end of this island experience, one might see the problem addressed and a new role in life possible. Along the way, much may go wrong. Most catastrophically, one might find the island to be a trap, not a liberating space at all. The shadings are very much what Frye speaks about when discussing the green world of archetypal comedy: it may be paradise; it may be hell; it may fade from the one to the other as one tries to negotiate its contours.

The island, as seen in the fiction written by many twentieth-century Canadian women, has many shadings. Nonetheless, it represents a compelling representation of the female experience. The shadings suggest its richness as trope; the shadings also remind us that fiction is after all storytelling and a narrative energy often does determine what is on the pages. The narratives discussed in this study are diverse: The characters are of different ages ranging from youth to middle age; the settings are varied ranging all across Canada and beyond; the stories *per se* range from that of an orphan to that of a near-spinster to that of a ill, fatigued jurist to those of writers. Despite this narrative diversity, however, a motif emerges. It does so because it so aptly captures the core female experience that the various stories are all variants of. Going "once more to the island" then becomes not a coincidence among these many literary texts but a way of capturing a need, a struggle, and — sometimes — a success in finding, like treasure, those things that give life and voice and connection.

Bibliography

Atwood, Margaret. *Bodily Harm*. 1982. Rpt. New York: Bantam, 1983.

——. *Surfacing*. 1972. Rpt. New York: Warner, 1983.

——. *Survival: A Thematic Introduction to Canadian Literature*. Toronto: Anansi, 1972.

Bader, Rudolf. "The Mirage of the Sceptr'd Isle: An Imagological Appraisal." *ARIEL* 9.1 (1988): 35–44.

Baer, Elizabeth R. "Pilgrimage Inward: Quest and Fairy Tale Motifs in *Surfacing*." *Margaret Atwood: Vision and Forms*. Ed. Kathryn VanSpanckeren and Jan Garden Castro. Carbondale: Southern Illinois UP, 1988. 24–34.

Bailey, Nancy. "Margaret Laurence and the Psychology off Re-Birth in *A Jest of God*." *Journal of Popular Culture* 15.3 (1981): 62–69.

Bartlett, Donald R. "'Fact' and Form in *Surfacing*." *The University of Windsor Review* 17.1 (1982): 21–28.

Barzalai, Shuli. "Who is He: The Missing Persons Behind the Pronoun in Atwood's *Surfacing*." *Canadian Literature* 164 (2000): 57–79.

Baum, Rosalie Murphy. "Artist and Woman: Young Lives in Laurence and Munro." *North Dakota Quarterly* 52.3 (1984): 196–211.

——. "Self-alienation of the Elderly in Margaret Laurence's Fiction." *NewPerspectives on Margaret Laurence: Poetic Narrative, Multiculturalism, and Feminism*. Ed. Greta M. K. McCormick Coger. Westport, Conn.: Greenwood, 1996. 153–60.

Beckman-Long, Brenda. "Authorizing Her Text: Margaret Laurence's Shift to Third Person Narration." *Studies in Canadian Literature* 24.2 (1999): 64–78.

Beeler, Karen. "Ethnic Dominance and Difference: The Post-Colonial Condition in Margaret Laurence's *The Stone Angel*, *A Jest of God*, and *The Diviners*." *Cultural Identities in Canadian Literature*. Ed. Benedicte Mauguiere. New York: Peter Lang, 1998.

Berryman, Charles. "Atwood's Narrative Quest." *The Journal of Narrative Technique* 17.1 (1987): 51–56.

Besner, Neil. "The Bodies of the Texts in *Lives of Girls and Women*: Del Jordan's Reading." *Multiple Voices: Recent Canadian Fiction.* Ed. Jeanne Delbaere. Sydney: Dangaroo, 1990. 131–44.

———. "A World Divided, A World Divined: Two North American Fictions." *New Perspectives on Margaret Laurence: Poetic Narrative, Multiculturalism, and Feminism.* Ed. Greta M. K. McCormick Coger. Westport, Conn.: Greenwood, 1996. 41–47.

Bicanic, Sonia Wild. "Dependence and Resolution in the Novels of Margaret Atwood." *Cross-Cultural Studies: American, Canadian and European Literatures: 1945-1985.* Ed. Mirko Jurak. Ljubljana: Filozofska Fakulteta, 1988. 79–83.

Bird, Michael. "Heuresis: The Mother-Daughter Theme in *A Jest of God* and *Autumn Sonata.*" *New Quarterly: New Directions in Canadian Writing* 7.1–2 (1987): 267–73.

Blais, Marie-Claire. *These Festive Nights.* Trans. Sheila Fischman. Toronto: Anansi, 1997.

Bok, Christian. "Sibyls: Echoes of French Feminism in 'The Diviners' and 'Lady Oracle.'" *Canadian Literature* 135 (Winter 1992): 80–93.

Bouson, Brooks. *Brutal Choreographies: Oppositional Strategies and Narrative Design in the Novels of Margaret Atwood.* Amherst: University of Massachusetts Press, 1997.

Boutelle, Ann Edwards. "Margaret Atwood, Margaret Laurence, and Their Nineteenth-Century Forerunners." *Faith of a (Woman) Writer.* Ed. Alice Kessler-Harris and William McBrien. Westport, Conn.: Greenwood, 1988. 41–47.

Bowen, Deborah. "In Camera: The Developed Photographs on Margaret Laurence and Alice Munro." *Studies in Canadian Literature* 13.1 (1988): 20-33.

Brydon, Diana. "'The Thematic Ancestor': Joseph Conrad, Patrick White and Margaret Atwood." *World Literature Written in English* 24.2 (1984): 386–97.

Buckman, Jacqueline. "Questions of Identity and Subjectivity: Audrey Thomas' *Intertidal Life.*" *English Studies in Canada* 2.1 (1996): 71–87.

Buss, Helen M. "Margaret Laurence's Dark Lovers: Sexual Metaphor, and the Movement toward Individualization, Hierogamy and Mythic Narrative in Four Manawaka Books." *Atlantis* 11.2 (1986): 97–107.

Butling, Pauline. "Thomas and Her Rag-Bag." *Canadian Literature* 102 (Autumn 1984): 195–99.

Cameron, Elspeth "Midsummer Madness: Marian Engel's *Bear.*" *Journal of Canadian Fiction* 21 (1977–78): 83–94.

Carolan-Brozy, Sandra, and Susanne Hagemann. "'There is such a place'—Is There? Scotland in Margaret Laurence's *The Diviners.*" *Studies in Scottish Fiction: 1945 to the Present.* Ed. Susanne Hagemann. Frankfurt: Peter Lang, 1993. 145–58.

Chlebek, Diana Arlene. "The Canadian Family and Female Adolescent Development during the 1930s: *Jane of Lantern Hill.*" *L. M. Montgomery and Canadian Cul-*

ture. Ed. Irene Gammel and Elizabeth Epperly. Toronto: University of Toronto Press, 1999. 145–52.

Clark, Meera T. "Margaret Atwood's *Surfacing*: Language, Logic and the Art of Fiction." *Modern Language Studies* 13.3 (1983): 3–15.

Cluett, Robert. "Surface Structures: The Syntactic Profile of *Surfacing*." *Margaret Atwood: Language, Text and System.* Ed. Sherrill E. Grace and Lorraine Weir. Vancouver: University of British Columbia Press, 1983. 67–90.

Coger, Greta M. K. "Margaret Laurence's Manawaka: A Canadian Yoknapatawpha." *Critical Approaches to the Fiction of Margaret Laurence.* Ed. Colin Nicholson. Vancouver: University of British Columbia Press, 1990. 228–46.

Coldwell, Joan. "Memory Organized: The Novels of Audrey Thomas." *Canadian Literature* 92 (Spring 1982): 46–56.

———. "Natural Herstory and *Intertidal Life*." *Room of One's Own* 10.3–4 (1986): 140–49.

Davidson, Cathy N. "Geography as Psychology in the Writings of Margaret Laurence." *Regionalism and the Female Imagination: A Collection of Essays.* Ed. Emily Toth. New York: Human Science, 1984.

Donaldson, Mara E. "Woman as Hero in Margaret Atwood's *Surfacing* and Maxine Hong Kingston's *The Woman Warrior*." *Heroines of Popular Culture.* Ed. Pat Browne. Bowling Green, Oh.: Bowling Green State University Popular Press, 1987. 101–13.

Drummond, Dennis. "Florentine Lacasse, Rachel Cameron, and Existential Anguish." *American Review of Canadian Studies* 19 (1989): 397–406.

Easingwood, Peter. "Margaret Laurence, Manawaka and the Edge of the Unknown." *World Literature Written in English* 22.2 (1983): 254–63.

Eldredge, L. M. "A Sense of Ending in *Lives of Girls and Women*." *Studies in Canadian Literature* 9.1 (1984): 110–15.

Engel, Marian. *Bear.* 1976. Rpt. Toronto: McClelland & Stewart, 1976.

Epperly, Elizabeth Rollins. *The Fragrance of Sweet-Grass: L. M. Montgomery's Heroines and the Pursuit of Romance.* Toronto: University of Toronto Press, 1992.

Ewell, Barbara C. "The Language of Alienation in Margaret Atwood's *Surfacing*." *The Centennial Review* 25.2 (1981): 185–202.

Fabre, Michel. "Words and the World: 'The Diviners' as an Exploration of the Book of Life." *Canadian Literature* 93 (Summer 1982): 60–78.

Fee, Margery. "Articulating the Female Subject: The Example of Marian Engel's *Bear*." *Atlantis* 14 (1988): 20–26.

Fiamengo, Janice. "'A Last Time for This Also': Margaret Atwood's Texts of Mourning." *Canadian Literature* 166 (2000): 145–64.

———. "Postcolonial Guilt in Margaret Atwood's *Surfacing*." *American Review of Canadian Studies* 29.1 (1999): 141–63.

Fredeman, Jane Cowan. "The Land of Lost Content: The Use of Fantasy in L. M. Montgomery's Novels." *Canadian Children's Literature* 1.3 (1975): 60–70.

Frye, Northrop. *Anatomy of Criticism: Four Essays*. Princeton, N.J.: Princeton UP, 1957.

———. *The Secular Scripture: A Study of the Structure of Romance*. Cambridge, Mass.: Harvard UP, 1976.

Gadpaille, Michelle. "A Note on 'Bear.'" *Canadian Literature* 92 (1982): 151–54.

Gandesbery, Jean. "Shaping Myths: The Manawaka Novels of Margaret Laurence." *Commonwealth Novel in English* 5.1 (1992): 65–72.

Gerstenberger, Donna. "Revisioning Cultural Norms: The Fiction of Margaret Atwood and Alice Walker." *Cross-Cultural Studies: American, Canadian and European Literatures: 1945–1985*. Ed. Mirko Jurak. Ljubljanna: Filozofska Fakulteta, 1988. 47–51.

Gilbert, Paula Ruth. "All Roads Pass Through Jubilee: Gabrielle Roy's *La Route d'Altamont* and Alice Munro's *Lives of Girls and Women*." *Colby Quarterly* 29.2 (1993): 136–48.

Godard, Barbara. *Audrey Thomas and Her Works*. Toronto: ECW, 1989.

———. "Caliban's Revolt: The Discourse of the (M)other." *Critical Approaches to the Fiction of Margaret Laurence*. Ed. Colin Nicholson. Vancouver: University of British Columbia Press, 1990. 208–27.

———. "'Heirs of the Living Body': Alice Munro and the Question of a Female Aesthetic." *The Art of Alice Munro: Saying the Unsayable*. Ed. Judith Miller. Waterloo, Ontario: University of Waterloo Press, 1984. 43–69.

———. "*The Diviners* as Supplement: (M)othering the Text." *Open Letter* 7.7 (1990): 26–73.

Gold, Joseph. "Our Feeling Exactly: The Writing of Alice Munro." *The Art of Alice Munro: Saying the Unsayable*. Ed. Judith Miller. Waterloo, Ontario: University of Waterloo Press, 1984. 1–13.

Goodwin, Ken. "Revolution as Bodily Fiction: Thea Astley and Margaret Atwood." *Antipodes* 4.2 (1990): 109–15.

Grace, Sherrill. "In Search of Demeter: The Lost, Silent Mother in *Surfacing*." *Margaret Atwood: Vision and Forms*. Ed. Kathryn Van Spanckeren and Jan Garden Castro. Carbondale: Southern Illinois UP, 1988. 35–47.

Greene, Gayle. "Margaret Laurence's *Diviners* and Shakespeare's *Tempest*: The Uses of the Past." *Women's Re-Visions of Shakespeare*. Ed. Marianne Novy. New York: St. Martin's Press, 1999. 165–82.

———. "Margaret Laurence's *The Diviners*: The Uses of the Past." *Critical Approaches to the Fiction of Margaret Laurence*. Ed. Colin Nicholson. Vancouver: University of British Columbia Press, 1990. 177–207.

Guedon, Marie-Francoise. "*Surfacing*: Amerindian Themes and Shamanism." *Margaret Atwood: Language, Text and System*. Ed. Sherrill E. Grace and Lorraine Weir. Vancouver: University of British Columbia Press, 1983. 91–111.

Hair, Donald S. "Marian Engel's 'Bear.'" *Canadian Literature* 92 (1982): 34–45.

Hales, Leslie-Ann. "Meddling with the Medium: Language and Identity in Audrey Thomas' *Intertidal Life.*" *Canadian Women's Studies* 8.3 (1987): 77–79.

Harger-Grinling, Virginia, and Tony Chadwick. "The Wild Animal as Metaphor in the Narrative of Three Examples of Canadian Fiction: Yves Theriault's *Agaguk*, Andre Langevin's *E'Elan D'Amerique* and Marian Engel's *Bear.*" *Canadian Studies* 44 (1988): 53–60.

Harris, Margaret. "Authors and Authority in *Lives of Girls and Women.*" *Sydney Studies in English* 12 (1986–87): 101–13.

Hartveit, Lars. "The Jester-Mask in Margaret Laurence's *A Jest of God* and *The Fire-Dwellers.*" *English Studies* 78 (1997): 342–54.

Heinemann, David. "Ironized Man: *A Jest of God* and *Life Before Man.*" *Canadian Literature* 154 (1997): 52–67.

Hinz, Evelyn J. "The Religious Roots of the Feminine Identity Issue: Margaret Laurence's *The Stone Angel* and Margaret Atwood's *Surfacing.*" *Journal of Canadian Studies* 22.1 (1987): 17–31.

Howells, Coral Ann. "Inheritance and Instability: Audrey Thomas' *Real Mothers.*" *Recherches anglaises et nord-amaericaines* 20 (1987): 157–62.

———. "In Search of Lost Mothers: Margaret Laurence's 'The Diviners' and Elizabeth Jolley's 'Miss Peabody's Inheritance.'" *ARIEL* 19.1 (1988): 57–70.

———. *Margaret Atwood.* New York: St. Martin's Press, 1996.

———. "Margaret Laurence: *The Diviners* and Audrey Thomas: *Latakia.*" *Canadian Women's Studies* 6.1 (1984): 98–100.

———. "Margaret Laurence's *A Jest of God.*" *Canadian Women's Studies* 8.3 (1987): 40–42.

———. "On Gender and Writing: Marian Engel's *Bear* and *The Tattooed Woman.*" *Narrative Strategies in Canadian Literature: Feminism and Postcolonialism.* Ed. Coral Ann Howells, Lynette Hunter, and Armando E. Jannetta. Milton Keynes, England: Open UP, 1991. 71–81.

———. "Storm Glass: The Preservation and Transformation of History in *The Diviners, Obasan, My Lovely Enemy.*" *Kunapipi* 16.1 (1994): 471–78.

———. "Weaving Fabrications: Women's Narratives in *A Jest of God* and *The Fire-Dwellers.*" *Critical Approaches to the Fiction of Margaret Laurence.* Ed. Colin Nicholson. Vancouver: University of British Columbia Press, 1990. 93–106.

———. "Worlds Alongside: Contradictory Discourses in the Fiction of Alice Munro and Margaret Atwood." *Gaining Ground: European Critics on Canadian Literature.* Ed. Robert Kroetsch and Reingard M. Nischik. Edmonton, Alberta: NeWest, 1985. 121–36.

Huggan, Graham. "Resisting the Map as Metaphor: A Comparison of Margaret Atwood's *Surfacing* and Janet Frame's *Scented Gardens for the Blind.*" *Kunapipi* 11.3 (1989): 5–15.

Hunter, Lynette. "Consolation and Articulation in Margaret Laurence's *The Diviners*." *Critical Approaches to the Fiction of Margaret Laurence*. Ed. Colin Nicholson. Vancouver: University of British Columbia Press, 1990. 133–51.

Hutcheon, Linda. *The Canadian Postmodern: A Study of Contemporary English-Canadian Fiction*. Toronto: Oxford UP, 1988.

———. "'Shape Shifters': Canadian Women Novelists and the Challenge to Tradition." *Amazing Space: Writing Canadian Women Writing*. Eds. Shirley Neuman and Smaro Kamboureli. Edmonton, Alberta: Longspoon, 1986. 219–27.

Hutchinson, Ann M. "Onward, Naked Puritans: The Progress of the Heroines of *Bear* and *The Glassy Sea*." *Canadian Women's Studies* 8 (1987): 63–68.

Irvine, Lorna. "The Here and Now of *Bodily Harm*." *Margaret Atwood: Vision and Forms*. Ed. Kathryn VanSpanckeren and Jan Garden Castro. Carbondale: Southern Illinois UP, 1988. 85–100.

———. "Sailing the Oceans of the World." *The New Quarterly* 7.1–2 (1987)): 284–93.

James, William. "Atwood's *Surfacing*." *Canadian Literature* 91 (1981): 174–81.

Jolly, Roslyn. "Transformations of Caliban and Ariel: Imagination and Language in David Malouf, Margaret Atwood and Seamus Heaney." *World Literature Written in English* 26.2 (1986): 295–330.

Jones, Dorothy. "'Waiting for the Rescue': A Discussion of Margaret Atwood's *Bodily Harm*." *Kunapipi* 6.3 (1984): 86–100.

Kadrmas, Karla Smart. "Owen Barfield Reads Margaret Atwood: The Concepts of Participatory and Nonparticipatory Consciousness as Present in *Surfacing*." *Margaret Atwood: Reflection and Reality*. Ed. Beatrice Mendez-Egle. Edinburg, Tex.: Pan American University, 1987. 71–88.

Kamboureli, Smaro. "The Body as Audience and Performance in the Writing of Alice Munro." *Amazing Space: Writing Canadian Women Writing*. Ed. Shirley Neumann and Smaro Kamboureli. Edmonton, Alberta: Longspoon, 1986. 31–38.

Keith, W. J. *Canadian Literature in English*. London: Longman, 1985.

———. "Margaret Laurence's *The Diviners*: The Problem of Close Reading." *Journal of Canadian Studies* 24.3 (1988): 102–16.

Kirtz, Mary K. "The Thematic Imperative: Didactic Characterization in *Bodily Harm*." *Margaret Atwood: Reflection and Reality*. Ed. Beatrice Mendez-Egle. Edinburg, Tex.: Pan American University, 1997.

Klovan, Peter. "'They Are Out of Reach': The Family Motif in Margaret Atwood's *Surfacing*." *Essays on Canadian Writing* 33 (1986): 1–28.

Kokotailo, Philip. "Form in Atwood's *Surfacing*: Toward a Synthesis of Critical Opinion." *Studies in Canadian Literature* 8.2 (1983): 155–65.

Kristeva, Julia. *Revolution in Poetic Language*. Trans. Margaret Waller. New York: Columbia UP, 1984.

Lacombe, Michele. "Woman and Nation: Epic Motifs in Margaret Laurence's *The Diviners* and Antonine Maillet's *Pelagie-La-Charrette.*" *Multiple Voices: Recent Canadian Fiction.* Ed. Jeanne Delbaere. Sydney: Dangaroo, 1990. 146–60.

Lamont-Stewart, Linda. "Order from Chaos: Writing as Self-Defense in the Fiction of Alice Munro and Clark Blaise." *The Art of Alice Munro: Saying the Unsayable.* Ed. Judith Miller. Waterloo, Ontario: University of Waterloo Press, 1984. 113–21.

Laurence, Margaret. *The Diviners.* 1974. Rpt. Chicago: University of Chicago Press, 1993.

———. *A Jest of God.* 1966. Rpt. Toronto: McClelland & Stewart, 1974.

Lecker, Robert. "Janus through the Looking Glass: Atwood's First Three Novels." *The Art of Margaret Atwood: Essays in Criticism.* Ed. Arnold E. Davidson and Cathy N. Davidson. Toronto: Anansi, 1981. 177–203.

Legendre, B. A. "Image Juxtaposition in *A Jest of God.*" *Studies in Canadian Literature* 12.1 (1987): 53–68.

Lewis, Paula Gilbert. "Female Spirals and Male Cages: The Urban Sphere in the Novels of Gabrielle Roy." *Traditionalism, Nationalism, and Feminism: Woen Writers of Quebec.* Ed. Paula Gilbert Lewis. Westport, Conn: Greenwood, 1985. 71–81.

Lindberg, Laurie. "Wordsmith and Woman: Morag Gunn's Triumph through Language." *New Perspectives on Margaret Laurence: Poetic Narrative, Multiculturalism, and Feminism.* Ed. Greta M K. McCormick Coger. Westport, Conn.: Greenwood, 1996. 187–201.

Little, Jean. "But What about Jane?" *Canadian Children's Literature* 3 (1975): 71–81.

Livesay, Dorothy. "Two Women Writers: Anglophone and Francophone." *Language and Literature in Multicultural Contexts.* Ed. Satendra Nandan. Suva, Fiji: The University of the South Pacific and The Association for Commonwealth Language and Literature Studies, 1983. 234–39.

Lozar, Tom. "America in the Canadian Mind." *Cross-Cultural Studies: American, Canadian and European Literatures: 1945–1985.* Ed. Mirko Jurak. Lgubljana: Filozofska Fakulteta, 1988. 379–85.

Mackenzie, Manfred. ""I am a place': *Surfacing* and Spirit of Place." *A Sense of Place in the New Literatures in English.* Ed. Peggy Nightingale. St. Lucia: University of Queensland Press, 1986. 32–36.

Martin, Mathew. "Dramas of Desire in Margaret Laurence's *A Jest of God, The Fire-Dwellers,* and *The Diviners.*" *Studies in Canadian Literature* 19.1 (1994): 58–71.

McCombs, Judith. "Crossing Over: Atwood's Wilderness Journals and *Surfacing.*" *Essays on the Literature of Mountaineering.* Ed. Armand E. Singer. Morgantown: West Virginia UP, 1982. 106–17.

Mendez, Charlotte Walker. "Loon Voice: Lying Words and Speaking World in Atwood's *Surfacing.*" *Margaret Atwood: Reflection and Reality.* Ed. Beatrice Mendez-Egle. Edinburg, Tex.: Pan American University, 1987. 89–94.

Meindl, Dieter. "Modernism and the English Canadian Short Story Cycle." *Recherches Anglaises et Americaines* 20 (1987): 17–22.

Montgomery, L. M. *Anne of Avonlea*. 1910. Rpt. New York: New American Library, 1987.

———. *Anne of Green Gables*. 1908. Rpt. New York: New American Library, 1987.

———. *Anne of Ingleside*. 1939. Rpt. New York: Bantam, 1981.

———. *Anne of the Island*. 1915. Rpt. New York: Bantam, 1987.

———. *Anne of Windy Poplars*. 1936. Rpt. New York: Bantam, 1987.

———. *Anne's House of Dreams*. 1922. Rpt. New York: Bantam, 1981.

———. *Emily Climbs*. 1925. Rpt. New York: Bantam, 1983.

———. *Emily of New Moon*. 1923. Rpt. New York: Bantam, 1983.

———. *Emily's Quest*. 1927. Rpt. New York: Bantam, 1983.

———. *The Golden Road*. 1910. Rpt. New York: Bantam, 1987.

———. *Jane of Lantern Hill*. 1937. Rpt. New York: Bantam, 1988.

———. *Magic for Marigold*. 1929. Rpt. New York: Bantam, 1988.

———. *Mistress Pat*. 1935. Rpt. New York: Bantam, 1988.

———. *Pat of Silver Bush*. 1933. Rpt. New York: Bantam, 1988.

———. *Rainbow Valley*. 1919. Rpt. New York: Bantam, 1985.

———. *Rilla of Ingleside*. 1944. Rpt. New York: Bantam, 1985.

———. *The Story Girl*. 1910. Rpt. New York: Bantam, 1987.

Morley, Patricia. "Margaret Laurence: A Canadian Tolstoy?" *Language and Literature in Multicultural Contexts*. Ed. Satendra Nandan. Suva, Figi: The University of the South Pacific and The Association for Commonwealth Language and Literature Studies, 1983. 254–63.

Munro, Alice. *Lives of Girls and Women*. New York: McGraw-Hill, 1971.

Murray, Heather. "Women in the Wilderness." *Amazing Space: Writing Canadian Women Writing*. Ed. Shirley Neuman and Smaro Kamboureli. Edmonton, Alberta: Longspoon, 1986. 74–83.

Nicholson, Colin. "'There and not there': Aspects of Scotland in Laurence's Writing." *Critical Approaches to the Fiction of Margaret Laurence*. Ed. Colin Nicholson. Vancouver: University of British Columbia Press, 1990. 162–76.

Osachoff, Margaret Gail. "The Bearness of *Bear*." *The University of Windsor Review* 15 (1979–80): 13–21.

Perrakis, Phyllis Sternberg, "Portrait of the Artist as a Young Girl: Alice Munro's *Lives of Girls and Women*." *Atlantis* 7.2 (1982): 61–67.

Pifer, Lynn. "'It Was Like the Book Say, But It Wasn't': Oral Folk History in Laurence's *The Diviners*." *New Perspectives on Margaret Laurence: Poetic Narrative,*

Multiculturalism, and Feminism. Ed. Greta M. K. McCormick Coger. Westport, Conn: Greenwood, 1996. 143–50.

Powell, Barbara. "The Conficting Inner Voices of Rachel Cameron." *Studies in Canadian Literature* 16.1 (1991): 22–35.

Prabhakar, M. "Margaret Atwood's *Surfacing*: Blue Print of Revolt." *The Literary Half-yearly* 36.1 (1995): 70-79.

Pratt, Annis. "*Surfacing* and the Rebirth Journey." *The Art of Margaret Atwood: Essays in Criticism.* Ed. Arnold E. Davidson and Cathy N. Davidson. Toronto: Anansi, 1981. 139–57.

Prentice, Christine. "Storytelling in Alice Munro's *Lives of Girls and Women* and Patricia Grace's *Potiki.*" *Australian-Canadian Studies* 8.2 (1991): 27–40.

Quartermaine, Peter. "Margaret Atwood's *Surfacing*: Strange Familiarity." *Margaret Atwood: Writing and Subjectivity.* Ed. Colin Nicholson. New York: St. Martin's, 1994. 119–32.

Radway, Janice A. *Reading the Romance: Women, Patriarchy, and Popular Literature.* Chapel Hill: University of North Carolina Press, 1984.

Rainwater, Catherine. "The Sense of Flesh in Four Novels by Margaret Atwood." *Margaret Atwood: Reflection and Reality.* Ed. Beatrice Mendez-Egle. Edinburg, Tex.: Pan American University, 1987. 14–28.

Relke, Diana M. A. "Pillar, Speaker, Mother: The Character of Calla in *A Jest f God.*" *Studies in Canadian Literature* 13.1 (1988): 34–46.

Rigney, Barbara. *Margaret Atwood.* Totowa, N.J.: Barnes & Noble Books, 1999.

Robinson, Sally. "The 'Anti-Logos Weapon': Multiplicity in Women's Texts." *Contemporary Literature* 19.1 (1988): 105–24.

Robson, Nora. "Alice Munro and the White American South: The Quest." *The Art of Alice Munro: Saying the Unsayable.* Ed. Judith Miller. Waterloo, Ontario: University of Waterloo Press, 1984. 73–84.

Rocard, Marcienne. "The Dispossession Theme in Margaret Laurence's *The Diviners.*" *World Literature Written in English* 21.1 (1982): 109–14.

———. "Margaret Atwood's *Surfacing* and Alma Luz Villanueva's *The Ultraviolet Sky*: The Spiritual Journey of Two Women Artists: One Anglo-Canadian and One Mexican-American." *Recherches anglaises et nord-americaines* 24 (1991): 155–61.

Roy, Gabrielle. *The Tin Flute.* 1945. Rpt. Toronto: McClelland & Stewart, 1980.

Rubenstein, Roberta. "Animal Idylls: Female Desire, Fantasy, and the Reconstructed Other." *LIT* 4 (1993): 123–25.

———. "Pandora's Box and Female Survival: Margaret Atwood's *Bodily Harm.*" *Journal of Canadian Studies* 20.1 (1985): 120–35.

Rubio, Mary, and Elizabeth Waterston, eds. *Selected Journals of L. M. Montgomery.* 4 vol. Toronto: Oxford UP, 1985, 1987, 1992, 1998.

Sheckels, Theodore F. "In Search of Structures for the Stories of Girls and Women: L. M. Montgomery's Life-Long Struggle." *American Review of Canadian Studies* 23 (1993): 523–38.

Smart, Patricia. *Writing in the Father's House: The Emergence of the Feminine in the Quebec Literary Tradition.* Toronto: University of Toronto Press, 1991.

Smith, Rowland. "Margaret Atwood and the City: Style and Substance in *Bodily Harm* and *Bluebeard's Egg.*" *World Literature Written in English* 25 (1985): 252–64.

Sparrow, Fiona. "'This place is some kind of garden': Clearings in the Bush in the Works of Susanna Moodie, Catharine Parr Traill, Margaret Atwood and Margaret Laurence." *Journal of Commonwealth Literature* 25.1 (1990): 24–41.

Spiet, Pierre. "A Retrospective Reading of *The Stone Angel* in Light of *The Diviners.*" *World Literature Written in English* 24.2 (1984): 312–27.

Staels, Hilda. *Margaret Atwood's Novels: A Study of Narrative Discourse.* Tubingen: Francke, 1999.

———. "The Social Construction of Identity and the Lost Female Imaginary in M. Atwood's *Surfacing.*" *Journal of Commonwealth and Postcolonial Studies* 6.2 (1999): 20–35.

Stein, Karen F. *Margaret Atwood Revisited.* New York: Twayne, 1999.

———. "Speaking in Tongues: Margaret Laurence's *A Jest of God* as Gothic Narrative." *Studies in Canadian Literature* 20.2 (1995): 74–95.

Stovel, Nora Foster. "Reflections on Mirror Images: Doubles and Identity in the Novels of Margaret Atwood." *Essays on Canadian Writing* 33 (1986): 60–67.

———. "'Sisters Under Their Skins': *A Jest of God* and *The Fire-Dwellers.*" *New Perspectives on Margaret Laurence: Poetic Narrative, Multiculturalism, and Feminism.* Ed. Greta M. K. McCormick Coger. Westport, Conn.: Greenwood, 1996. 63–79.

Strobel, Christina. "On the Representation of Representation in Margaret Atwood's *Surfacing.*" *Zeitschrift für Anglistik und Amerikanistik* 40.1 (1992): 35–43.

Tausky, Thomas E. "'What Happened to Marion?': Art and Reality in *Lives of Girls and Women.*" *Studies in Canadian Literature* 11.1 (1986): 52–76.

Thieme, John. "Acknowledging Myths: The Image of Europe in Margaret Laurence's *The Diviners* and Jack Hodgins's *The Invention of the World.*" *Critical Approaches to the Fiction of Margaret Laurence.* Ed. Colin Nicholson. Vancouver: University of British Columbia Press, 1990. 152–61.

Thomas, Audrey. *Intertidal Life.* 1984. Rpt. Toronto: General, 1986.

Thomas, Clara. "'Planted firmly in some soil': Margaret Laurence and the Canadian Tradition in Fiction." *Critical Approaches to the Fiction of Margaret Laurence.* Ed. Colin Nicholson. Vancouver: University of British Columbia Press, 1990. 1–15.

Thomas, Susan. "Mythic Reconception and the Mother/Daughter Relationship in Margaret Atwood's *Surfacing.*" *ARIEL* 19.2 (1988): 73–85.

———. "Reading Female Sexual Desire in Alice Munro's *Lives of Girls and Women.*" *Critique* 36.2 (1995): 107–20.

Tiger, Virginia. "The I as Sight and Site: Memory and Space in Audrey Thomas' Fiction." *Canadian Women Writing Fiction.* Ed. Mickey Pearlman. Jackson: University Press of Mississippi, 1993.

Tschachler, Heinz. "The Reconstruction of Myth in James Dickey's *Deliverance* and Margaret Atwood's *Surfacing*, or, The Ideology of Form." *Cross-Cultural Studies: American, Canadian and European Literatures: 1945–1985.* Ed. Mirko Jurak. Ljubljana: Filozofska Fakulteta, 1988. 65–77.

Verduyn, Christl. "Contra/diction/s: Language in Laurence's *The Diviners.*" *Journal of Canadian Studies* 26.3 (1991): 52–67.

VanSpanckeren, Kathryn. "Magic in the Novels of Margaret Atwood." *Margaret Atwood: Reflection and Reality.* Ed. Beatrice Mendez-Egle. Edinburg, Tex.: Pan American University, 1987. 1–13.

Wachtel, Eleanor. "An Interview with Audrey Thomas." *Room of One's Own* 10.3–4 (1986): 7–61.

Wagner, Linda W. "Margaret Laurence's *The Diviners.*" *The University of Windsor Review* 16.2 (1982): 5–17.

Wainwright, J. A. "You Have to Go Home Again: Art and Life in *The Diviners.*" *World Literature Written in English* 20.2 (1981): 292–311.

Ward, David. "*Surfacing*: Separation, Transition, Incorporation." *Margaret Atwood: Writing and Subjectivity.* Ed. Colin Nicholson. New York: St. Martin's Press, 1994. 94–118.

Warwick, Susan. "Growing Up: The Novels of Alice Munro." *Essays on Canadian Writing* 29 (1984): 204–25.

———. *River of Now and Then: Margaret Laurence's* The Diviners. Toronto: ECW, 1993.

Waterston, Elizabeth. "Double is Trouble: Twins in *A Jest of God.*" *Critical Approaches to the Fiction of Margaret Laurence.* Ed. Colin Nicholson. Vancouver: University of British Columbia Press, 1990. 83–92.

———. "Lucy Maud Montgomery, 1874-1942." *Canadian Children's Literature* 1.3 (1975): 9–26.

Whitaker, Muriel. "'Queer Children': L. M. Montgomery's Heroines." *Canadian Children's Literature* 1.3 (1975): 50–59.

Wilkins, Peter. "Defense of the Realm: Canada's Relationship to the United States in Margaret Atwood's *Surfacing.*" *The Yearbook of Research in English and American Literature* 14 (1998): 205–22.

Wilson, Sharon. "Camera Images in Margaret Atwood's Novels." *Margaret Atwood: Reflection and Reality.* Ed. Beatrice Mendez-Egle. Edinburg, Tex.: Pan American University, 1987. 29–57.

———. *Margaret Atwood's Fairy-Tale Sexual Politics.* Oxford: University of Mississippi Press, 1993.

Woodcock, George. *Introducing Margaret Atwood's* Surfacing: *A Reader's Guide.* Toronto: ECW, 1990.

York, Lorraine M. "Lives of Joan and Del: Separate Paths to Transformation in *Lives of Girls and Women* and *Lady Oracle.*" *The University of Windsor Review* 19.2 (1986): 1–10.

———. "The Rival Bards: Alice Munro's *Lives of Girls and Women* and Victorian Poetry." *Canadian Literature* 112 (1987): 211–16.

Index

Studies on Themes and Motifs in Literature

The series is designed to advance the publication of research pertaining to themes and motifs in literature. The studies cover cross-cultural patterns as well as the entire range of national literatures. They trace the development and use of themes and motifs over extended periods, elucidate the significance of specific themes or motifs for the formation of period styles, and analyze the unique structural function of themes and motifs. By examining themes or motifs in the work of an author or period, the studies point to the impulses authors received from literary tradition, the choices made, and the creative transformation of the cultural heritage. The series will include publications of colloquia and theoretical studies that contribute to a greater understanding of literature.

For additional information about this series or for the submission of manuscripts, please contact:

Dr. Heidi Burns
Peter Lang Publishing
P.O. Box 1246
Bel Air, MD 21014-1246

To order other books in this series, please contact our Customer Service Department:

800-770-LANG (within the U.S.)
212-647-7706 (outside the U.S.)
212-647-7707 FAX

Or browse online by series at:

www.peterlangusa.com